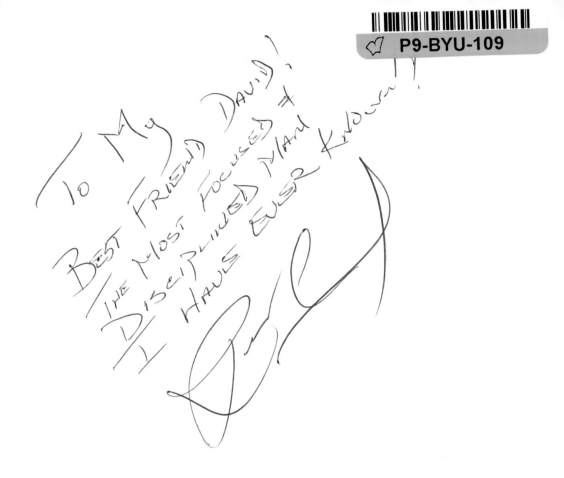

To My Friend David!
Best Friend David!
The Most Focused &
Disciplined Man and
D/I Have Ever Known!

CISO SOFT SKILLS

SECURING ORGANIZATIONS IMPAIRED BY EMPLOYEE POLITICS, APATHY, AND INTOLERANT PERSPECTIVES

CISO SOFT SKILLS

SECURING ORGANIZATIONS IMPAIRED BY EMPLOYEE POLITICS, APATHY, AND INTOLERANT PERSPECTIVES

RON COLLETTE MIKE GENTILE SKYE GENTILE

CRC Press
Taylor & Francis Group
Boca Raton   London   New York

CRC Press is an imprint of the
Taylor & Francis Group, an **Informa** business
AN AUERBACH BOOK

Auerbach Publications
Taylor & Francis Group
6000 Broken Sound Parkway NW, Suite 300
Boca Raton, FL 33487-2742

© 2009 by Taylor & Francis Group, LLC
Auerbach is an imprint of Taylor & Francis Group, an Informa business

Library of Congress Cataloging-in-Publication Data
Collette, Ron.
CISO soft skills : securing organizations impaired by employee politics, apathy, and intolerant perspectives / Ron Collette, Michael Gentile, and Skye Gentile.
p. cm.
Includes bibliographical references and index.
ISBN 978-1-4200-8910-3 (alk. paper)
1. Business--Data processing--Security measures. 2. Computer security. 3. Information technology--Security measures. 4. Data protection. I. Collette, Ronald D. II. Gentile, Skye. III. Title.
HF5548.37.G462 2009
658.4'78--dc22   2008040279

Visit the Taylor & Francis Web site at
http://www.taylorandfrancis.com

and the Auerbach Web site at
http://www.auerbach-publications.com

Contents

Foreword xi

Acknowledgments xiii

About the Authors xvii

Overview xxi

Chapter 1   What's Not Right 1
Overview 1
What Is Security? 3
Why Is All This Important? 6
Measuring Security 8
    Security Program Strategy 8
    Mission and Mandate 11
    Security Policies 14
    Roles and Responsibilities 16
    Training and Awareness 19
    The Security Risk Project Portfolio 21
    Other Methods of Measurement 23
    Security Constraints (Apathy, Myopia,
        Primacy, and Infancy) 29
    The Con of Security 35
    Conclusion 39

Chapter 2   True Security Model 41
True Security 41
    Part I—The Tangible Elements of True Security 42
    Part II—Modeling the Intangible Elements
        of True Security (The Hard Part) 43
    The Two "Step-Children" Groups of the Model 47
    Tying It All Together 49
    True Security Summary 51

Using the Model 51
    Introduction to Systems Theory 53
    Components of Systems Theory 53
    Overlaying Security onto Systems Theory 54
    Putting It All Together 55
Summary 57

Chapter 3   Apathy **59**
Overview—What We Are Going to Cover 59
Causes 60
    Causes of Apathy in Humans 60
    Causes of Apathy within a System 62
    Causes of Apathy within an Organization............................. 64
    Causes of Apathy within a Security Program 69
    Equilibrium of Accountability and Authority........................75
    Security Interaction Points within an Organization 76
    Eating the Elephant in One Bite 78
    Missing Tangible Items of a Security Program 79
    Communication—The "Why" 79
    Causes of Apathy Section Summary.......................................80
    Cause and Effect of Apathy on the True Security Model.......80
Apathy and the True Security Model 82
    Apathy and the Board of Directors...83
    Apathy and the Executive Team 84
    Apathy and Middle Management...86
    Apathy and the Supervisory Team..86
    Apathy and Employees 87
    Apathy and Consumers 88
    Effects Summary 89
Solutions to Apathy 89
    Security Solutions..92
Chapter Summary 96

Chapter 4   Myopia **97**
Overview 97
Causes of Myopia within an Organization...103
    History and Myopia 104
    Complexity of Systems 105
    Those Who Perform the Work 106
    Professional Fraud 108
    Knowledge Management...109
Causes of Myopia within a Security Program 110
    What Is Security? 111

Techno-Centric Security 111
It's a Game of Inches 112
Pedigree Matters.. 113
The Generalist versus the Specialist.. 113
No Hablas Security 114
Life is a Wheel 114
Buyer Beware 115
Security Training 116
Causes of Myopia Section Summary 116
Cause and Effect of Myopia on the True Security Model 118
Myopia and the True Security Model 118
Myopia and the Board of Directors 119
Myopia and the Executive Team 120
Myopia and Middle Management 122
Myopia and the Supervisory Team 122
Myopia and Employees 123
Myopia and Consumers 123
Effects Summary 125
Solutions..125
Security Solutions...126
Chapter Summary 134

Chapter 5   Primacy...**135**
Overview 135
Primacy Tune-Up...136
Causes of Primacy within an Organization.......................................141
Organizational Culture 141
Causes of Primacy within a Security Program 148
Walk Softly in the Land of the Giants...153
Summary 153
Cause and Effect of Primacy on the True Security Model.................155
Effects of Primacy 155
Solutions..160
Security Solutions 163
Step #1: Assess Your Own Situation 163
Step #2: What's in The Message?..165
Step #3: Be Gentle with Your Knowledge.......................................168
Step #4: Power Flows from the Top...169
Conclusion...170

Chapter 6   Infancy **171**
Overview 171
Infancy within an Organization 181

Summary 184
Infancy within a Security Program 184
    Nature of Security 185
    Lack of Credibility 185
    Pedaling Doom (or How Chicken Little Found
        His Calling in Security) 187
    Summary 187
True Security Model and Infancy 189
    True Security Model 189
    Board of Directors 190
    Executive Management 191
    Middle Managers 191
    Supervisory Team 192
    Employees 193
    Consumers 193
    Summary 195
Security Solutions 195
    First Things First 198
    No One Likes Big Brother 199
    Find Good Sources 199
    Do Not Blindly Trust Sources Just Because They Appear
        Authoritative 199
    Educate Yourself and Then Teach Others 201
    Organize Your Messages 202
    Be Patient 204
    Summary 204

Chapter 7   Tying It All Together **205**
Tales from the Security Consultant 205
Overview 206
Warning: Awareness and Comprehension of Previous
    Chapters Are Necessary to Read Past This Point 208
How to Measure Constraints within Your Environment 209
    Localized Security Constraint Identification 209
    Identification of Security Constraints within
        the True Security Model 211
    Summary 214
GAP the True Security Model 214
    The Tangible Elements of the True Security Model 215
    Measuring the Intangible Elements of the
        True Security Model 216

Organizational GAP Analysis within the
    True Security Model 218
  Summary 220
Filling the Gap 220
  R.E.A.P.—Security Success Model 220
  Final Steps 231
  Summary 233

Chapter 8   Closing Thoughts 235
The Final Tale from the Security Consultant 235
Concept 1: Recognize That the Security Constraints Are
    What Leads to All of the Failures on Security Initiatives
    and in Security Programs 236
Concept 2: Be Reasonable in Your Approach
    to Mitigate the Security Constraints 236
Concept 3: True Security Is an Ideal 236
Concept 4: Treat Security Personally 237
Summary 237

Appendix 239
Exercise 8: Apathy 239
Exercise 9: Apathy 240
Exercise 10: Myopia 242
Exercise 11: Myopia 243
Exercise 12: Myopia 244
Exercise 13: Primacy 245
Exercise 14: Primacy 246
Exercise 15: Primacy 247
Exercise 16: Infancy 248
Exercise 17: Infancy 249
Exercise 18: Tying It All Together 250
Exercise 19: Tying It All Together 253
Exercise 20: Tying It All Together 257
Exercise 21: Tying It All Together 260
Exercise 22: Tying It All Together 263
R.E.A.P. Templates: Exercises 24 to 30 266

References 271

Index 273

Foreword

The brief histories of many information security teams are littered with abandoned projects, ineffective policies, ill-acquired technologies, and the blood of well-intentioned security staff and consultants. What is it that keeps so many of these programs from gaining ground even with dedicated staff members, widespread regulatory pressure, executive support, and financial backing? Let's see if we can find the answer in a book.

What we will find in most of the numerous books on my professional reading shelves will probably be useful. However, none of these books in my experience delve into some of the fundamental deficiencies that organizations, security or otherwise, often exhibit—until now. Ron, Mike, and Skye have covered the fundamentals of an effective information security program with the True Security Model, but what really stands out in this book is the careful consideration of the formidable, though often overlooked, constraints that hinder an organization's security program. Far from just considering these constraints, the authors provide some tangible and practical examples of how to deal with them.

What are these constraints? Well, that's for the book to explain, but I'll give you a hint. They aren't problems with the overall organization, they have nothing to do with budget, and there will be no whining about unsupportive executives. The constraints have everything to do with flaws within the security program itself. It's probably worthwhile to toughen up your skin because this book is taking aim squarely at us security professionals as the cause of these problems.

The refreshing perspective of self-examination in this book makes me certain that I will find myself back among its pages when tough questions need to be answered.

Michael Boyd, CISSP

In 2006, Verisign conducted a lighthearted, unscientific survey with people on the busy walkways of San Francisco's Market Street to determine how many people would divulge their computer password for a $3 Starbucks gift card. The result was an astonishing 85 percent of those surveyed easily divulged their password. For the equivalent of two cups of coffee, these individuals gladly compromised one of the most important security controls of their organization.

In the same year, 26.5 million veterans' records were stolen from an employee's home, marking the largest loss of confidential information in U.S. government history. According to the inspector general's findings, the employee who lost the information acknowledged that he took the security of the data for granted. This loss of information spurred a dramatic request to Congress for over $500 million in emergency federal funds to address not only the technical controls, but also the cultural and leadership issues facing veterans' affairs with protecting sensitive files and systems.

What do these two stories have in common? They clearly illustrate that the overriding issue in security today is managing the "people element" as part of a security program. A quick search on the Internet for major security breaches or loss of sensitive information over the past few years supports this assertion; it reveals that the vast majority were due to people rather than technical control failures.

Though this is obviously a concern, most security magazines and books barely cover the topic. That is why I was pleasantly surprised when I was asked to review this book.

The writers of *CISO Soft Skills* analyze this sociological and often oversimplified component of security—people—its effect on security programs, and then deliver intuitive solutions that can help even the most seasoned security professional.

They take on this topic with a tongue-in-cheek approach that made potentially dull and dry material amusing and easy to understand. This is definitely a book for the security reference section in my library.

If you are looking for another security technical book to protect yourself from hackers and malware, please put this book down now. For the rest of us who want to understand this overlooked challenge to implementing security programs and attaining tools to achieve true security, turn to the next page.

Enjoy!

Christopher Chock, CISSP

Acknowledgments

Team Acknowledgment

We would like to thank humankind and our incredibly mixed-up sense of social interaction, without which there would not be a book.

Ron Collette Would Like to Thank the Following People and Organizations:

- My wife, Alice, for her patience, support, and friendship during this project.
- My mother, father, sister, and brother-in-law, all of whom have been infinitely supportive.
- My co-authors for their insights, determination, and support.
- All of our clients for the experience they provide us.
- My dog, Mimi, who constantly reminds me that life is really about the next meal, the next nap, and finding things to make your tail wag.

Mike Gentile Would Like to Thank the Following People and Organizations:

- My wife, Tiffany, for supporting me on this second book after she knew how time-consuming the first one was to complete and for only charging one pair of Jimmy Choo shoes to edit for us this time.
- My family for support during this process.

- My fellow authors, Ron, for putting up with my obsessive compulsive ways on just about a daily basis, and Skye, for providing me with a different perspective to view this project and the world.
- Dr. Lawrence B. Werlin and the Coastal Fertility team for helping give my family the most important reason to write this book.
- Sam (Bean), for teaching me all you need to be happy are two walks per day, family and friends nearby, and that a T-bone now and then doesn't hurt.

Skye Gentile Would Like to Thank the Following People and Organizations:

- My husband, Alfred, and my two daughters for their patience, support, and love throughout the duration of this project.
- My parents, Mike and Lorraine, for their unwavering confidence in my abilities.

Organizations We Would Like to Thank:

- Rich and the rest of the Auerbach Team.
- The makers of Advil™. This book gave us a headache.
- Brewing companies around the world for providing the necessary sedation when necessary.
- The makers of Emergen-C™.

Book Reviewers We Would Like to Thank:

- Mike Boyd, CISSP
- Sheri Camuso
- Biljana Cerin, CISA, CISM, CBCP, PMP
- Chris Chock, CISSP
- Sal Cornejo, CISSP, CISM
- Tiffany Gentile, CPA
- Jay Houlden
- John Kelly, CISSP
- Keith Maxon, CISSP, GSEC
- Stephen Northcutt, Founder GIAC Certification
- Marcus J. Ranum

- Ben Rothke, CISSP, PCI, QSA, CISM, CCO, SITA
- Frank Scavo, CFPIM, CIRM
- Ehab Sheira, CISSP, CIPP

Art and Cover Designer

- Shelli Reiter

About the Authors

We have provided our biographies for three reasons:

1. This book is about people, so we should probably introduce ourselves.
2. To provide a mechanism for our security peers to get in touch with us. We enjoy getting comments, feedback, and questions that can help us learn more about these concepts.
3. To show how different the backgrounds are for each author. We thought this level of diversity was essential in this type of book; we hope you agree.

> "In an insane society, the sane man must appear insane."
>
> **Stokely**

Ron Collette, CISSP

Ron Collette, CISSP, is a principal in the southern California security consultancy Traxx Consulting. Traxx works with Fortune 500 organizations, designing and building security programs and large-scale security control sets. He is a member of the board of advisors for Savant Protection, an anti-malware product.

Ron is also co-author of *The CISO Handbook, A Practical Guide to Securing Your Company.* When he is not penning the next action-packed security treatise (yawn), he works as an editor and analyst for the security portal www.cisohandbook.com developing tools and templates for security professionals. Additionally, he writes articles for the *ISSA Journal, Secure World Expo,* and is a senior research analyst for *Computer Economics.*

Yes, sports fans, he does have a real life. He lives in the hills of Orange County, California with his wife, Alice, and demented dog-child, Mimi. When there isn't any snow for skiing, he can be found surfing with co-author and business partner, Mike, making furniture, or beating on a heavy bag at the boxing gym.

Send Ron an e-mail at ron@cisohandbook.com.

"Tacos, anyone?"

Mike Gentile, CISSP

 **Mike Gentile,** CISSP, is cofounder and managing partner with Traxx Consulting in Newport Beach, California. He is also co-founder of www.cisohandbook.com. When designed by the factory, they somehow made a mistake and gave Mike's skills to become the next striker for Manchester United to someone else, instead leading him to seek a career in his other passion: information security. Mike has made the best of this mix-up and as a result spends most of his time working with organizations to solve this riddle we all call "security." He has performed security program development, security architecture, and project management services for countless organizations ranging from government entities to some of the largest within the Fortune 500. Mike is also co-author of *The CISO Handbook, A Practical Guide to Securing Your Company.*

In his personal life, Mike is blessed with a beautiful wife, Tiffany, a newborn son, Jack, and a crazy dog, Sam. They split their time between awesome San Clemente, California, when the weather is warm and the surf is good, and high in the pines of Arizona when Orange County becomes too stressful. He was a competitive soccer player, is now a weekend warrior, and is still learning the ropes as a novice surfer. Oh, and he loves to eat tacos!

Send Mike an e-mail at mike@cisohandbook.com.

"In every being there exists a seed of perfection; however, it takes compassion to activate that seed inherent in our heart and mind."

Dalai Lama

Skye Gentile

Professor **Skye Gentile** has twenty years of experience creating and implementing on-site training programs and initiatives for corporate, nonprofit, and academic climates. During her career, she has taught at California State University East Bay, Chabot College, Ohlone College, and is currently teaching at Cabrillo College in Santa Cruz, California.

Skye's teaching philosophy rests in the belief that individuals learn best in a climate that is active, stimulating, and relevant to the learner. Her academic area of study embodies multiple facets of interpersonal and intercultural communication, actively engaging students with diverse perspectives and teaching styles.

In addition to teaching full-time and acting as an advisor for Alpha Gamma Sigma Honor Society, Cabrillo Chapter, she is active in college governance and instructor training, helping colleagues improve their teaching strategies in hopes of better meeting the changing needs of the student population.

When she is not teaching, she enjoys coaching her daughter's soccer team, spending time with her husband and two children, and exploring the beautiful scenic beaches of Santa Cruz with her dog, Buddy. Skye enjoys running, biking, swimming, and boxing, and was a sponsored triathlete for active.com, until being diagnosed with lupus in 2005 and cancer in 2007 (both in remission). Her perspective holds firm: see every challenge as an opportunity for reflective growth and change helping both self and others effectively scaffold the life they want to live and the people they desire to become. This is a lifelong process with a discreet beginning, many chapters in between, and a story that never ends.

Send Skye an e-mail at skye@cisohandbook.com.

Overview

Here we go, time to write the second book. It has been several years since the first one: *The Chief Information Security Officer (CISO) Handbook, A Practical Guide to Securing Your Company*. The reason it has been a while is simply because we did not want to write another book just to write another book. We wanted to try to find a topic that we believed could add the most value for our peers. We think the time has arrived and we found our topic: *CISO Soft Skills: Securing Organizations Impaired by Employee Politics, Apathy, and Intolerant Perspectives*. We hope you agree.

Fair Warning!

If you are looking for a sterile, perfect-state approach that can only be utilized in a fictional organization, this book is not what you are looking for. Instead, this book reflects experiences and solutions of those who are in the trenches of modern organizations. To achieve that objective, we have tried to be brutally direct, honest, and realistic in developing this material. In addition, to keep ourselves honest regarding the material that is presented, this book employs the use of research and survey data to further support many of its positions. The goal of all of this is to present practical ideas that can make a difference in the daily lives of security practitioners, specifically security leaders.

The Challenge (or opportunity for you positive folks)

Recently, it has become apparent that many organizations are implementing security in a manner that is designed to provide the appearance of security, rather than actual security. It is the embodiment of spin-doctoring security to elicit a feeling of safety. This concept was originally coined as "security theatre" by Bruce Schneier in his book, *Beyond Fear* (Schneier, 2003). In our experience, and through the experiences of our peers, this particular trend is becoming commonplace and is actually on the rise in many organizations. We agree that, though there is plenty of "security stuff" occurring in organizations, most of it appears to be geared toward presenting a perception of diligence and improved security rather than actual security. In other words, many of us see a lot of activity masquerading as productivity.

Though this stuff makes for great conversation over a beer or martini, the realization that organizations are not doing enough to secure themselves is alone probably not worth your time to read or our time to write in another book. However, when you step back and take a closer look, many more important questions begin to come to mind. These questions were the inspiration to spend the last five months writing, and two years researching, what you will find in these pages. Below, we have identified these questions, which we believe are bookworthy. In addition, we have provided a reference to the area within this book that addresses each question. If none of these questions, or our approach to answering them, interests you, then this book is probably not for you.

- Why are organizations claiming they are getting better at security while objective assessment demonstrates that they are not?

Chapter 1 explains that most organizations are measuring the wrong things. This faulty measurement causes skewed results about success.

- Why should a Chief Information Security Officer (CISO) care?

Chapter 2 answers by saying that many CISOs are getting caught in the middle between the claimed security level at their organizations and what is reality. This difference causes two things to occur. First, it makes it difficult for a CISO to get the support and momentum needed to truly secure their enterprise. Second, it at times influences those security professionals to participate in also perpetuating this false sense of security. We have coined this second concept the "security con."

- What should organizations be measuring to identify the success of their security efforts?

Chapter 2 presents a tangible approach, which we call the "True Security Model," that is designed to clearly illustrate all of the intangible requirements that are needed by a healthy security effort.

- What are the root causes that negatively influence both a CISO and an organization's ability to truly secure itself?

Chapters 3 through 6 discuss these causes, which are called the four security constraints:

1. Employee Apathy
2. Employee Myopia (or tunnel vision)
3. Employee Primacy (often exhibited as office politics)
4. The Infancy of the Information Security Discipline

■ What can a CISO do about the Security Constraints?

At the end of Chapters 3 through 6, we have provided numerous practical and actionable exercises, tools, and techniques to identify, limit, and compensate for the influence of the security constraints in any type of organization.

■ What are some proactive techniques that CISOs can utilize in order to effectively secure challenging work environments?

Chapter 7 discusses some proactive techniques that CISOs can utilize in order to effectively secure challenging work environments. One of these techniques is called the "R.E.A.P. Security Success Model," which is designed to help aid the efforts of a CISO. This practical approach is designed to aid a CISO with solving these complex intangible constraints within an organizational environment. In addition, though it is specifically designed for a CISO, for the most part it can also be applied by just about anyone who is focused on security, regardless of his role within the security function of an organization.

If you are still with us, then we can assume that all or at least some of these questions resonate with you. When reviewing these questions, it should start to become clear why many organizations and CISOs are struggling with security. For the most part, it is because many of the core issues that are causing the problem have little or nothing to do with security. This particular fact makes them very easy and, in some cases, desirable to overlook. After all, CISOs want to deal with security, not all that other stuff.

So our challenge (or opportunity) in this book is, first, to present tools that can help our readers try to identify these intangible negative influencers of security that plague most organizations. Our second objective is to then provide tangible tools and techniques for CISOs to identify, minimize, and overcome these issues within their own unique situation.

Now that premise is certainly a topic worth exploring and conquering.

Before moving on to the next section, please keep in mind that our intent is not to point fingers or affix blame, rather it is to have a blatant, honest conversation about a difficult subject that many of our colleagues care deeply about and that affects everyone in the security community, including us.

Why Do We Care?

We understand that it is uncommon for most authors to project their rationale for developing an article or book. And there are certainly valid reasons for this practice. But in the name of honesty and full disclosure, we feel that our motivations are fair game in this instance. Here is the story.

We had just finished an engagement to build a brand new security program from the ground up for a large organization. We followed our own advice, putting into practice the concepts and methods outlined in our first book, research from our Web site, lessons learned from our peers in the security community, and lastly our own experience. Everything went according to plan, yielding the desired results during each step in the process.

When the project concluded, it was labeled as a success by all parties! The board of directors was happy because it had a functioning security program. Executive management was happy because it felt that it had demonstrated due diligence on a difficult issue. The project sponsor, the CISO, was ecstatic because his political capital had increased along with the budget. We should have been happy because, as consultants, we got paid—with emphasis on "we should have been happy." We weren't! Something just did not seem right.

It would have been easy to dismiss that feeling as a one-time occurrence. Cash the check and move on to the next project. But this was not a one-time occurrence. We had seen this result on countless projects prior to this one, but were still unable to quantify what it was. After consulting with some of our colleagues, we found that we were not alone with our dilemma. Our peers were seeing the same thing and though they could identify with it, they were having difficulty identifying the root causes of the problem. We had continuously heard the same issues repeated in places of unquestionable empirical study such as the hotel bar after a conference presentation (the place where you can really find out what people think). What was going on? What was the answer to this little mystery?

In order to answer that question, we proceeded to review several years, even decades, worth of projects. What we learned is that regardless of the methods, models, or approaches to building a security program the final product often could not be considered optimal for the organization. It was not optimal in terms of true security, cultural fit, organizational maturity, or business needs. The finished product—an effective customized security program—would start out as a beautiful intricate ice sculpture, but would always end up being reduced to a puddle of its former glory (we reserve the right to wax poetic from time to time)—diminished and marginalized by constraints, individuals, and decisions that had little to do with security, risk reduction, threat mitigation, or what best served the organization. Ouch! We were feeling the anguish of watching all of the hard work evaporate as the apathy, primacy, myopia, and infancy of a situation diminished what was once an effective strategy.

Perhaps even more fascinating (fascinating as a car accident) was the fact that everyone involved in the project would stand back and look at the "puddle" and comment on the beauty and magnificence of the "sculpture." The auditors, the executives, and the board had their own reasons for viewing the "puddle" as a "masterpiece." The point to be taken in this situation is that perception of the results was skewed by the self-interest of each group, none of which happened to coincide with what was best for the organization. Folks, we hate to say it, but the emperor is still naked, yet everyone is still marveling at his new suit of clothes.

That was the breaking point. No longer is the status quo good enough for our organizations, our families, or us. We can and should be doing better as a discipline. The question is what should be done and who should do it?

The Target Audience of This Book

We have written this material with a focus on the security professionals within an organization who generally have the biggest effect on making changes within a security program. Because that it is often the CISO, or a similar leadership role, this book is most applicable for that audience. Of course, since many of the concepts that we will discuss, particularly the security constraints, affect all security professionals regardless of their role, this book can be enjoyed by just about any member of a security program. Now that we know who is involved, let us move on to how we plan to help fix the problem.

The Book's Approach

As you can see, this book is certainly different than our first one. Though we still firmly stand behind the concepts, techniques, and principles in our first book, there are a number of new considerations that can be used to augment that material. These items are far more esoteric and in many cases far outside the accepted domain of security. As a result, a couple of things are going to change with how we present this material. Most noticeably, we will not use a purely linear model in the chapters of this book. The only two caveats to this are that we highly recommend that you start by reading Chapters 1 and 2, and that you have read Chapters 3 through 6, regardless of order, before taking on Chapter 7.

Another change in this book is that throughout various chapters we have employed the use of survey data and statistics in order to provide substantiation for the positions taken within the chapter. We decided on this approach since many of the concepts in this book are generally nebulous by nature. Though the survey data cannot be taken as absolute proof, we feel that it provides enough substantiation to give the topic credibility.

We are big fans of survey data, provided the surveys are conducted with the proper controls and parameters. The survey results used in each chapter were collected from the diverse membership from around the world of our security portal at www.cisohandbook.com. This survey represents responses from more than 100 individuals, primarily CISOs located worldwide. Figure 0.1 is an example of some

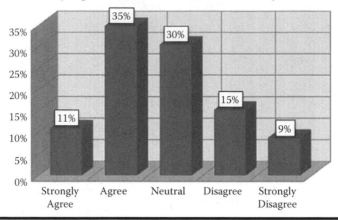

There Is a Discrepancy between the Security Posture That My Organization Presents and Its True Security Posture

Figure 0.1   CISO handbook survey. As evidenced in Figure 0.1, nearly half of the respondents in the www.cisohandbook.com survey indicated that there is a discrepancy between the real security posture of their organization and that which is presented. What does that mean? What we take away from this is that nearly half of the organizations whose products and services we use in our daily lives are not accurately representing their true state of security. In other words, as consumers we are being misled and as security professionals we are in many cases misleading.

of the data that we will be presenting throughout the book. Where applicable, you will also see a quick observation regarding the survey information.

Another change is that we have enlisted the aid of a professional in the field of sociology: Professor Skye Gentile. Since we will be delving into the realm of human interaction, Skye will be furnishing some of the theory and practices to help clarify and substantiate the material within the following chapters. Depending on the sociological issue, she will provide a gateway to some of the applicable research that can shed light on the security issue we are attempting to address. Of these theories, the one that she will utilize the most is a sociological model known as "systems theory."

This is a foundation concept that will be used throughout the text. In order for us to build on this concept later and give you some context, we will give you your first lesson on systems theory here. The other reason for injecting this portion is to demonstrate how a seemingly unrelated concept can be associated with security. This is a mindset that you need to be prepared for, as the entire book will bring things in from left field, tie them to security, and then explain their effect on your efforts. As a side note, the next paragraph is in gray. When you see this, as you continue to read on further in the book, it means that this information is coming from Skye.

YOUR ORGANIZATION AS A LIVING, BREATHING HUMAN SYSTEM

Systems theory is not new. The roots of systems theory can be traced to Georg Hegel's work in the nineteenth century. Hegel's vested interest in systems theory was based on his observations of the world being controlled by the tension created by opposites. Thus systems theory can help us understand a variety of physical, biological, social, and behavioral processes. Systems theory was later codified by biologist Ludwig von Bertalanaffy, who established a multidisciplinary approach to knowledge known as "general systems theory (GST)." Other pioneers such as Gregory Bateson also furthered research in the systems theory arena, researching various communication scenarios between humans. Following pioneers such as Gregory Bateson, Paul Watzlavick, Janet Beavin, and Don Jackson in their book, *Pragmatics of Human Behavior*, specifically highlight patterns of human communication. Their findings were innovative and have been studied further by scholars of psychology, sociology, and communication studies, in addition to scientists.

WHAT IS A SYSTEM?

1. A system is a set of things that affect one another within an environment and form a larger pattern that is different from any of the parts.
2. If you change one part of the system, the entire system changes.
3. One distinction that can be made to systems is whether they are open or closed systems.
   a. A closed system has no interchange with its environment, which causes it to move toward chaos, disintegration, and death (for example, physical systems such as stars, that do not have life sustaining qualities).
   b. An open system receives matter and energy from its environment and passes matter and energy to its environment.

Figure 0.2 illustrates the nature and the associated attributes of systems based on their relative position along a continuum from open to closed.

Applying systems theory to social organizations (humans) is not new. In addition, recently some in the security field have also begun to conduct research in this area. However, considering the intricacies of how systems operate when humans are involved, as well as the impacts this has on the security constraints of apathy, myopia, primacy, and infancy, is new and something we believe is of the utmost importance for securing your organization.

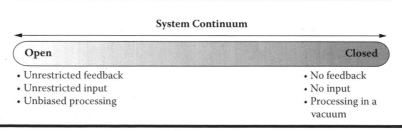

System Continuum

Open	Closed
• Unrestricted feedback	• No feedback
• Unrestricted input	• No input
• Unbiased processing	• Processing in a vacuum

Figure 0.2   Figure 0.2 illustrates the nature and the associated attributes of systems based on their relative position along a continuum from opened to closed.

How Is This Book Organized?

The first two chapters of this book provide a great deal of fundamental information that will be used and expounded upon in the remaining chapters. We will address the concept of security and the difficulty that some have comprehending its scope. We then plan on discussing the methods and criteria by which your security efforts are measured and deemed as a success or failure. During this conversation, we will address the decision-making processes of security officials and how those determinations impact the people, their organization, and in many instances their communities. During this section, we will also take a closer look at the causal relationship between the definition of success for security and the impact that has on an organization. Though that sounds a bit existential, a common understanding of items as basic as security and success has a tremendous bearing on the next topic of environmental constraints.

After spending time exploring the ramifications and importance of having an appropriate definition of success for your security effort in Chapter 1, Chapter 2 will introduce our model of what we believe a successful security effort should look like. We believe that a successful security effort is the attainment of a concept we call "true security." The goal of this chapter is to make the intangible components of true security tangible, so that they can be utilized as a benchmark through the rest of the book. With a tangible point of reference explained, the next four chapters will focus on the constraints within most organizations that hinder the attainment of true security.

We believe that the four constraints that will be explored in this book have more of an impact on an organization's ability to achieve true security than any other factor. The topic is substantial enough to dedicate an entire chapter to each of the constraints: apathy, myopia, primacy, and infancy.

The first portion of each constraint-specific chapter will be used to identify its root causes. We will perform this from human, system, organizational, and security program perspectives. Each perspective will build on the one from before. After all, security programs reside in an organization, which is a system that is comprised of humans. After looking specifically at causes, we will then focus on the correlation between the root cause and the effect this has on achieving true security.

Each chapter on constraints will conclude with actionable solutions for their identification, remediation, or compensation. This is where we start to make the intangible very tangible. We will provide tools and techniques that as a CISO you can use in almost any organizational situation. The goal is to provide tools, techniques, and solutions for managing these issues without compromising yourself or the integrity of your security effort.

After a thorough review of the constraints in isolation, the next chapter will tie all of them together. After all, you will often see more than one of them within an organization. We will also introduce the R.E.A.P. Security Success

Model. The goal of this model is to provide CISOs with actionable techniques for mitigating security constraints while enhancing their ability to achieve true security.

After providing a tangible toolkit, we will use the final chapter for some final closing thoughts. These opinions will provide some final recommendations for how to use many of the concepts we will discuss during your security travels. Figure 0.3 illustrates each chapter's layout in this book.

So, fasten your seatbelts and break out your moral compass. Ready ... Set ... On with the show!

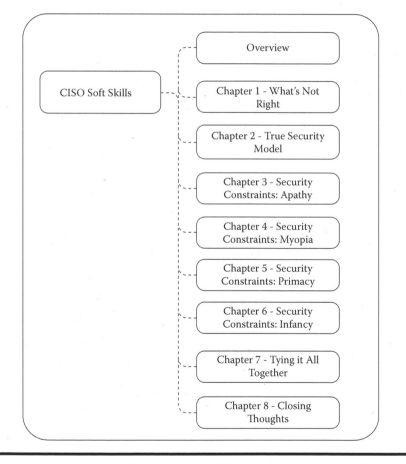

Figure 0.3   Illustrates the chapter layout of this book.

Chapter 1

What's Not Right

Overview

There are two base assumptions that were introduced in the preface that we plan to explore deeper within this chapter.

1. Most organizations are not doing enough to truly secure themselves.
2. Not only are organizations not doing enough, they are convincing themselves and the people around them to the contrary.

This chapter will illustrate what we believe to be the underlying or root causes behind these issues in an organizational setting. We are beginning with these concepts because they will serve as foundation principles that will be carried on throughout the remainder of the book. The first of these issues that will be discussed will focus on how the varying interpretations of what people believe "security" to represent impact their ability to successfully implement it. We will conclude by showing the relationship between the use of inconsistent definitions of "security" within organizations and how they are used to measure success or failure—many times producing misleading results. Of course, inconsistent definitions of the term "security" are not the only factors that are creating faulty measurement within organizations. The next section of this chapter will introduce a myriad of items that are contributing to an organization's ability to accurately measure its success with security.

The approach will be to use tangible, relatable examples in order to prepare you for the primary concepts that are defined later within this chapter. In many of the examples, you will see the sentence or paragraph followed by a set of parentheses that enclose the name of the concepts that the example illustrates. Though this may seem a little unorthodox, we feel that a demonstration of the symptoms will aid you later in diagnosing your own situation. After all, as any doctor would say, you cannot make a diagnosis

1

if you cannot recognize the symptoms. The following section will provide our diagnosis and the core root causes of the problem: what we refer to as "the security constraints."

These discussions will provide additional information and context about each of the security constraints (myopia, primacy, apathy, and infancy) and its impact. After introducing and exploring each security constraint, we will introduce a related concept: the security con.

The final portion of this chapter will focus on defining the phenomenon that we have labeled as "the security con." We will define this concept, how it is manifested, how to identify it, and its implications to your organization. This is a foundation concept that is necessary to illustrate how some organizations are compensating for the difference between the portrayal of their security efforts and the true state of security.

As you can see, we have a number of interesting and potentially foreign concepts to introduce in this chapter. These concepts will evolve and grow as we proceed through each chapter thereby building your knowledge, understanding, and most importantly your recognition of them. Our objective is to raise your level of awareness toward these concepts, as well as explain how and why these issues stifle the execution of many security efforts. Further, we are hopeful that this understanding will aid you in coping and addressing these issues within your own organization. Prior to beginning, we want to provide one disclaimer for this chapter. To be honest, this was a difficult chapter for us to write because we like to present solutions, not merely complain about the way of the world. However, these are fairly difficult and complicated concepts that require some time to establish the necessary foundation before we can get to the solutions. Rest assured, that is where we are going.

Let us start with the linchpin for all of these concepts: the definition of security. After all, how can you measure anything without an established benchmark as a reference? Defining the concept of security may seem overly simplistic, but, as you will see, appearances can be deceiving (see Figure 1.1).

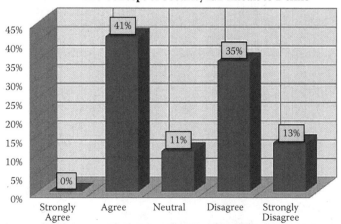

The Concept of Security is Difficult to Define

Figure 1.1   **The results in this figure illustrate that even most security professionals have difficulty defining security.**

What Is Security?

Before we answer that question, here is your first homework assignment. Tomorrow at work, take ten minutes and perform the following exercise:

Exercise 1

This is a simple exercise designed to demonstrate the relativity of a concept or idea. Within your organization, independently ask ten people, from various departments and levels of the organization, for their definition of security. Take note if their responses are varied based on their relative perspective. This should not surprise you. Security is a concept. As a concept, it becomes a container for whatever someone wishes to place in it. For example, is the response "police department" incorrect when discussing security? Or is it incorrect to think of a firewall when discussing security? You get the idea.

The most fundamental aspect of security, a functional definition, is generally the most ambiguous and the most frequently missing in most organizations. As security professionals, we struggle amongst ourselves to establish a common criterion for defining security, let alone one we can share with others outside of the profession. We try, get frustrated, and then we fall back on our "safety blanket": the CIA triad. For those of you who are not familiar with this concept, it refers to information security as the protection of confidentiality, integrity, and availability (Ouch! CISSP exam flashback ... sorry!). Why the CIA triad?

The CIA triad is one of the few formal definitions that can be applied to security. It is the most recognized by security professionals and has become a de facto standard. Because of this it definitely is valuable. However, it is an information security definition rather than a general security definition. And for the purposes of this book, we were looking for a definition that was applicable to both information and physical security, but we could not find one that was generally recognized, which speaks volumes.

With that said, think of all the times that you have attempted to explain the CIA triad to someone outside of the world of information security. Why was it so difficult for you to explain, and more importantly, for others to understand?

We believe that the difficulty lies in the difference between the definition that the rest of the world uses and that of the security field. First, we do not believe that the average person has a working definition for security (people probably have better things to do). They probably have more of an idea or feeling about what constitutes security rather than a working explanation. However, if they did have a fully functional definition it would probably be one that is more akin to that found in a dictionary. Therefore, to illustrate the differences, we will present the definition of security as found in the dictionary:

Security (definition 1): "Freedom from risk or danger; safety."
The American Heritage® Dictionary of the English Language, Fourth Edition

The reason we needed to introduce this dictionary definition is, either consciously or subconsciously, this is the concept that the average person is operating under. Since this definition relies on the feelings of the individual, security will always inherently be subject to interpretation. Whether it is the customer, employee, executive, stockholder, etc. their view of risk and danger, and the freedom from it, will be a moving target.

Now look at the CIA triad. What does confidentiality, integrity, or availability have to do with the definition listed above? Do not get us wrong, as we mentioned above we like the CIA triad. It is useful as an analysis tool that provides common ground for our profession. But, this definition does little to foster communication between our profession and the rest of humanity. Why is there such a difference between the varying definitions? What is so hard about defining security?

We are glad you asked. The reason that there is such an extreme variation between definitions is illustrated in the following list. Also, note that we have begun incorporating the root cause labels to each section below. These are the words within the parentheses: primacy, apathy, myopia, or infancy. These tags have been associated to the idea to tell you of their importance and relation.

- Though security is an abstract concept, most individuals view it as an absolute. To clarify, what constitutes being rich? If you ask the Internal Revenue Service in the United States, it is any entity, company, or individual making more than $200,000 per year. If you were to ask someone who is currently making $200,000 per year, he or she would probably view Bill Gates, Warren Buffet, and the like as the threshold for being rich. Security is very similar in that everyone seems to know what it is, but the definition varies dramatically based on one's own perception. As such, people will gravitate to, and define security as, the aspects of security that are important or beneficial to them. (Myopia)
- Defining security is difficult. It forces you to manage the perceptions of individuals and in some cases challenge strongly held beliefs. It takes work to get it right, and many people are just not up to the task. (Apathy)
- Various people within an organization will want or need security to mean different things for differing reasons. (Primacy)
- Security touches everything within an organization. It affects processes, employees, technologies, and the buildings in which the organization resides. But it goes even further, affecting the laws of our country and the individual consumer. In short, it is big. So big, in fact, that it can be very difficult for people to grasp the magnitude and nuances with a definition. The result is a definition or concept that makes the concept mentally consumable. (Myopia)
- Security can be incredibly inconvenient and expensive. Isn't it easier to simply exclude elements of security because of political expediency or because it is beyond your control? (Apathy and primacy)

- Exact definitions have a tendency to hold individuals and organizations accountable. This is generally considered undesirable by lawyers, politicians, and executives. (Primacy)
- The concepts of security have been around for a long time, but the concepts in relation to organizational security are much newer. Often, people just do not know how to describe, let alone define, the domain in its entirety. (Infancy)
- Let us face it. Most people are just not interested in security as long as nothing bad happens to them. As a result, most people do not care what definition is being used (what does that say about us?). We believe that this occurs for the simple fact that "most people do not know what they do not know." How could they? For example, as security consultants, we have done work in some of the largest banks, government agencies, health care providers, etc.; therefore, we have seen the actual security stance that is implemented by these entities. We like to think we know what to look for and understand the ramifications caused by these security deficiencies. If the general public had the same vantage point, we believe that they would think twice before using an ATM card or boarding an airplane. It should be noted that we are not proponents nor are we practitioners of fear, uncertainty, and doubt (FUD) to sell security. Unfortunately, given the current state of security from our perspective, one should be scared, times are uncertain, and we have major doubts. (Apathy and infancy)
- The result of developing a functional definition of security can produce undesirable results for individuals in authority. For example, say your organization chooses a highly comprehensive definition of security. What will that mean to different roles within that entity? Perhaps the chief executive officer (CEO) has to spend even more time explaining security to the board of directors—an act that would compel the sanest of individuals to contemplate removing their eye with a ballpoint pen as an alternative. The result of such a definition could also result in a doubling of accountability for the chief information security officer (CISO) when compared with a meaningless or trivial definition. (Primacy)
- Taking on this endeavor has many pitfalls. Maybe it is easier to just leave the definition vague or nonexistent? Well, that is exactly what most organizations are doing. (Primacy and apathy)

We found the results for Figure 1.2 to be very interesting, if you consider that we have never been in an organization that has provided a written definition of security (and we have asked for this item). We believe that this metric addresses the confusion regarding how we define security in general. All of this is fascinating, but why is it so important?

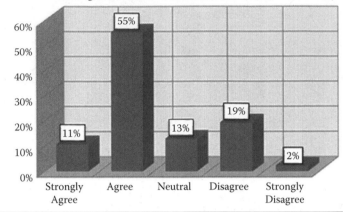

Our Organization Has a Documented Definition of Security

Figure 1.2 **We found the results for Figure 1.2 to be very interesting, if you consider that we have never been in an organization that has provided a written definition of security (and we have asked for this item). We believe that this metric addresses the confusion regarding how we define security in general. All of this is fascinating, but why is it so important?**

Why Is All This Important?

It would be rather difficult, if not impossible, to successfully secure an organization when there is no consensus for what constitutes security. How would you ever define success? If you are one of the souls tasked with security for your organization, these reasons should resonate with you as well. As with any project or initiative, a shared vision of the end state is required to meet the needs and expectations of all the consumers and stakeholders.

To clarify, take the individual who believes that security is a firewall. To that individual, a successful security effort would be the implementation of a firewall. After the firewall is in place that person is likely to believe that the organization is now secure. We commonly refer to that as a "false sense of security" since it only addresses one aspect of security (technology) and only one element of that aspect (network); therefore, that belief is clearly erroneous. If your organization produces enough of these situations, the false sense of security becomes distributed throughout the enterprise. Now everyone is drinking the Kool-Aid®.

Further, our example only addressed the perception of one individual: the person with the myopic view of firewalls. Most organizations have a large number of stakeholders (executives, employees, customers, stockholders, etc.) each with his or her own unique perception. Each of these perceptions must be acknowledged, addressed, or shaped. The management of these perceptions is as much a job of a security professional as any of the more obvious activities. How you choose to address this issue is the variable. Your choices are either to:

■ Shape the perceptions through a shared vision.
■ Ignore the majority of perceptions and address those of which you are aware or care about.
■ Address each individual's perception on an ad hoc basis.

In our travels, we have found that most organizations are opting for ignoring the majority of perceptions. So you might be asking yourself how are these organizations able to just ignore their stakeholders or, returning to the prior concept, get away with manufacturing a false sense of security? The first way it is accomplished is through the improper application or faulty interpretation of measurement information.

Figure 1.3 clearly illustrates that there is not one accepted means of measuring security. We as a discipline are still searching for the tool that resonates with our audience.

The most obvious way in which the majority of organizations are measuring security is by assessing the various components of what many have termed as a "security program." It is ironic how this is another term, born from security, that is also highly subjective and ambiguous. We have had more conversations trying to explain the concept of a security program with people outside of our field. In

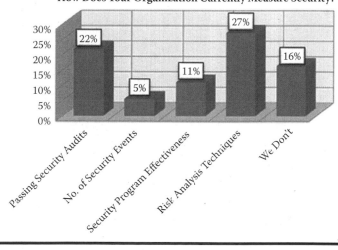

Figure 1.3   This figure clearly illustrates that there is not one accepted means of measuring security. We as a discipline are still searching for the tool that resonates with our audience.

one instance, we literally spent 30 minutes with a person who was unable to grasp that we were not talking about software. After that incredibly painful experience, combined with countless others, we like to believe that we have developed a decent 30-second elevator pitch for what defines a security program.

Our first book was on the development of a formal organizational security program, so we do not plan on reinventing the wheel in this book. Instead, we will take a little time and identify some of the major components within a security program to help us out in the context of measurement. It is important to note that all of these components, whether taken from our methodology for security program development presented in our first book or the existing security frameworks that are available (e.g., ISO27001-2, NIST), will always identify components in the same manner using different names. Here is a listing of each category, with a quick description:

- Security program strategy: the means by which your security organization will achieve its overall mission.
- Mission and mandate (M&M): the goal of the security office as well as its associated level of authority to reach that goal.
- Security policies: the documented and ratified rules by which the security office applies security to the organization. In most methodologies, they represent the ideal security state of the organization—a benchmark from which to measure everything.
- Roles and responsibilities: the identification and definition of each position on the security office team and its individual role for providing security to the organization.
- Training and awareness: the strategy and tactics for educating nonsecurity personnel on security concepts.
- Security risk project portfolio: the mechanism by which your security organization approaches the prioritization and execution of its responsibilities based on risk.

Now that we have established the common elements of a security program and common definitions, let us expand on the common aspects of an organization's security efforts and how they are measured. Figure 1.4 illustrates the various components of a complete security program.

Measuring Security

Security Program Strategy

As we mentioned above, security program strategy is the means by which your security organization will achieve its overall mission.

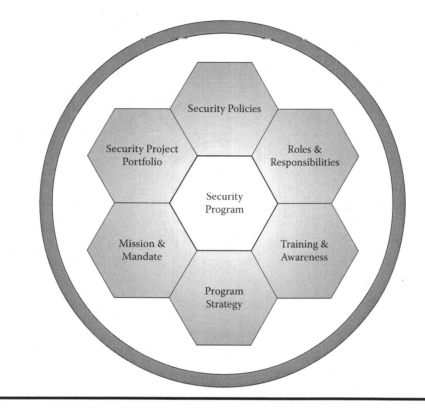

Figure 1.4 This figure shows the various components of a complete security program.

Figure 1.5 illustrates that only 24 percent of security programs bother to document their strategy. No wonder that most security programs are either failing or struggling.

The concept of measuring program strategy success is foreign to most organizations. The success or failure is generally measured in terms of projects completed (something tangible), rather than the overall strategy (something intangible). That is analogous to measuring the success of the D-Day strategy in World War II by the outcome of the Omaha Beach Landing: one battle in a much larger theater of operation.

Why Is This Happening?

When organizations measure the effort or success of their security program, it is usually done under the guise of their annual budget planning. The strategy in this case is actually a side effect of the budget process. Budgeting requires planning, which passes for the annual security strategy. We have rarely witnessed the

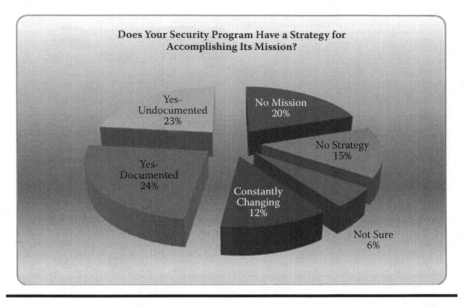

Figure 1.5 This figure shows that only 24 percent of security programs bother to document their strategy. No wonder that most security programs are either failing or struggling.

opposite, where the security strategy is determined and the budget is derived from that strategy.

How Does This Support Faulty Measurement?

Once the budgets have been approved, the success of the security program is now associated to the amount of budget allocated for security and the number of projects to be executed during the year. Simply stated, an organization that spends one million dollars on security is generally viewed as more secure than a company that spends half that amount. It is almost as though the goal of the security program is to acquire funding, not secure the organization.

We feel that there are a number of reasons for this phenomenon. The first reason is that most security efforts are operating in a highly reactive manner due to the fact that they are understaffed and are often relying heavily upon audits for direction. This approach leaves very little time or resources available for planning. The other reason, one which is far more nebulous, is the entire concept of security.

Oh no, here they come again with security as a concept! Yep, that is exactly where we are going, again. Security is this great big hairy amorphous blob that is very difficult to comprehend in its entirety. As such, most organizations struggle to build cohesive plans that consider all of its aspects.

How Does This Lead to a False Sense of Security?

This approach can lead to a false sense of security since activity does not always equate to productivity. Do not get us wrong, we are not asserting that the work completed in this manner is without merit, but we do question whether the projects, proposed or completed, address the most critical needs of the organization or whether these projects were working toward achieving a larger goal.

Before wrapping up this section, we have a true story to relate that underscores this concept. While working with a government agency, we had the opportunity to see one of the more bizarre methods for determining the annual security strategy. This entity's sole method for determining its security strategy was to identify which items it could get funded from the Department of Homeland Security (DOHS). You can see the logic in this approach, the acquisition of government funding for security, but this certainly is an odd means for developing a security strategy. (Apathy and infancy)

Exercise 2

If you have access to your security program budget information, review your past three budget cycles and identify whether strategy drove your budgetary request or vice versa.

Mission and Mandate

As we mentioned above, mission and mandate is the goal of the security office as well as its associated level of authority to reach that goal.

With more than half of the security programs (Figure 1.6) lacking a formal mission and mandate, how do they truly know what their objectives are and what constitutes success?

This may sound odd, but we have found that staff level is the most common means by which success is determined when measuring the mission and mandate of the security program. It can be as simple as the fact that an individual has been assigned or hired as the security officer for the organization. However, the mission and mandate has nothing to do with staffing. It speaks to the objective of the function and the power that it has to achieve that objective. We have often found that the mission of a security program is undocumented, operating by some vague understanding of its objective. Something like, "Secure the organization." (Do not laugh, this is a real-world example.) What the heck does that mean? With a mission statement like that, what would the mandate look like?

These two items are discussed together because it is virtually impossible to have one without the other. Assigning power for no particular reason generally does not happen in most organizations. Further, too much authority can actually be counterproductive. It needs to be balanced against the goals and objectives of the function.

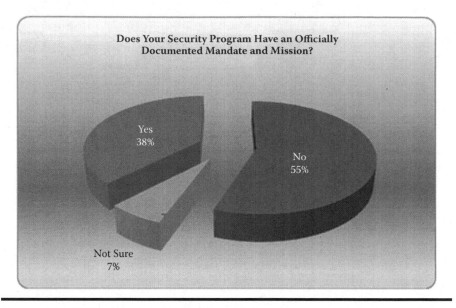

Figure 1.6 With more than half of the security programs (Figure 1.6) lacking a formal mission and mandate, how do they truly know what their objectives are and what constitutes success?

Why Is This Happening?

Definitions are not fun. We established that fact at the beginning of the chapter when discussing the definition of security. They require individuals to take a position on a subject and accept responsibility for those positions. The mission represents the definition of your organization's security initiative. Building definitions is difficult and requires discipline and diplomacy. These are the fundamentals of the security program. Unfortunately, most organizations have neither the patience nor the inclination to spend resources in this manner. They want security and they want it now. However, this is analogous to writing a book without an outline—something only a fool would try (we know because we tried once ... fools that we are!). Now, if organizations do not spend the time defining a clear mission, how can they develop the appropriate mandate? The answer is that they do not. The mandate is usually derived by looking at the organization chart, not driven by the mission; more on this later.

Figure 1.7 clearly illustrates why security is viewed as a "black box" to most within an organization.

How Does This Support Faulty Measurement?

This should be fairly obvious. Without a solid mission and mandate (M&M) as a benchmark, how can you measure the success of a security initiative? Let us use the M&M statement from above: secure the organization. Using that criterion,

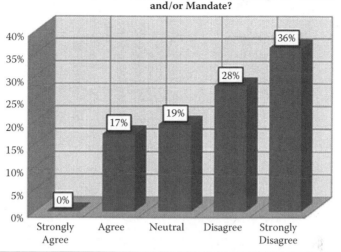

Figure 1.7   This figure clearly illustrates why security is viewed as a "black box" to most within an organization.

combined with the tendency of individuals to make themselves look good, how do you think the rating will turn out? Our guess is that the assessment of the security program's success will be less than accurate.

How Does This Lead to a False Sense of Security?

The false sense of security comes from the tainted metric that will inevitably be used to determine success. Since the M&M statement is so vague, the criterion can change as frequently as necessary in order to demonstrate success, regardless of the actual state of security for the organization.

A vague M&M will also lead to a false sense of security since it serves everyone's perceptions of security. Huh? We know that sounds counterintuitive, but think about it. Since "secure the organization" can mean anything to anyone, everyone's perception is addressed whether their definition of security is a firewall or a lock on the door.

The Costs

Inefficiency and execution difficulty are often the costs to this situation. When you do not have a clearly defined M&M, there is a limited understanding of what the security team is supposed to be doing and the level of authority that has been granted to achieve the specified mission. This generally leads to situations where the group is expected to achieve a great deal without a reasonable level of authority to make these things happen. For example, a security group that is expected by the organization to handle all security issues but is only a one-person team with the authority of a department supervisor. In order for any security program to be successful and cost effective, the authority of the program must be commensurate with its accountability. A nonexistent, weak, or poorly vetted M&M is generally the root cause for creating the imbalance between the two.

If you need evidence of this issue, stop by the pub at your next security conference and keep your ears open. You will hear statements such as, "I can't get anything done," "I can't get any support for my initiatives," "I don't know how they expect me to secure the company, when they won't even let me secure the floor."

Exercise 3

Select ten people who regularly interact with the security office and ask them if they believe that the accountability and the authority of the security program are in balance.

Security Policies

As mentioned above, security policies are the documented and ratified rules by which the security office applies security to the organization.

Figure 1.8 continues the theme of missing security fundamentals with more than half of the respondents declaring that they do not have fully documented security policies. How would our country operate if fewer than half of the laws were documented?

How do most organizations measure success for security policies? This one is easy. If they have a binder entitled "security policies," they have been successful. The applicability or thoroughness of the policy set generally does not seem to matter; what matters is just that they have them. We find that most security policies are not written very well. Either they are collections written by different people over different time periods or they are written at different or misrepresented altitudes. The result is a fairly convoluted set of documents that generally miss the mark of serving as a benchmark for appropriate security within the organization.

Why Is This Happening?

Most organizations recognize that security policies are required in today's business climate. All you have to do is review a few well-chosen pieces of legislation to determine that need. As an example, we have listed a couple of statements from the Health Insurance Portability and Accountability Act (HIPAA) and the Payment

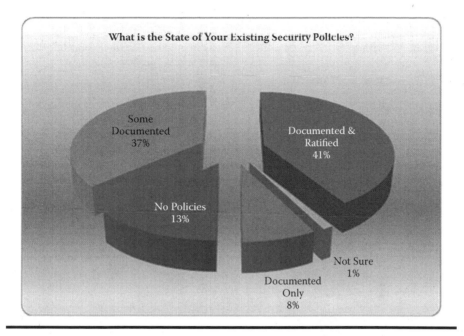

Figure 1.8 **Figure 1.8 continues the theme of missing security fundamentals with more than half of the respondents declaring that they do not have fully documented security policies. How would our country operate if fewer than half of the laws were documented?**

Card Industries Data Security Standards (PCI DSS) that address the need for security policies:

- HIPAA: Identify the security official who is responsible for the development and implementation of the policies and procedures required by this subpart for the entity.
- PCI DSS: (Requirement 12) Maintain a policy that addresses information security.

What the legislation does not say is whether the policies have to be any good or whether they need to be applicable; it merely says that they should exist. As a result, most organizations do not spend a great deal of time or energy developing their policies. They are merely looking for the check in their to-do list leading to an audit conversation that looks like this:

> *Auditor:* "Do you have security policies?"
> *Organization X:* "Yes we do, they are in that binder entitled 'Security Policies'."
> *Auditor:* "Great … check! That's all I needed." (Infancy)

How Does This Support Faulty Measurement?

This example is an obvious oversimplification of the issue, but the conclusion should be the same. Since most organizations determine their security readiness based on the audit process, this produces a simple equation:

Weak Security Policies + Audit = Potential for Faulty Measurement

How Does This Lead to a False Sense of Security?

The mere existence of security policies and compliance to those policies generally suggests that the organization is doing the right thing in its efforts to secure itself. That may be true, but only if the security policies are reflective of the needs and issues of the organization. In our experience, this is often not the case, but this goes undetected because the quality of policies is not what is usually being measured.

The Costs

Security policies are one of those items that force you to "pay me now or pay me later." You can either spend the time up front creating sound applicable security policies or live with the pain that inappropriate policies will yield. Bad, weak, or inappropriate policies create inefficiencies, friction, and costs to the organization. This certainly is not the way to win the hearts and minds of the people you work with.

Exercise 4

Read your organization's security policies and identify:

1. The number of statements that are <u>not</u> applicable to your organization
2. The number of statements that are actually standards, not policies
3. The number of statements that are actually procedures, not policies
4. Whether they address people, process, technologies, and facilities

Roles and Responsibilities

As mentioned above, roles and responsibilities are the identification and definition of the security office team and its responsibilities.

With only 32 percent of security programs having fully documented roles and responsibilities (Figure 1.9), it is no wonder that there is confusion regarding what constitutes security for an organization.

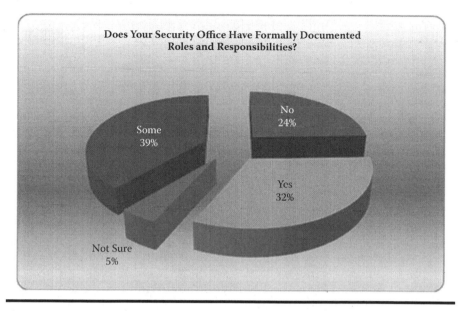

Does Your Security Office Have Formally Documented Roles and Responsibilities?

No 24%

Some 39%

Yes 32%

Not Sure 5%

Figure 1.9 With only 32 percent of security programs having fully documented roles and responsibilities (Figure 1.9), it is no wonder that there is confusion regarding what constitutes security for an organization.

Once again, we have found that the mere existence of a roles and responsibilities document signals success in this area. If this document has been translated into a spot on the organization chart, you should consider yourself wildly successful. If you are part of the latest trend (within the past 2 years), then the organization will be divided by large areas of responsibilities such as risk management, compliance, disaster recovery, business continuity, physical security, or information security. To take things further, you are up for sainthood if you have taken the time to build a departmental organization chart, outlining each position's responsibility. There is not necessarily anything wrong with what we have described so far; however, there are some caveats.

The first concern is the applicability of the roles and responsibilities to the organization. Is it the structure that the organization needs or the one which it is willing to accept (primacy)? Generally, it is the latter of the two. We are not complaining, we understand that there are resource limitations in every organization. The problem though is that there is often a big gap in effectiveness between what is needed and what is implemented. This can impact effective measurement and overall understanding of what people are really doing for the organization. The other prominent concern is the vague titles and job descriptions of the positions within a security organization.

We have found that most positions within security have fairly indistinct titles such as security analyst or security engineer. Once again, since security is a concept, using it within a title does not necessarily provide a clear description of the role that individual has within the organization unless of course you have taken the time to define security. This issue is compounded by the job descriptions of the positions.

We have all read job descriptions. They often more closely resemble a five-year-old child's letter to Santa Claus for every toy ever made. These descriptions will ask for a wide ranging set of skills and talents that are usually beyond the realm of possibility for most individuals.

Why Is This Happening?

This issue is a simple cause and effect model. Without a strong M&M, combined with a security strategy, there is often a lack of direction and focus. That lack of focus is manifested in the direction that is, or is not, provided to the security team. Vague job titles and descriptions are a warning sign of potential flaws in the fundamentals of the security program.

How Does This Lead to a False Sense of Security?

No one ever measures whether people within a security office are actually performing the tasks and roles that are identified within their job descriptions, only that they have job titles and descriptions. Granted that most employees receive annual performance reviews, but the criterion is generally subjective and administered by the same individuals who were assigning the tasks during the year. (Primacy and infancy)

The Costs

This enables the security program to participate in issues that are outside of its core focus or not perform the work it is supposed to be doing. This is often attributed to a lack of true core focus stemming from a missing or poorly formed fundamental component such as security strategy or M&M. This means of operation provides a wonderful sense of ambiguity around security, so no one is really sure what he or she is supposed to be doing.

This often leads to a duplication of effort within the organization. Since security touches everything, many groups within the organization will attempt to address various security issues while the security program is attempting to address the same thing.

Exercise 5

Go to a job posting Web site and perform a search using either "security analyst," "security architect," or "security engineer" as the search term. Now read each job description that is returned from the search. Aren't the differences amazing when looking at different descriptions for the same job title? Now, do the same thing for your organization. Get the job descriptions for all of the positions that are staffed within security. Look at the job titles and descriptions. Are they reflective of the positions and responsibilities as they are assigned within the company?

Training and Awareness

As mentioned above, training and awareness is the strategy for educating nonsecurity personnel on security concepts and practices.

Both Figures 1.10 and 1.11 illustrate that only a quarter of security programs are making full use of training and awareness as a security tool. This continues to baffle us, especially considering the relatively low cost and high return associated with security training.

This is an area where we find mixed results. However, many will consider themselves successful if their organization has conducted any type of security training over a reasonable time period—usually a year. Once again, the quality or applicability is not necessarily an issue. What matters is that the training has occurred. The amount of training conducted by an organization is usually less than two sessions per year and is often only during new-hire orientation. These trainings generally do not have an overall strategy where each training initiative is part of a larger and more cohesive training goal, rather a disconnected ad hoc approach.

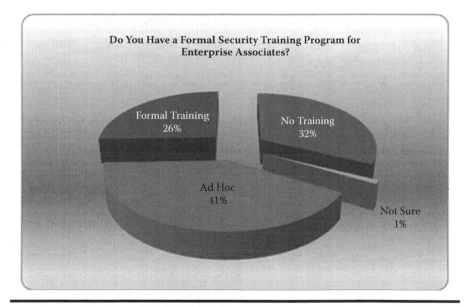

Figure 1.10 This figure illustrates that only a quarter of security programs are making full use of training and awareness as a security tool. This continues to baffle us, especially considering the relatively low cost and high return associated with security training.

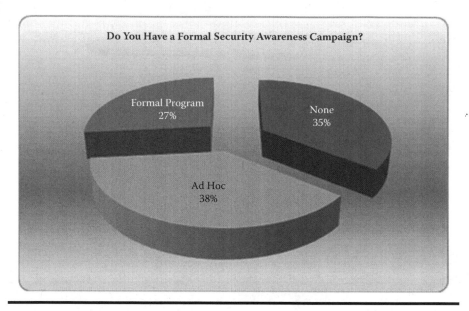

Do You Have a Formal Security Awareness Campaign?

Figure 1.11 **This figure illustrates that only a quarter of security programs are making full use of training and awareness as a security tool. This continues to baffle us, especially considering the relatively low cost and high return associated with security training.**

How Does This Lead to a False Sense of Security?

First, any training is better than no training. It is one of the most efficient, cost effective security controls available. However, there is not a single training course in the world that delivers all of the material required for educating employees on the topic of organizational security. Further, we have yet to encounter an individual capable of absorbing 100 percent of the material presented, even if such a course existed. However, there is a common misconception that these security courses cover all of the material to achieve that very goal. As a result, from an organizational perspective, most feel comfortable that a disjointed, ad hoc security training approach is still sufficient to meet the organization's needs. (Infancy and apathy)

The Costs

The cost to administering training by rote or in an ad hoc manner manifests itself in terms of opportunity cost. As we said above, training is one of the most cost-effective security controls with one of the highest returns on investment if approached in a logical manner. As a result, the opportunity cost associated with a weak training curriculum is very high.

Exercise 6

Review the training curriculum and course materials within your organization. Are the materials sufficient to achieve the tactical objectives of the course? Are the materials sufficient to achieve the strategic objectives of the training and awareness program?

The Security Risk Project Portfolio

As mentioned above, the security risk project portfolio is the mechanism by which your security organization approaches the prioritization and execution of its responsibilities based on risk.

Figure 1.12 illustrates that only about one quarter of security efforts uses a structured approach to prioritizing its work. Why prioritize the work effort when it's so much more fun to thrash? This one baffles us.

The list of projects or initiatives that the security effort will address in a given year is usually the result of the budget planning process (see the section on security strategy) rather than strategic multiyear planning. That said, most of the "portfolios" that we see are nothing more than a task list derived from various locations. The most common sources for these lists come from previous security audits, vulnerability assessments, or the current "hot" issue.

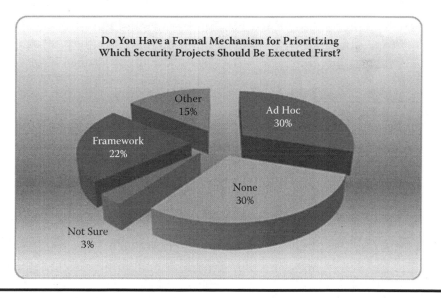

Figure 1.12 **This figure shows that only about one quarter of security efforts use a structured approach to prioritizing their work. Why prioritize the work effort when it's so much more fun to thrash? This one baffles us.**

The concept of a project portfolio is derived from the discipline of project management where each project has a defined scope, forecasted budget, estimated resources, and schedule. It also incorporates the concept of risk rating each initiative to determine its relative priority to the organization. This is a great deal more complicated than maintaining a list in a spreadsheet since it attempts to quantify all of the aspects necessary to successfully execute each portion of the portfolio. The reason it is a portfolio is that it is the representation of the security strategy, as well as the M&M for a given year or series of years. This understanding is important when explaining the costs associated with a simplified version of a security risk project portfolio.

How Does This Support Faulty Measurement?

The faulty measurement aspect of a simplified list comes from the perception of the list itself. It suggests that a certain amount of proactive due diligence has been performed. Heck, it probably has. What it fails to recognize is whether any of the items are actually accomplished and in what timeframe. Compare and contrast that to the full version of the security risk project portfolio that was described above where there are costs, schedules, and resources associated with each initiative. Using that type of tool can give a true reflection of the success or failure of a security effort.

How Does This Lead to a False Sense of Security?

This is the same issue as stated above. The list, any list, creates a perception that some type of due diligence has been performed and that the organization is aware of its security issues. Further, the "list" assumes that something is being done about those deficiencies. Lastly, it assumes that the issues currently receiving attention are the most important to the organization. If you consider the sources for many of these lists, that is questionable.

We have found that the majority of items found within the "list" are findings from prior audits. Audits are fine for measuring the implementation or effectiveness of a security control, but they are a poor substitution for strategic planning. In our experience, most audit findings, whether conducted internally or externally, address the symptoms of an issue rather than the root cause. This often results in a reactive approach for a tool that is designed to be proactive in nature.

The Costs

There are a number of costs to managing your security projects as described above. The first is the reactive position that is often created from a heavy reliance upon audits and assessments. The second is that simple lists do not provide an accurate picture of how the end state will look or how to achieve it. This becomes a problem when it is time to get the funds or political support that may be necessary to undertake the effort.

Exercise 7

Get your security risk project portfolio. Does it separately quantify the scope, schedule, budget, and risk for each project? Is it prioritized in some manner that is associated with risk? Lastly, how many items are on the list from prior years?

Other Methods of Measurement

The prior section on "Measuring a Security Program" is gaining traction within the security community, but it is not the only manner in which many organizations are measuring success. There is a wide range of approaches that stretch from the simple and ridiculous to the complicated and obscure. We will start by addressing the simple and ridiculous; it is more fun.

Security Is Invisible, Let's Count Stuff Instead

The section title says it all: let's count stuff. The latest trend that we have witnessed is to present management with the count of "something" that is related to security to demonstrate how competent or successful the security effort is for the organization. The "something" ranges from security devices to professional certifications as long as it is tangible and associated with security. The strangest "count" that we have ever seen is the security device count.

Counting Security Widgets

This is the strangest and most ridiculous concept, but we love it. It is the practice of counting security devices and using it as a criterion of success or failure for the organization's security efforts. Organizations that embrace this measurement approach believe that effective security can be defined and demonstrated by the quantity of security devices that are implemented: "We have 3 ga-zillion security widgets ... we are now secure." This is just plain weird! However, we see it and executive managements that accept it. Not quite as strange as counting security widgets are the practices of counting events.

Counting Events

Another means by which organizations are measuring the success of security is by counting the number of events that occur in a given timeframe. On the surface, it seems logical. After all, "no news is good news," right?

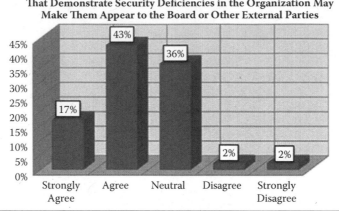

Executive Management Concerned with How Security Assessments That Demonstrate Security Deficiencies in the Organization May Make Them Appear to the Board or Other External Parties

Figure 1.13   No one who has worked in security should be surprised with the information in Figure 1.13.

However, if your organization lacks any detective controls or worse does not know what to measure, how does it know that it has not had an event? Simply because no one has identified an issue as an event does not mean that it did not happen. We can assure you that the best exploit is the one that no one ever discovers. So, once again, "No news is good news?"

No one who has worked in security should be surprised with the information in Figure 1.13.

Counting Certifications

Another means by which organizations rate their security prowess is by the number of professional certifications and accreditations that their staff possesses. The advent of the CISSP, CISM, CISA, GIAC, etc. has been good for our industry, but not as a sole criterion for evaluating the effectiveness of an organization's security efforts. Security certifications are nothing more than a tool to determine the experience and competencies of individual team members. Granted, a competent team is a necessary ingredient to a successful security effort, but we do not believe that it is a legitimate means of measuring success.

Audit … After All, Everyone Understands Audit

Figure 1.14 is a shining example of why most security programs are often reactive.

We are no strangers to audits. How can you work in the field of security and not come across an audit or two? We have had the good fortune to have participated on

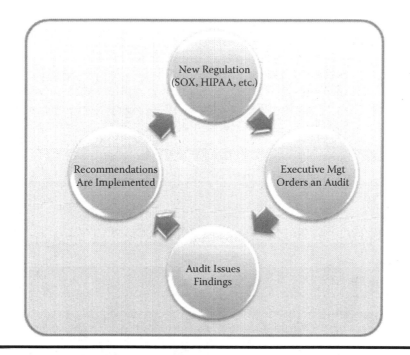

Figure 1.14 **This figure is an example of why most security programs are often reactive. Figure 1.14 demonstrates the endless cycle of regulations, audits, and remediation. All of this is driven by the comfort level that executives have developed for the audit process as a decision support tool.**

both sides of an audit both as the "auditee" and the "auditor." We have also come in after a completed audit to work on the remediation of audit findings. The perspective that is of the most interest to us, in this section of the book, is the use of audit as a measurement tool for determining the level of security within an organization. This method of measurement is valuable when properly used and in the correct context. However, in our opinion, it has recently been overused as a panacea for evaluation. The key to a useful and proper application of the audit tool is an established criterion of measurement.

An audit is the measurement of the effectiveness of a control or set of controls as prescribed within an established benchmark or standard. For internal audits, the evaluation is generally against internal requirements, such as the organization's security policies. External evaluations generally use established frameworks, such as ISO27001-2, as their requirements. In either case, the applicability of the benchmark in relationship to your organization determines the validity of the audit findings. For example, applying the Federal Information Security Management Act (FISMA), a regulation for U.S. government agencies, to that of a commercial organization based in Brazil will substantially alter the relevancy and applicability of the assessment. Most organizations struggle with using applicable and relevant benchmarks, thus impacting the ability to get an accurate vehicle for measurement.

If your organization does possess the necessary baseline criterion to fuel an audit, we hope that you love the audit benchmark that is selected because the audit process will often force the implementation of its standards regardless of their applicability. The reason is that an unanswered or unaddressed audit finding is a legal liability for the organization. This is specifically the case if the audit has been performed by an independent third party.

These two ideas are fairly important due to the fact that the sheer number of security audits is on the rise. We attribute this phenomenon to something we refer to as the "regulatory effect" (Figure 1.14). So, if you are comfortable with the baseline criteria for an audit, here are some of the other caveats that impact their effectiveness as a measurement tool. The first issue is the maturity and qualifications of the security audit discipline.

Figure 1.14 demonstrates the endless cycle of regulations, audits, and remediation. All of this is driven by the comfort level that executives have developed for the audit process as a decision support tool.

Let us begin by stating the obvious: security auditing is not financial auditing. However, many of the major consultancies and internal audit functions have borrowed the credibility from the time-tested and accepted practice of financial auditing. Contrasting financial and security auditing, you find that there is a high degree of consistency with the items included within a standard financial audit: general ledger, chart of accounts, balance sheet, etc. This is not the case when evaluating the security environment of an organization. There is no "one-size-fits-all" in security. The security requirements of a Baskin Robbins* are much different than those for the Boeing Corporation. However, more often than not, both have the same financial components: general ledger, chart of accounts, balance sheet, etc. This consistency allows for more standardized rules for a financial audit—consistency that just does not exist in the world of security. As you can see, we are discussing apples and oranges. However, executive management in most organizations has been conditioned that all audits possess the same level of credibility. This practice provides a false sense of security in that it generates a belief that all deficiencies have been identified and can now be addressed. This can be exacerbated when considering the level of experience, competency, and credentials of the individuals performing the audit.

The majority of security auditors that we have worked with have their professional roots in accounting. There is nothing wrong with that until the audit has to address technically or sociologically complicated security controls. We understand that many of the principles used in audits insolate the auditor from the need to have an in-depth understanding of these issues, but in many cases it is the nuances that make a control set effective or deficient. Another factor that impacts the audit, specifically in large consultancies, is the tendency of today's professionals to be specialists instead of generalists.

The large consultancies that perform audits, like many companies, tend to have individuals who are specialists. Though specialization certainly has its place, particularly in financial auditing, it can be highly detrimental in the field of security. Like many aspects of security, security auditing benefits from a global perspective since security touches many facets of an organization. Think of it this way: a specialist can assess his or her specialty very well and everything else will always come from that perspective. This leads to results that are myopic. Myopia is kryptonite to security, but we will talk more about that in the following section and future chapters. The problem is that organizations do not train generalists; it just is not cost effective. So, how are generalists created? It is usually accomplished by the individuals themselves over time.

It is not unusual to find that the individuals tasked with the security audit of an organization have only been out of college for a few years, usually with a degree in accounting and maybe some work experience conducting financial audits. This type of experience and education presents an issue when evaluating the results of such an audit. This almost guarantees a myopic result for the audit findings.

We do not want to discourage the use of audits when they are applied correctly. However, the credibility given to this practice, when framed with the issues presented above, has the high potential for presenting a skewed picture of the security profile for the organization. This is when a security effort can head out into the twilight zone where fantasy becomes reality. This skewed reality is a slippery slope for organizations in search of true security. Though audits are an issue that is full of excitement, let us move on to the next common measurement tool that is being utilized.

Threat Du Jour

Threat du jour, or threat of the day, is measuring security by your organization's reaction time in addressing the latest threat or trendy security news release. It goes like this: you turn on NBC Dateline with Stone Phillips. He reports on an unusually large breakout of the ABC123 virus and how it is decimating organizations worldwide. Upon arriving at work the next day, you immediately launch a full investigation into the company's preparedness for the ABC123 virus, knowing full well that your organization has a full deployment of antivirus for all of the computing assets. As expected, the company is in no danger from this threat. However, now you begin to market the death-defying feats that were undertaken to save the organization from the villainous ABC123 virus, once again proving the value and success of the organization's security program. Good job. The other variation within this form of measurement is that we were not proactive in preparing for the potential of a computer virus within the organization (what can we say, we are lame security guys). Upon hearing the deep and thoughtful presentation of Stone Phillips, we decided to look into this antivirus software thing and make a purchase. Once antivirus is installed and the risk of damage from the ABC123 virus has been quelled, it is assumed that the organization is now secure (myopia). That is until the next trend or issue is printed in *The Wall Street Journal* or presented on *60 Minutes*.

As sad as this may sound, we have actually been in organizations where people are charged, within the security office, to do nothing but search for these types of trends and report to management on the potential impact. Perhaps this would work except this is the only task that the group was permitted to work on. In these organizations, their measurement for success is based on the number of potential threat assessments that they author.

Security Framework Correlation

Security framework compliance or alignment is another popular method of measuring the success of security within an organization. It works like this: select a framework such as ISO27001-2 or NIST, distill your interpretation of the required elements, construct those elements, and then complete the associated certification process if desired. We actually do not have a problem with this as a starting point or approach for a security program; in fact, we recommended the use of frameworks in our first book. Where frameworks can fall down is that they are frameworks, only providing an outline upon which to base the requirements of a security program. They fail to take into consideration the specific elements and attributes of the target organization thus requiring interpretation and customization in order to avoid a situation that is either under- or overcontrolled. With that said, the use of frameworks generally leads to one of three outcomes:

1. The frameworks are employed as intended … hurray!
2. There is an attempt to use the frameworks correctly, but contention arises between the direction of the frameworks and the cultural constraints of the organization.
3. The frameworks are used as a political "trick bag" where the security program is instructed to pursue the certification for a specific framework without the intent to improve security. The true intent is to give the security program something to do that will keep it occupied with something that is not annoying. We call this the "security now you see them, now you don't (for two years) maneuver." This is particularly diabolical in that it provides executive management with the appearance of extreme diligence in the area of security without having to spend money or change practices (primacy). Sweet deal for them! The message from executive management to the board or newspapers will look like this: "We are fully committed to achieving the highest standards in security. Our security team is diligently pursuing an ISO security certification." In the meantime, the security office is so busy with the bureaucracy of achieving the certification that it does not have any time available to bother the executive team with issues that would improve the true security of the organization.

Adding complexity to this issue is that all three of these outcomes look identical to the untrained eye. Even worse, all of them are often tagged as successful efforts. The differentiator in all of these situations is the impact they have on the true security of an organization.

Closing Thoughts on Measuring the Success of Security

As you can see, there are a number of issues that are impacting the ability of many organizations to accurately measure how successful or unsuccessful they are when addressing security. Though we have presented the cause and effect for these various methods, the question is, "Why is it so difficult to accurately measure the success of security?" Measuring success of security within an organization should not be any more difficult than measuring anything else:

1. Establish the requirements of success.
2. Determine the criteria of measurement.
3. Establish a benchmark for acceptability.
4. Evaluate the conformance of the final product to the benchmark.
5. Result: binary decision—success or failure.

That is the formula. Why does it not consistently work for security? We are glad you asked. We believe there are four major constraints that consistently affect the measurement and application of security within an organization. We have been giving you hints throughout this chapter as to the identity of the culprits, now it is time to officially reveal the villains in our story. Drum roll ... introducing ... the villain ... security constraints.

Security Constraints (Apathy, Myopia, Primacy, and Infancy)

A "security constraint" is the label that we have given to a number of sociological elements that inhabit every organization that employs human beings. We became aware of them through observation while working on various security-based initiatives. It began as a joke that revolved around the eminent sage and social satirist: Dilbert.

We have all been astounded by the incredible poignancy that Dilbert has when addressing the social systems within the workplace. We would witness something that was "Dilbertesque" and manage to find a cartoon that addressed the situation. As we said, it was just fun and games at the beginning.

Since we are nerds, we felt that it might be interesting to systematize the Dilbertesque behavior to determine the level of frequency and predictability. That is when the security constraints were born. Not only was it noticeable, but once we really started looking, it could not be avoided. We did this by simply labeling behavior with one or more of the labels that you have seen throughout the book (apathy, myopia, primacy, and infancy). For example, we would see a watered-down security report destined for the board (primacy) or the security manager whose definition of security was an incident response process (myopia). As you can see, the game was simple and harmless, but it was becoming an effective tool. No matter what oddity we saw that was harmful to the organization attaining true security, it always managed to fit into at least one of the four categories. We like to refer to these items as constraints because their sole function appears to be nothing more than adding barriers and complexity to a complex topic: security.

These are the issues and forces that we believe need to be measured and evaluated within any organization because they have a greater effect on your ability to achieve true security than all of the firewalls and antivirus that you could ever purchase. Our mission in this book is to explore each of them and provide insight and direction for addressing the barriers that they create. We will spend the next few pages briefly introducing each constraint and expand on each one within its own chapter later on.

Figure 1.15 illustrates the pressure that the security constraints put on a security program.

We felt that a quick primer would be useful for providing some context for these ideas. More importantly, they are necessary precursors for introducing the

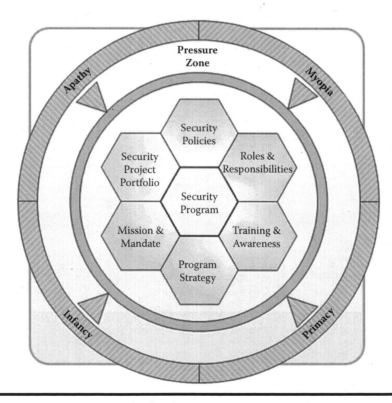

Figure 1.15   This figure depicts the pressure that the security constraints exert on the necessary elements of a security program.

last concept in this chapter: the security con. The security con is the result when these factors are allowed to manifest within an organization. Do not worry, if you still have questions at the end of this section, we will be spending four chapters elaborating on these and other concepts. The first constraint on the list is apathy.

Apathy (definition 1): "Lack of interest or concern, especially regarding matters of general importance or appeal; indifference."
The American Heritage® Dictionary of the English Language, Fourth Edition

Unfortunately, apathy is not unique to security. It is found within many organizations regardless of size or industry. However, the effect that it has on security is far more pronounced due to the necessity that security has for individual diligence. Though diligence is required for security, it is not always necessary for performing regular daily tasks. This difference goes unnoticed until there is a security event that can be directly associated to the behavior.

For example, Joe has been charged with transferring the backup tapes of the organization to the pickup location for off-site storage. Since Joe works for Big-NukeBombMaker (BNBM), Inc. (a subsidiary of HappyTime Ice Cream), the information contained on the tapes is both important to the business and sensitive. This daily job that Joe regularly performs has little if any impact on the business; therefore, every day he takes his tapes to the appointed location and waits for the pickup. This is definitely a task that he considers to be dull and monotonous. One day, Joe decides that he really does not need to wait for the vendor's agent to pick up the tapes. He begins to simply leave the tapes at the appointed location and goes back to work. This occurs for several months until, one day, the vendor contacts Joe inquiring why there had not been any tapes to pickup for the past three weeks (the vendor was apathetic as well). Joe panics. Joe's boss panics. The chief executive officer (CEO) panics. The U.S. Nuclear Regulatory Agency panics. The CISO for BNBM appears on CSPAN answering questions posed by Congress!

It should be noted that this type of behavior was allowed to propagate until there was an event. That is how it generally works. But, closing the barn door after the horse has gotten out does not work well in the world of security.

Myopia (definition 2): "Lack of discernment or long-range perspective in thinking or planning."
The American Heritage® Dictionary of the English Language, Fourth Edition

Myopia is a type of tunnel vision or the inability to see beyond that which is right in front of you. It is almost a type of obsession. In terms of security, it is the idea that people lock onto one or two concepts to the detriment of everything else.

Referring back to our prior example of BNBM, it would not be difficult to extrapolate some of the fallout from the tape-loss event and how that could produce a form of myopia for the organization. After the event and the drama of the lost tape had passed, the corporate executives were fixated on everything associated with tape backups (an impromptu Congressional prostate exam will do that to an organization). From that point on, the M&M for the security office was to secure the backup process. For all intents and purposes, security at BNBM began and ended with protecting tape backups.

As you can see, myopia is not limited to the techno-folks or security jockeys, it was practiced by the executive management of BNBM in this instance. Also, note that we chose to illustrate event-driven myopia—a fixation resulting from an event or series of events—rather than domain-boundary myopia—a fixation based on a limited frame of reference or the inability to visualize interaction of an entire system. We will discuss these concepts in greater detail in the chapter devoted to myopia.

> Primacy (definition 1): "The state of being first or foremost."
> *The American Heritage® Dictionary of the English Language, Fourth Edition*

Primacy involves all aspects of being first, whether we are referring to being selfish (putting yourself first), political (putting your career or professional power first), or a general lack of altruism. This constraint is highly prevalent and the hardest with which to address. After all, we are delving into the human ego, concepts of morality, and the sociological phenomenon of politics.

Returning to our example from BNBM, a subsidiary of HappyTime Ice Cream, let us look at how primacy played a part in this situation. Several months prior to Joe's mishandling of the backup tapes, the chief security officer had commissioned a penetration study to identify weaknesses in the security practices at BNBM. During the study, the penetration team was able to make use of the time window created by Joe to obtain a set of backup tapes and extract critical information, thereby circumventing a number of security measures. This issue was noted in the findings report prepared by the team along with half-a-dozen other major issues. After reviewing the findings, the CISO determined that the report would place several prominent executives in an awkward situation because of the fact that Joe is the son of BNBM's CEO. Therefore, the penetration test and its findings were rewritten so as to minimize the issue. This decision was not made to improve the security of the organization, rather to avoid embarrassing powerful people.

We picked this as our example because it is a familiar situation for most of us where the politics of a situation supersedes what is best for the organization. This particular example also highlights one of the moral crossroads that we mentioned earlier in the chapter: career or conscience? We will discuss this topic, along with some suggestions on how to minimize these agonizing (we assume agonizing; for you evil people, please disregard) decisions, in the following chapters.

> Infancy (definition 3): "An early stage of existence."
> *The American Heritage® Dictionary of the English Language, Fourth Edition*

For the purposes of this book, we are only referring to organizational security when referring to infancy. We are not professing that the subject or concept of security is new. After all, people have been building walls and moats around castles for a very, very long time. However, organizational security, outside of the military or defense industry, is a fairly recent phenomenon. Further, the intricacies and complexities associated with it have increased exponentially as the domain continues to evolve. This influence has been further fueled by computer and telecommunication advances, changes in the geopolitical structure, the nature of warfare (terrorism), and global commerce.

As a result, the "art and science" of security has little resemblance to the field of security 30 years ago. This rebirth or reinvention of security is currently in its infancy. This level of "infancy" or perceived "infancy" poses tremendous obstacles for the security professional in terms of selecting an approach to security.

Wrap-Up

If you accept the basic premise of these items, how come they are never acknowledged or measured? Hmmm, good question! It is certainly not the lack of funds, though more money is always nice! It is not the fact that we do not have enough resources; no one ever does! Let us turn to some of the leading research agencies. They must have analyzed these concepts and their impact on security. Nope, we must have missed that one somewhere between the common headlines at most research firms, "the death of intrusion detection" and "the synergistic convergence of physical and logical security."

But the elements that we have just described are what we believe is truly hindering the security efforts of most organizations. Since we started our little game, we have seen these constraints present themselves, obstruct progress, and in many cases, kill what was originally a good idea that was intended to improve security. So, if these issues are so important to the success of security why doesn't anyone talk about them?

What Prevents Us from Discussing These Issues?

There are a number of answers to this question, but we believe the most compelling reason for this is that once again the topics are intangible. In other words, it is very touchy-feely stuff. Issues such as interpersonal communications and group dynamics can be absolutely mystifying to people within a business or government organization. Take something as simple as ordering a pizza with a group of six people. The pizza can only have two toppings. You will see demonstrations of:

- Apathy: "I don't care ... anything is fine."
- Primacy: "I must have sausage on my pizza!"
- Myopia: "Anything, as long as I do not have to make the call and order it."

These brief categorizations are merely a sample of the reactions that you would probably see or have seen before. Also, keep in mind that this is only for something as trivial as ordering a pizza. Having ordered pizza for the group on many occasions, we can attest to this situation, but how many times have we stopped, reviewed, and analyzed it? (The answer is never…you have a real life.) If we were all sociologists or clinical psychologists, we would analyze it. We would write papers in journals about the subject. We would speak, lecture, and who knows what else. It would be the stuff dreams are made of. For the rest of us, it is just ordering dinner for the group. The challenge is taking the topic, that is so enticing to the sociologist, and making it real, tangible, and relatable for the security professional in order to facilitate true security.

It is human nature to gravitate toward concrete, relatable ideas and materials. When discussing these ideas within the context of business organizations, quantifiable information is always preferred over the esoteric. Though there are models for quantifying these subjects, they are generally regarded as voodoo or pseudoscience by the majority of the business community. Lacking the foundation of these modeling tools or belief in their validity creates an impasse to understanding, measuring, or reporting on them. For example, without these items, how do you measure the political health or the political volatility of an organization? Or how do you measure the emotional maturity of an individual? Or how do you measure individual or cultural apathy? You get the point.

If Only I Could

Let us assume, for argument's sake, that you are able to employ some of the models or tools for measuring the organizational constraints. You locate the appropriate model, diligently record and chart your data, and set up your presentation to management. If you can get management to actually attend this presentation (they tend to be very busy individuals, especially when these types of topics are added to their calendar), our experience has been that management's response to these types of presentations falls into one of three categories:

1. Acceptance: "We had no idea that this is what was holding back our organization. What can we do?" (This never happens.)
2. Bury It: "The executive ostrich maneuver." Stick your head in the sand and wait until it goes away. (This is the most typical response.)
3. Discredit It: Attack the basic philosophy or conditions under which the information was gathered. "We don't believe in the basic premise that your charts are based upon." (Congratulations, you just committed professional suicide! It is time to move to another state or country. At a minimum, change professions. We understand that the morgue is hiring for the graveyard shift.)

Generally speaking, few individuals have the courage (or insanity) to actually attempt something this formal and wide-sweeping in the first place. There is little personal upside to such a venture with a tremendous amount of professional risk.

The Fox Is Guarding the Hen House

OK, hold on to your melon! The fact is that the constraints themselves prevent the measurement of the constraints in the first place. How is that for irony? The politics of an organization often prevent a change to the political environment (primacy). The inability of executive management to understand the interrelation of elements creates a hindrance (myopia). In many cases, things never change because it takes energy and commitment to change them (apathy). And lastly, there are too few individuals who are well versed in the intricacies of organizational security (infancy) to provide direction and guidance for this type of conversation.

Summary

We have certainly covered a lot of material and you may be asking yourself, "Isn't this a security book?" The answer to that is, "Yes." The reason we are discussing all of this stuff is to demonstrate how these concepts are impacting the ability for you as a CISO to bring security to an organization. Since we have covered so much material to this point, we feel it would be beneficial to quickly recap. Here are the major concepts we have covered thus far:

- The definition of security is perceived differently by different people in many organizations.
- The manner in which we are measuring the success of security in many organizations is flawed.
- There are constraints within many organizations that are hindering the success of security.
- The constraints (apathy, myopia, primacy, and infancy) are also very difficult to measure within most organizations.

All of these factors contribute to a less than ideal environment for anyone who is trying to implement true security within an organization. The situation is made worse for individuals who can discern between the false sense of security that many organizations are putting forth and the implementation of true security. This gap is the topic that we will address next; we call it the "security con."

The Con of Security

> Con (definition 4): "To swindle (a victim) by first winning his or her confidence; dupe."
> *The American Heritage® Dictionary of the English Language, Fourth Edition*

What Is the Security Con?

The security con is what results from the effects of the factors that we have described up to this point within the chapter. It is our way of describing the act of adjusting the results, opinions, or information to match an objective or desired perception rather than to present the actual state of security. As we have discussed, many struggle with how to define, measure, and implement effective security. In the case of security, people are willing to accept the security con because everyone wants (or hopes) to be secure. This is true whether we are talking about our online identities or airline travel. In a post-9/11 world, there is a heavy emphasis for all entities to employ the appropriate levels of security. This growing emphasis for organizations to be more secure, combined with the increasing weight of the security constraints, has produced a breeding ground for the "security con." The easiest way to clarify this concept is with the following example.

Example: The Security Con

The GetMHigh Pharmaceutical Lab, a medical marijuana laboratory, is required to meet certain criteria under HIPAA since it handles protected health information (PHI). One aspect of this law requires that the organization have an individual designated specifically to address the security and privacy of PHI. This company, like many, is resource constrained for qualified security professionals. After a review of the available resources, the company determined that Bob Smith, the janitor, is the right person for the job. So, Bob Smith is officially designated as the HIPAA security and privacy officer. Bob is thrilled, but needs to get back to emptying the waste paper baskets.

As with any organization bound by HIPAA, another requirement is regular reviews for compliance. Therefore, GetMHigh Pharmaceutical Lab engages a local consultancy, OverBillUnderDeliver Inc., to perform the review. Though there are many aspects of a HIPAA review, below is the conversation regarding the requirement of the assigned security official:

> *Auditor: "Who is the security officer for the company?"*
> *Response: "Oh, that would be Bob Smith!"*
> *Auditor: "Check."*
> *Auditor: "Who is the privacy officer?"*
> *Response: "That is also Bob Smith."*
> *Auditor: "Check."*

Example Analysis

There is obviously more to a HIPAA review than we have illustrated, but for the verification of the security official, this is fairly common. The regulations are not necessarily specific enough for a more detailed examination. They do not specify the required qualifications for the role, just that it is assigned.

We do not want to digress too far. After all, we are attempting to illustrate the "security con." Let us look at all of the affected parties and review how each participated in the con.

The Authors of HIPAA

The regulation only requires that someone be designated for the position, not be qualified to perform the function. This is part of the con in that the federal government has issued a law to protect everyone's PHI, yet it allows for loopholes such as the one described. Do not fool yourself, there are plenty of others as well. We merely selected the low-hanging fruit for our example.

The U.S. Government

We have performed a number of HIPAA assessments and sadly few organizations have received passing marks for their security and privacy efforts. Now unless we have only reviewed the "bad apples," we must assume that compliance to this regulation is low. Yet, there have been very few investigations or penalties for organizations that fail to comply with the law. Since this is a federal law, it is up to the federal government to enforce it. They seem good at enforcing certain laws like the Internal Revenue Code. Why not this one? Simple, the law is too vague to be enforceable.

Therefore, the government's participation in the con is twofold:

1. They enacted a law that is not specific enough to be effective.
2. They fail to enforce a law that has been enacted.

Members of Congress

We do not believe that you can talk about a con and the federal government without including the politicians that we elect. How have the politician's participated? In the case of HIPAA, they got to demonstrate their commitment to your security and privacy by drafting a law and enacting it, regardless of the quality, applicability, enforceability, or any of a hundred issues that would make the law effective.

The Management of GetMHigh Pharmaceutical Lab

This one is easy. The management of the company knowingly assigned an unqualified person as the security official to oversee security and privacy. Enough said.

The HIPAA Consultants

This is a sore point because we, as consultants, fall into this category. We can identify with the fictitious consultants due to the fact that we have been in similar situations. Though the consultants conducted the assessment according to the HIPAA guidelines, they certainly did not uphold the spirit of the law in their review. What could have been done? There really is not much recourse. Our solution was to write a book instead of standing by and continuing to participate in the con.

Good Old Bob Smith

Come on, Bob knows that he is not qualified to do anything toward furthering the security of the organization or protect the PHI of the customers. He went along because he was told to do so.

The Consumer

Yes, we are also adding our community at large. Though consumers could be construed to be the victim in all of this, they have a part in perpetuating the con—they blindly accept what they are told in the HIPAA privacy notifications that they receive in the mail. That is if they even read it.

This is a simple example that we made ludicrous to illustrate a point. Though it is unlikely that a company would assign this responsibility to a janitor, we have seen a number of examples where it was given to an individual not even close to qualified by background or training. This behavior is not unusual. Actually, we would consider it to be the norm, specifically when dealing with smaller organizations. The medical company in our example was merely attempting to fulfill a requirement that incurs expenses without any corresponding revenue generation.

The security con, in this particular case, could be considered a defensive measure to something that was mandated. This was identified as a small organization that did not necessarily have the resources to accommodate the requirement. This is often the case, when an organization needs to achieve compliance in an area of security, but lacks the ability to achieve the objective. It is doubtful that anyone within the medical company felt that they were committing fraud.

Many of these decisions occur in the normal course of business and in our experience the meetings surrounding these topics are generally geared to addressing the issue. These are not malicious acts perpetrated by evil people; rather, they are regular folks who are just trying to get a job done like the rest of us. The problem is that whether it is intentional or not, the results are the same: the security posture of the organization was not improved, yet an illusion of security was created instead.

We in the security community have been given a "free" pass to participate in the con, though we should know better. Of all of the participants in the con, we are the ones who should have the best perspective on how to avoid this circumstance.

After many years of development, the security profession is beginning to understand what needs to be done in order to attain real security progress versus what is purported by most organizations. We should understand the ramifications of participation and the potential risks that these situations expose. That said, we understand the challenges that we all face in security.

The domain of organizational security is still developing. It lacks strong definitions, and is highly influenced by issues that are difficult to measure and control (constraints). This is leading to a professional, ethical, and moral dilemma for our profession. On one hand, we are getting smarter about what truly needs to be accomplished in order to achieve true security. On the other hand, we have mounting constraints and pressures that are encouraging us to perpetuate the con. Our goal with this book is to increase your awareness of the constraints, and in doing so, reduce their effect and power to hinder your security efforts.

Conclusion

Within this chapter, we have established the issues and challenges associated with achieving true security within an organization. Further, we have introduced the factors that are allowing organizations to "con" themselves into believing that they have achieved their security objectives. Lastly, we have identified the basic sociological constraints, common to most organizations, which are at the heart of this dysfunctional behavior, thus enabling the persistence of the con.

Now that we have whetted your interests and created a foundation to provide some context to support your understanding of the issues at hand, we must create a tangible baseline in order to add clarity and substance. The baseline we are going to introduce is our definition of "true security." It is only fair considering that we have spent the bulk of this chapter presenting the dangers of leaving security concepts in an undefined state. Therefore, in order to really get us moving, we will now focus on defining "true security." We think that this definition is so important that we have dedicated the entire next chapter to its exploration. After all, how can anyone achieve it if no one knows what it is? With a thorough understanding of true security, we will then move on to an in-depth analysis of each of the major elements that can affect your attainment of this state (the security constraints). You will notice, as we leave this chapter and move forward, a gradual shift from trying to illustrate the problems to how we can all start to solve them. We promised you we would get there.

Chapter 2

True Security Model

True Security

Up to this point we have used the term "true security" freely within the book to help support some of the foundation concepts we have introduced thus far. Our goal was to support the concepts we have presented while not bombarding the reader with too many concepts at a time. With that said, we also spent a large portion of the last chapter talking about the dangers of not providing definitions around security concepts. After all, if you do a Google™ search on the term "true security," you will see varying topics presented ranging from approaches to social security to achieving energy independence. So, the time has come for us to take our own advice and provide our definition of true security. We think it is important to get us all on the same page since your perception of true security may or may not coincide with ours. So, what is true security?

Our definition of true security is the idea that all of the necessary elements to secure an organization are present, balanced, and as free as possible from the constraints introduced in Chapter 1. We are not saying that this state eliminates every risk or threat from an organization; we would probably label that as "uber security" or "absolute security." What we are saying is that organizations that have achieved true security have a healthy and functional mechanism to identify, rate, prioritize, and manage risks in an orderly and effective manner. Think of it as the antithesis of Bruce Schneier's concept of "security theater" where instead the intent of all activity is to be productive in addressing and reducing security risk.

The key to identifying true security is in recognizing that it possesses both tangible and intangible components. In our first book, we discussed how to methodically develop the tangible pieces. As such, that book was easier to write (as easy as

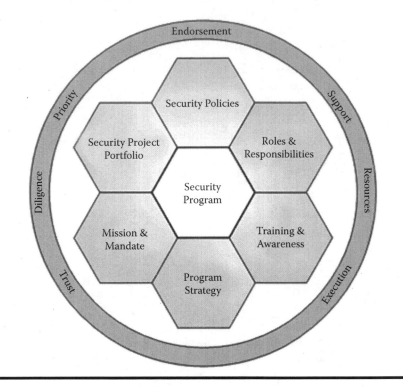

Figure 2.1 This figure overlays the intangible components of the True Security Model with the necessary elements of a security program.

a book can be to write). Other references, such as ISO27001-2 and NIST, have also described the tangible elements of a security effort. However, each of these frameworks has overlooked something that we feel is just as important, the intangible aspects of developing a sound security effort. This would include presenting a viable model for accurately measuring and predicting the most random elements in any organization: the sociological actions of people. This is an easy issue to overlook since they are intangible! Since the focus of this book is helping you cope with some of these softer elements, we believe now is as good a time as any to introduce this model. So, what does it take to attain true security? Figure 2.1 overlays the intangible components of the True Security Model with the necessary elements of a security program.

Part I—The Tangible Elements of True Security

The tangible aspects of true security are the six required elements of a security program outlined within the National Institute of Standards and Technology (NIST), the International Organization for Standardization (ISO), etc. We gave a quick review of them in Chapter 1; however, they are important and have a strong bearing on this topic so we will provide a quick refresher. The six essential elements are:

1. Security strategy
2. Mission and mandate (M&M)
3. Roles and responsibilities
4. Security policies
5. Training and awareness
6. Security risk project portfolio

We admit that it is simple to list the six items, but it takes far "more" to establish and use these tools within any organization. The "more" is what often is overlooked and certainly never measured. The "more" is what gets influenced by the constraints. The "more" in this case is the hearts and minds of the people within the organization. That certainly is a wonderful platitude, but is nevertheless true. In writing this book, we realized that the "more" would need to be quantified and modeled in order to provide a useful, consumable tool for our readers.

Part II—Modeling the Intangible Elements of True Security (The Hard Part)

The foundation for the model is a standard organizational structure for a corporation that depicts various roles ranging from the board of directors down to the average employee. These are the same type of things that you would find on any corporate organizational chart. It should be noted that our selection of a corporate organizational structure to illustrate the various groups is for demonstrative purposes only. This model will also work within nonprofit entities, government agencies, or any other type of organization that can map its management hierarchy as a vertical in the distribution of its power structure. Within each of the groups below, we have then associated the one or two "things" that are desired from each group in order to achieve a healthy and successful security effort. These items are referred to as the desired actions or behaviors we will attempt to solicit, demand, or coerce from each group.

Though we believe that there are many platitudes that pass for wisdom in security, we do agree with the statement that the most successful strategy for attaining these "things" is always to begin from the top of an organization and work your way down to the lower levels. This strategy works on the concept of social momentum.

Just as a sports team gains new fans as it becomes successful, your security efforts can also exploit this sociological phenomenon. As a viable functional security effort garners the desired items from each target group, it in turn produces more momentum and energy to attain the desired item from the subsequent group. As one victory is attained, the effects are cumulative with each subsequent group inheriting the "thing" (desired action or behavior) from the groups above it within the organization hierarchy. The following table illustrates the desired actions or behaviors ("things") that we want from each group. After introducing each behavior, we have also identified why we believe that you need each one in order to attain true security. Essentially, this represents the "what" and the "why" for the intangible elements of the model.

Organizational Group	Desired Action or Behavior
Board of directors	Endorsement
Executive management	Priority
Middle management	Resources
Supervisory management	Support
Employees	Diligence

To aid in making this more straightforward, we have included our definitions for each of the group stratifications within the model. Following that list, we have provided a listing of the desired actions we need with associated definitions. We have also provided a brief description of why we need this desired action.

Organizational Groups

Below are the definitions for each organizational group.

Board of directors: A group of individuals chosen to govern the affairs of a corporation or large entity.

Executive management: A group of individuals that represent the highest level of organizational management that have responsibility of determining the strategic direction of the organization.

Middle management: A management layer within an organization whose primary responsibilities include the development of tactical plans along with the coordination and monitoring of subordinate activities.

Supervisory management: A group of individuals within an organization who have been granted limited authority over a small group of employees. This role often resides as a layer between middle management and regular employees.

Employee: A group of individuals hired by an employer to perform a specific function for an organization.

Desired Action Definitions

Below are the definitions for each desired action, as well as why we need it for true security.

Endorsement (definition 2): "Something, such as a signature or voucher, that endorses or validates."
The American Heritage® Dictionary of the English Language, Fourth Edition

Why You Need Endorsement to Achieve True Security

The desire or need for validation at the highest level of an organization—what we refer to as "board level"—seems as though it should be obvious. But we are not interested in presenting simply the obvious.

We believe that there are three primary reasons for needing or desiring an endorsement from the highest authority within an organization. The first is the fact that security touches everything within an organization and permeates all levels of management. That makes it critical that you have the explicit approval to pursue the issue of security with the most powerful and influential group within an organization. This provides you with a skeleton key to the organization to pursue any matter regardless of your title or pay grade.

The second reason that we feel security requires an endorsement at the highest level of an organization is the issue we mentioned above: social momentum. We realize that this is a type of mandated momentum, which is never as desirable as momentum garnered through voluntary participation or true enthusiasm, but in the beginning of a security effort we will take what we can get and be thankful. The alternative is a much tougher road.

Lastly, a high-level endorsement induces a certain level of responsibility to the management of the organization. This is in part due to the reporting requirements that are generally associated with board-level management groups. These requirements are usually fairly stringent in terms of motions, actions, initiatives, and direction. This fact makes it difficult to have an endorsed initiative simply vanish from the face of the Earth because it is inconvenient, difficult, or expensive. This is important since these are traits generally associated to organizational security.

Priority (definition 1): "Precedence, especially established by order of importance or urgency."
The American Heritage® Dictionary of the English Language, Fourth Edition

Why You Need Priority to Achieve True Security

We have seen organizations where they have a virtually limitless budget available for security, but are unable to make any real progress. Upon review of hundreds of organizations, it almost always comes down to the same thing: a lack of executive level priority. Priority at this level translates directly into support and action at the subordinate levels within the organization. The challenge is that executives are constantly barraged with a multitude of issues that are competing for their attention, action, and resources. However, the all-encompassing nature of security requires the executive team to consistently focus its attention and energy for it to be successful. That is if the goal is true security.

> Resource (definition 2): "An available supply that can be drawn on when needed."
> *The American Heritage® Dictionary of the English Language, Fourth Edition*

Why You Need Resources to Achieve True Security

For the sake of this topic, we are referring to people and budget when discussing resources. It is simple: if you do not have them, little if anything gets done. We apply this "thing" to middle management because it is the group who is usually charged with the direct management and assignment of tactical duties to staff. For all intents and purposes, middle management "owns" the resource pool that we will need to borrow.

> Support (definition 7a): "To aid the cause, policy, or interests of."
> *The American Heritage® Dictionary of the English Language, Fourth Edition*

Why You Need Support to Achieve True Security

We are getting pretty low in the food chain of most organizations when discussing supervisory staff, but this by no means diminishes their importance; receiving their support is critical. They are like the noncommissioned officers in the military. These are the people who work down in the trenches with the troops dealing with the myriad of problems and issues that arise during the course of any initiative. As such, the manner in which this work is approached and the zeal with which it is accomplished can be tied directly to the level of support that this level of management has for the initiative and the overall strategy of security. Their support in clearing the way for resources to perform the necessary tasks at hand is crucial to overall security success. Lastly, these are also the people who are selecting the individual resources. Their support can be the difference between getting the right resource for the job versus any old body.

> Diligence (definition 1): "Earnest and persistent application to an undertaking; steady effort; assiduity."
> *The American Heritage® Dictionary of the English Language, Fourth Edition*

Why You Need Diligence to Achieve True Security

We have said it a thousand times, "Good security is just good design or execution." If employees carry out their daily roles with attention and care, much of the intangible elements of security can be attained.

Inheritance and the Model

We have now provided the what and the how at each level within an organization, but there is another key piece to this puzzle: the relationship and inheritance that goes on between each group. For example, if the security effort for your organization gains the "endorsement" from the board of directors, then that "support" is inherited by the next group: executive management. After gaining "priority" from executive management, we now believe that this group possesses both "endorsement and priority." Thus, each successive group continues to aggregate its own desired actions and behaviors, as well as those inherited from all the groups above it.

The Two "Step-Children" Groups of the Model

There are two groups, which we will now include in the model, that are different from the other groups, but are still integral to providing a comprehensive analysis tool. They are unique in that they do not inherit the desired actions and behaviors of any of the other groups. These are the organization's customers and consumers and the internal security office.

The amount of media exposure that security has received in the past five years has increased the awareness of the average individual. Unfortunately, most of this exposure has been negative, which does nothing more than promote fear. Fear is diametrically opposed to the desired behavior that we wish to illicit from our customers. We want them to trust us, not question our every action as a result of fear or anxiety. We want them to have confidence that we are going to handle their confidential information correctly or that we are going to ensure their personal safety when they board an airplane. And most importantly, we want them to trust us so they will buy more of our organization's goods or services. As a result, we feel that the consumer is a critical component to our model.

> Trust (definition 1): "To have or place confidence in; depend on."
> *The American Heritage® Dictionary of the English Language, Fourth Edition*

Why You Need Trust to Achieve True Security

One of the most powerful things that security can bring to an organization is to build trust in its consumers or customers. If your consumers trust you, there is a strong likelihood that they are going to buy more of your widgets. We frequently hear many in our profession utter that security is a business enabler. In many ways, we think that this idea is pure bunk (different book). But the one true area where security can be a business enabler is through the development of trust with a consumer. We believe this is something that can directly translate into revenue for an organization, thus, making it one of the few areas of security in which we can actually enable business. We look at the consumer in our model as the outsider. A group that can only be cared for by proxy since it has little, if any, direct impact on the security decisions of an organization. At least, that is what we often see in most organizations from a security perspective. It is only logical that if we include an "outsider" view, we need to add the converse view of an "insider." We felt that for the True Security Model the "insider" would be represented by the organization's security office.

Organizational Group	Desired Action or Behavior
Consumer	Trust

A consumer is a person who uses goods or services.

The security office is comprised of individuals who are tasked with the various aspects surrounding an organization's security effort. Since we are assuming that most of the people reading our book are security professionals, and more specifically probably leaders of this group, this view will enable them to evaluate their own situation, and that of their team. Hopefully, this view will enable the development of insights into how to address their own unique situation. So, what is the "thing" that we need from a security office? Execution!

> Execution (definition 2): "The act of performing; of doing something successfully; using knowledge as distinguished from merely possessing it."
> *Word Net* 3.0

Why You Need Execution to Achieve True Security

Yes, security is everyone's responsibility within an organization, but implementing the six, core, tangible elements of a security effort is usually the responsibility of a security office. In order to attain and maintain a state of true security we require this group to "execute." Without execution, there is a good chance that the six required tangible items will never materialize. Further, if they are in existence, those items will slowly wilt if they are not exercised and maintained. As such, the continued desire and ability of the security office to "execute" is a critical component.

Organizational Group	Desired Action or Behavior
Security office	Execution

Tying It All Together

We feel that these desired actions from each group are the critical items that require attention in most organizations. It is very difficult to achieve the six fundamental elements of a security program without them. The lack of one of these items at any level results in an impaired security effort. In our experience, most organizations are struggling to get the six tangible items implemented, let alone focus any energy on the intangible elements. Unfortunately though, most security programs can trace their weaknesses to a lack of one or more of these invisible "things."

Transportation Security Agency (TSA) Example

If you have taken a trip that required the use of a commercial airline flight, then you are familiar with efforts by the TSA to "secure" airline travel. We get in line, place all of our liquids in a zip lock bag, remove our shoes, and proceed to be herded across filthy floors through metal detectors prior to boarding the aircraft. Not only do we have these concentration camp procedures, but there are a number of security personnel that include TSA employees, private security, police, canine units, and in some cases soldiers from various branches of the armed services.

Though we cannot deny that these precautions improve the security of airline flights, their greatest contribution is not security, but instead the trust that they generate for travelers. Each of the controls that we described above is highly visible and personal. Are they thorough? No, we have accidently managed to get through security with a bottle of water or hand sanitizer (hand sanitizer ... the preferred addiction for the obsessive compulsive). Could the process be more effective? Of course it could. But it is very effective at achieving the primary thing we need from consumers: "trust."

We used this example because it clearly demonstrates one of the intangible components in our model: trust. If we are only looking at the tangible, we would agree that these security controls are a pain in the behind. But when you use this example within the True Security Model, it becomes apparent why these security practices become important. Can these processes be made better from a risk perspective? Absolutely! But that does not mean that the intangible element of "trust" that these processes do provide consumers should be forgotten either.

By the way, if you want a demonstration of what it looks like when consumers do lose trust, try flying at any airport on September 11th. It is almost completely empty!

Board of Directors—Security Committee Example

We have found that a typical demonstration of board endorsement is the formation of a committee to oversee the security efforts of an organization. We selected this as an example because it clearly demonstrates endorsement, involvement, and continued interest for security from the highest level of the organization. However, the objective of these groups is usually to provide oversight to ensure that the organization shows consistent progress in identifying and reducing risk. Unfortunately, we have seen very few board level security oversight committees that are actually effective in executing its primary objective. This is often attributed to the items that we discussed in Chapter 1. Specifically, most organizations are measuring the wrong things and then reporting the wrong information to these committees. You cannot blame them for making bad decisions if they are getting bad information. That said, the secondary effect of demonstrating its endorsement is far more useful to the organization in that it fosters true security.

As we have said, each of these groups plays a role in the security of any organization. But this is meant to be a general model. Your organization may not have as many structural levels to negotiate, but the desired actions or behaviors are the same. Therefore, we believe that you still need endorsement, priority, resources, support, diligence, trust, and execution for your security effort. However, it is important to keep in mind that these items may reside with one person instead of many.

Public Corporation	Private Organization	Government Agencies
Board of directors	Owner	Director
Executive management	Vice-president	Deputy director
Middle management	Manager	Station chief
Supervisory management		Section chief
Employees	Employees	Associate

If you are able to gain these actions or behaviors and combine them with the six tangible components of your security program, we believe that you have achieved true security. With this understanding of our True Security Model, we are now going to put it to work. After all, what good is a model that cannot be used?

True Security Summary

Before moving on in this chapter, let us touch on some of the important points we have covered thus far.

1. Most organizations that are developing or running a security program are focused on the six elements outlined within the major frameworks.
2. The security industry is moving toward the evaluation and measurement of the six elements outlined within the major frameworks to determine success or failure of a security program.
3. The intangible aspects of a security program are the lubricant that allows for the six elements outlined within the major frameworks to operate in a state of true security.
4. Most organizations are missing one or more intangible elements that are impairing the ability of the security program to operate effectively and have no idea why.
5. Most organizations are marketing their security efforts as wildly successful when they are not even close to achieving true security.

Using the Model

Let us continue building on the concepts from the prior section. The intangible elements of a security program that we just introduced are influenced or directly affected by the intangible security constraints. You may be saying to yourself, "What?" That's the hard part in all of this, so it deserves repeating:

The intangible elements that allow for true security are negatively impacted by the intangible influences that we have labeled as the security constraints!

That is what makes the attainment of true security such a mind bender. We are working with a bunch of invisible stuff that is getting messed up by the other invisible stuff, and are asked to report on a bunch of invisible stuff that is labeled as security (see Figure 2.2). As you may have noticed, each of the security constraints is fairly shapeless. Though we can witness their effects, directly viewing something like myopia or apathy is challenging.

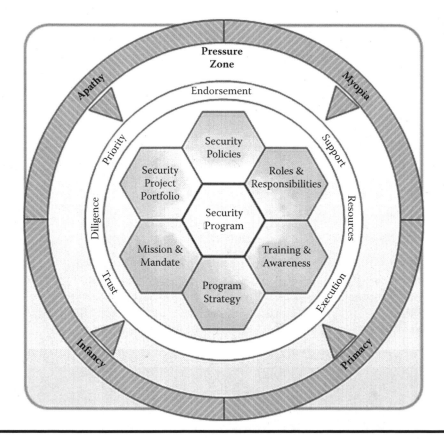

Figure 2.2   This figure illustrates how true security is pressured by the security constraints.

However, to be successful in our security efforts, we have to force ourselves to work with all this invisible stuff. This is something that most people are not necessarily accustomed to addressing in their daily work lives, at least not consciously.

That is why we needed the model. We needed a tool that would provide a controlled environment that would allow us to look at each constraint in the context of its ability to negatively impact security. The way we plan to achieve this is to take our True Security Model, assuming that we have obtained all of the required aspects of true security, and introduce one of the security constraints to one group and examine the results. From that point, we can place these reactions into context by applying systems theory and discuss the means to reduce their influence or mitigate their effects. To facilitate that approach, the next step is to familiarize you with the fundamentals of systems theory.

Introduction to Systems Theory

The tendency when discussing any concept, such as security, is to do so assuming a perfect, static state environment. We discuss issues in isolation with little thought given to the idea of component interaction (myopia). This practice is useful for simplifying complex models during their design, but is somewhat limiting when we attempt to place our designs into practice. This is where the concepts of systems theory become very useful for our purposes.

The fundamental truth of any organization is that it does not operate in a vacuum. Systems theory is an elegant means of demonstrating that fact within an easily consumable model. It clearly illustrates that each aspect of your system affects every other aspect of the system. Thus, if there is a breakdown within one part of your system, it can have a negative ripple effect throughout the entire organization!

Components of Systems Theory

We chose systems theory for two major reasons: it is highly applicable as we have already explained, but more importantly it is easy to grasp by those who do not have a Ph.D. in organizational dynamics. It is comprised of five major components, which are listed below:

1. Environment: The universe in which the system exists. The surroundings that provide stimuli to the system (e.g., information, changes in the organizational structure, customers, etc.).
2. Input: Materials to be consumed and transformed by the system (e.g., actions, behaviors, information, tools, etc.).
3. Throughput: The means by which stimuli (information and resources) are processed by the system.

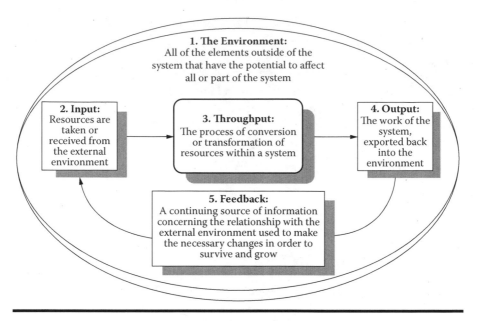

Figure 2.3   This figure demonstrates the primary components of a system and the fundamentals of systems theory.

4. Output: Everything produced by the systems (e.g., product, perception, communication, training, etc.). All perception of effectiveness in achieving mission by other members within the organization.
5. Feedback: Information from both inside and outside the organization.

These elements interact in a predictable process to form a never-ending process loop as illustrated in Figure 2.3.

Overlaying Security onto Systems Theory

At its core, applying systems theory to any organization means you must view the organization as an open system, meaning that it freely interacts with the surrounding environment. Our purpose here is for you to assess how effective your system is functioning when you objectively analyze it in terms of the True Security Model.

If you think of your organization as the ENVIRONMENT which the security program needs to affect (No. 1 in the diagram), the desired actions and behaviors from the target groups as the INPUT (No. 2 in the diagram), the security program as the SYSTEM (No. 3 in the diagram), the results of all of the security efforts as the OUTPUT (No. 4 in the diagram), and the measurement that is done regarding effectiveness of the efforts as the FEEDBACK (No. 5 in the diagram), then applying systems theory as a reference model is highly suitable to our purpose of addressing the ideal of true security.

Putting It All Together

In a perfect world, your security program (system) will receive all of the intangible inputs (endorsement, priority, resources, support, diligence, and trust) that it requires from each organizational group (board of directors, executive management, middle management, supervisory management, employees, and customers). It will consume and transform those inputs as part of the system's throughput, producing both a tangible product—mission and mandate (M&M), security policies, training and awareness, security strategy, and a risk rated project portfolio—along with a perception of effectiveness in achieving its stated mission as some of the outputs. These outputs get recycled as part of the feedback loop in the form of input.

The feedback loop can assume three potential states: positive, negative, or bipolar. In our approach to systems theory, the ideal is to achieve and maintain a positive feedback loop for a security program, meaning that we only want to feed our system the correct inputs that optimize the processing and maximize production and output. It is exactly how your body operates. If you are serious about your health, you only eat and drink foods that produce the optimal performance from your body. Using that analogy, introducing a fifth of vodka would be considered a negative input and a Screwdriver (orange juice and vodka) would be a bipolar input. The bottom line is that we want to feed our security program the best "foods," but of course that is not always realistic. Chances are we will always still get a little vodka in the mix.

If your security program operates in an environment that furnishes pure inputs, thus maximizing its throughput and output, then put down this book and go get a drink. You do not need to read any further. (If you are living there, give our best to Cinderella, the Seven Dwarfs, Dorothy, the Scarecrow, and the Tin Woodsman … no hello for the Lion, he kind of freaks us out.)

For those that are still reading, we will now proceed with explaining how the True Security Model will be applied to help us with this issue. In many situations within systems, if your inputs are flawed then your outputs will also be flawed— "garbage in, garbage out" certainly applies. Therefore, we want to focus our attention on the items that cause our system inputs to be undesirable to the development of a healthy system. We have already introduced these items. They are the villains in our tale: the security constraints.

To clarify this thought, let us take one of the inputs that we need for true security: endorsement from the board of directors. Now, let us inject one of the security constraints, such as apathy, and see what happens. If your board of directors is apathetic toward security, then your chances of getting a pure endorsement are jeopardized, thus creating a flawed input that will harm the health of your system.

So, in the upcoming chapters we will go through this exercise for each constraint and the various intangible inputs that we need for a successful security effort. The goal of this will be to get your security program system into a positive feedback cycle. We will accomplish this by using systems theory and other various tools to achieve three objectives.

The first objective will be to help identify how the constraints manifest themselves within most organizations. This will be illustrated by showing how a particular constraint can negatively affect a particular input to your security program system. The other objective will then be to show how to reduce or, in some cases, mitigate the influence of the constraint on the various security program inputs. The final objective will be to provide tools that you can use to help make changes in your actions that both aid in reducing constraints and promote your ability to achieve true security.

The primary applicability for these tools will be for the security manager, but others within a security program should also be able to attain value from them. This is made possible by a couple of items. First, any security role within an organization will be impacted by the security constraints as long as they interact within the system (organization). So, that is just about any security role you can think of. Second, we are going to provide exercises and techniques that will train you to assess your own individual situations. The focus will be on how your actions within these situations impact and are impacted by the security constraints. We are on a mission to take all of this information and present it in a manner that will allow you to make these techniques actionable within your environment.

Global Considerations When Using Systems Theory

There are some global concepts from systems theory that can be used to provide guidance in building a healthy security program system.

An effective system seeks to create homeostasis. When something changes within the system, the system will usually adapt, reestablishing a sense of stability. All systems will constantly adjust to achieve stability. However, if a system is not amenable to change or if the change is not properly controlled, resulting in too much change, the system will not be able to compensate rapidly enough creating an unstable state, the result of which is for the system to operate in a closed state.

All systems are judged based on how effectively they interact with the environment. The degree of perceived effectiveness is judged by all levels of employees, other organizations, and customers. To reiterate, the level of effectiveness (throughput and output), is judged by employees (feedback), competition (feedback), and customers (feedback). Furthermore, the resources available (input) to the organization also influence how the system interrelates with the environment.

If you are assessing aspects that are of insignificance to the concept of true security, then your system will become unstable and naturally begin to move toward chaos or ultimately death. This is a major reason why we spent the first chapter illustrating the importance of measuring the wrong things in security.

If the organization is lacking resources or the resources are disproportionately distributed, it will adversely affect the system. This will directly affect team throughput by starving the system, resulting in reduced production, and thus creating a negative feedback cycle.

Summary

In this chapter we have expanded on the concept of true security by discussing the required components and the intangible factors that promote its successful operation. Further, we introduced the model that will provide the foundation throughout the majority of the book.

Our purpose for introducing and using the True Security Model is to illustrate the effects of the security constraints on your security efforts. Using this model, combined with systems theory and other tools, we can analyze the effects of the security constraints among the various stakeholder groups. This will provide an understanding of how they inhibit our ability to elicit the desired actions or behaviors from each of them.

This chapter also is the end of the preparation material. From this point forward we will now begin to apply these concepts and tools to help you with making decisions that promote both individual success and your ability to attain a state of true security. More specifically, we will address the intangible aspects of true security and how to identify, measure, and mitigate the effects of the security constraints through your actions.

Though the constraints are intangible, they do not operate well when they are identified and understood. They are most effective when ignored and allowed to spread unhindered. Therefore, our first prescription to address this affliction is awareness and education.

The next four chapters will be dedicated to each of the four constraints. We will examine each one in depth by answering the following questions:

1. What is the cause of the constraint in humans?
2. What is the cause of the constraint in systems?
3. How does the constraint affect each of the target groups?
4. How does the constraint manifest or present itself for each of the groups?
5. How does the constraint contribute to the security con?
6. What are the strategies and techniques for mitigating the effects on each group?
7. How can you assess your own unique situation?
8. What are some practical techniques that can be used to reduce each constraint?

With that said, we will begin this adventure by taking a closer look at the security constraint that we call apathy.

Chapter 3

Apathy

"We wanted to write this chapter on apathy, but we just didn't feel like it!"

Overview—What We Are Going to Cover

Not a day goes by with any of our clients where we do not see obvious demonstrations of apathy. From people who take three-hour lunches to executives who spend the day shopping for their next golf club. Heck, we worked in one place where the executive team actually instructed the operational security team to configure the Web-filtering software to explicitly permit any Web sites related to golf. In fact, we could spend the next 50 to 100 pages presenting story after story, as we are sure you could too. So, from our point of view, it is safe to say that apathy is alive and well within public, private, and government related entities across the globe.

Just like the stories we mentioned above, apathetic behavior often presents itself in some very humorous ways. But, it is important to note that while many of these situations make you laugh, they still often have real consequences within most organizations. As a result, the goal of this chapter is to explore the causes of apathy, its effects, and some solutions for preventing it from impacting your organization's system and security.

The chapter will begin with a look at some of the causes of human apathy. Since apathy is a behavior, we will start at the source: perception of human behavior. This section will look at the root causes of apathy in humans and whether this behavior is something we are born with or something that we learn. From there, we will widen the focus and examine the causes of apathy from a system view perspective. The causes section of the chapter will conclude with a look at the common causes of apathy within organizations and then within an organizational security program (we have not forgotten that this is a security book). After looking specifically at causes, we will move on to the cause and effect relationship between apathy and our True Security Model. This area will detail how apathy is caused within the various organizational groups that we require support from within the True Security Model. This information will focus on tangible impacts that we have all faced at one time or another in our quest for true security. With the causes and effects of apathy clearly identified, we have a perfect lead to explore some tangible solutions. This section will present strategic and tactical items that will serve as a personal guide for both alleviating the impacts of apathy and attaining true security.

As you can see, we have a fairly ambitious agenda in this chapter and a lot of ground to cover, so let's get started. We will begin with a look at the causes of apathy in humans.

Causes

Causes of Apathy in Humans

Before we started writing this book, if you asked us—the security folks Ron and Mike—what causes apathy, our answer would have been very simple: "Some people are just born with a drive to be productive, while others are not." It is just that easy. Boy, were we wrong on this one! It sure is a good thing we have our co-author, Skye, to ensure we continue to stick to what we do best, which is security, and leave the sociological elements to her. We are going to let her handle the next sections, which fall within her realm of expertise. Run with it, Skye! So, what causes apathy in humans?

In order to answer this question, we must look to research within the realm of psychology. Since the primary composition of most organizations is made up of humans, it is imperative that we look at the human behaviors (the good, bad, and apathetically ugly) that profoundly determine the success or failure of any organization. The root of the word *apathy* is derived from a Greek word literally meaning "without feeling."

When dealing with human emotions, or lack thereof, the most important thing to remember is that communication behaviors are learned. Depending on the role models we had as a child, coupled with formal education and life experiences, will determine the multiplicity and complexity of human emotions. Although some might argue that parts of our personality are predisposed, there is no research to support that theory and this is not the venue to argue the nurture versus nature debate. However, the moment we are born (and some would argue even sooner) humans are actively responding to stimuli from the environment. So, if human behavior is learned or a result of adaptation to the environment, then it is fair to say that some of us had better teachers growing up than others. We must factor in education, life experience, cognitive complexity, culture, economics, age, etc.; in short, diversity in behaviors is enormous.

This does not mean that there are not some strong innate influencers in humans that lead to apathetic behavior. Most influencers have to do with the levels of power that are felt by individuals within various situations and how they react to those associations. One of the primary means by which humans establish their level of power within a situation is through the manner in which they communicate. In his book, *Pragmatics of Human Communication*, Paul Watzlawick (1968) suggests that all communications between humans contain both a content and relational component within each message. The content component represents the literal meaning of the message, while the relational component defines the nature of the relationship between the people communicating. Let us consider an example of a high-level executive telling a middle-management employee that she needs to get her team ready for an inspection this week. The content component of that message is just to "get your team ready for inspection this week." The relational component is often unspoken, but the message is heard loud and clear: "I have the authority to tell you to prepare your team for inspection." It is within this level of metacommunication that power dimensions are defined. This is important when discussing apathy in that a subservient position is one of reduced power within the relationship. If that level of powerlessness exceeds the individual's threshold for caring, the result could be apathy.

Of all the influences that cause apathy, most importantly apathy is influenced greatly by an individual's attitude and response toward change. Change is another stimulator of feelings of being helpless or powerless, which in turn is a catalyst for apathetic behavior, creating a self-sustaining downward spiral.

Another common cause of apathy in humans is the individual's perception of futility toward tasking. If someone feels that his or her work is dull or meaningless (e.g., busy work or impossible objectives) he or she is more likely to become apathetic when accomplishing it. These feelings encourage emotional withdrawal from the situation, including an overall lack of interest or ownership.

To summarize, humans are more likely to become apathetic if:

1. They perceive their required tasking as futile, meaningless, or dull.
2. They feel helpless or powerless regarding a specific situation.
3. There is too much change too fast.

Sweet, we are safe! Everybody knows that organizations are static (like the world is flat), so we do not need to worry about change. All that new technology, the emergence of the global economy, and the changing threat landscape … hey, wait a second … yikes! Maybe we do need to consider that organizations are constantly influenced by external factors that require adaptation or change.

Whoops! It would appear that we need a little more information regarding apathy, but this time, we need to direct our background information of the causes of apathy within a system. Again, we will call on our expert, Skye, to provide a primer on the subject.

Causes of Apathy within a System

As we discussed earlier, a system processes input, produces output, and receives feedback from the environment as an input for the next cycle. A healthy, open system will adapt to positive and negative feedback

and modify or change its method or means of processing throughput in order to maintain a stable environment
(homeostasis). This processing of change by system components (humans) within the system (the organization)
feeds into the basic nature of human beings to become
apathetic in the face of change.

Another cause of apathy within a system can be
attributed to the effects of the wholeness that every system represents. Within an organization, this wholeness
causes each organizational member to be interdepen-
dently related to every other member. The members at
the bottom of the organization make the folks at the top
look good, or vice versa—they are mutually dependent
on one another. This effect leads to the realization that
the sum of the whole is greater than the sum of the individual parts. In systems theory, this concept is known as
"nonsummativity."

Another aspect of systems theory that must be considered when evaluating apathy is the idea of synergy.
Though the term "synergy" has been brutally abused by
most people within organizations over the years, it is a
very powerful concept when used properly.

Synergy incorporates the interaction of two or more
agents or forces (energy) so that their combined effect is
greater than the sum of their individual effect. For example, two people working together will create more output
than each of them will when working independently.

When thinking about this definition, it becomes
apparent that there is a synergistic nature to organizations, which further supports the idea of wholeness and
nonsummativity within systems. Synergy can be either
positive or negative. Using apathy as our constraint is
akin to negative synergy. Apathy is a human emotion
and emotions are contagious. For example, if someone
smiles at you or is jovial, you too tend to feel lighter and
more pleasant. Conversely, if someone is continuously
grouchy or negative, you too tend to feel less than pleasant, and might even unintentionally pass that behavior
forward. This phenomenon happens subtly, to the point
where you might not even be aware of that interchange
or "transfer of attitude." The negative transfer of attitude
can have profound effects on a system.

> If you consider that one social loafer or apathetic employee (perceived or real) can stonewall an organization's ability to adapt to change, begin to multiply that number and you can begin to understand the profound effects negative synergy has on a system. This phenomenon within a system could be considered as perceived or real resistance to change, which ultimately moves the system toward the closed side of the continuum, leading the system to ultimate chaos and death.

Are we mistaken or did we just read about the concept of synergy in one of our books. You see, we have a list of banned words and "synergy" has definitely been near the top of the list. Words or phrases such as "holistic," "defense-in-depth," "security as a business enabler," and "convergence" are often brutally overused or applied incorrectly, usually by the consulting community first, then by marketing, and then by all the go-along folks. Therefore, in our circles, these terms have been strictly prohibited for speaking, writing, and general use.

In order to use the word "synergy" in this book, we had to hold an emergency tribunal where many beers were consumed and much debate was had. Eventually, we got bored with the topic and gave the word "synergy" a weekend pass to appear in this book … but only a couple of times.

Before moving on, let's have a quick recap. So far, we have addressed some of the causes of apathy in humans and have reviewed the primary driver of apathy within systems. Of course, this cursory information should serve us well as we move forward in this book, but we highly recommend that if you are interested you take a further look on your own at these concepts. There are volumes of research on both of these items waiting for you to explore. With that said, we now need to redirect the conversation toward the causes of apathy within a typical organization.

We have just learned that change is a major catalyst in the development of apathy, and the manner in which that change is managed determines the propensity toward apathy. It seems logical to next look at the various forms of management structures to examine how change is likely to occur and be managed. We plan on accomplishing this using a cultural archetype model.

Causes of Apathy within an Organization

A cultural archetype model is a simple linear progression that demonstrates all of the various types of cultures that are possible. An example of an archetype model would be one that illustrates a person's politics: conservatives to the far right and

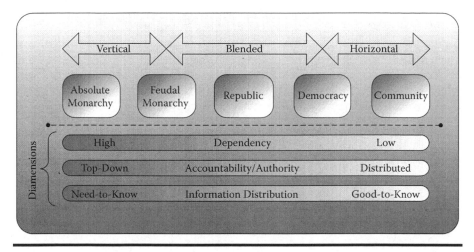

Figure 3.1 This figure is a continuum of cultural archetypes that can be used to model the culture of an organization.

liberals to the far left. But in this case, the model that best suits our needs is one that demonstrates governance or power distribution within an organization. Figure 3.1 is a continuum of cultural archetypes that can be used to model the culture of an organization.

Our continuum stretches from an authoritarian organization on the far left to a purely communal organization on the right, or another way of looking at it is a purely vertical power structure on the left that gradually moves to a pure horizontal power structure on the right. The authoritarian organization is denoted by a purely vertical power structure with absolute power resting at the top with graduated levels of diminished power below it. A prime example of a pure authoritarian model would be a dictatorship. Dictators wield absolute power and loan small amounts to those around them maintaining power by trusting few and closely monitoring those who use it. Power in this type of arrangement is generally derived by one's proximity to the dictator, not necessarily according to one's "rank." Where the authoritarian model is purely vertical, the communal model, in its purest form, is a completely horizontal example of an organizational structure.

Figure 3.2 illustrates something that should be of no surprise to anyone. Most people do not like their management and it is no wonder that apathy is on the rise.

In the communal model, power is distributed horizontally across the organization. The idea is that those with the greatest stake in the success for an area are those that are closest to it. This idea is best exemplified by the hippie communes in the late 1960s. The idea was to live in harmony with the environment and your fellow man. The means by which they attempted to accomplish this objective was the elimination of any hierarchy and basing their self-governance on the group as a whole. Their intent was to eliminate competition, share everything, and allow

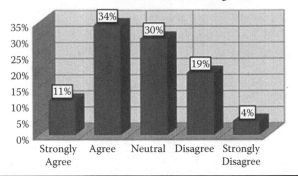

Figure 3.2   Figure 3.2 illustrates something that should be of no surprise to anyone. Most people do not like their management and it is no wonder that apathy is on the rise.

everyone to benefit and participate in all aspects of the community. All decisions were made on a consensus basis allowing everyone an equal voice in the decision-making process.

Hopefully, we have provided you with a visual representation that will resonate: Adolph Hitler on the left with his fascist regime and those whacky, peace-loving hippies of the 1960s with their attempt at the utopian society through communal living on the right. These two extremes will represent the boundaries of our organizational model. And though we understand that this is a far more complicated topic, these simple examples will do nicely for our discussion. Now let's combine our newfound knowledge of sociological theory with the organizational model to illustrate how the culture can produce apathy.

Positives Aspects to the Extreme Cultural Archetypes

As with most things in this world, the various organizational archetypes that inhabit the continuum have positive and negative aspects associated with them. The phrase "Your greatest strength is also your greatest weakness" is also applicable when discussing organizational archetypes. Since we are going to be focusing on the negative aspects that are created by the extremes of the continuum, we felt that it was only fair to address some of the positives that can be achieved through their use. First, we will address some positive aspects of an authoritarian model.

Authoritarian models can be incredibly efficient due to the centralization of power and control. The direction and focus of the organization can be altered very quickly. This creates the potential for a very nimble and agile organization that can achieve tremendous objectives.

On the communal side of the fence there are also some positives that can be derived. Specifically, since the model is collaborative, the final work product is often based on the ideas and input of many, not just the perspective of one person. This model also fosters communication amongst the group, which can strengthen the relationship of the members. This level of involvement can foster a sense of personal ownership and responsibility for the overall success of the organization.

As you can see, both extremes of the continuum have the potential to influence an organization in a positive manner; however, these positive aspects are only possible if these models are carefully tended and managed. The reason for this is that both models in extremes tend to marginalize the individual. Without careful management, both will exhibit entropic effects on the participants, one of which is apathy.

The Authoritarian Model and Apathy

We will begin with the far left of the spectrum with the authoritarian model. The roots of apathy in this model are based on the perceived lack of power that an individual feels when functioning within this structure. It is not much of a stretch to imagine that if an organization employs a purely authoritarian model, very few within the organization will actually have any power. If you recall what we said earlier, feeling powerless is a fundamental factor in the creation of apathy in humans. Therefore, within a pure authoritarian model, apathy is inevitable without the introduction of corrective factors. Feelings of apathy are magnified when the environment is perceived to be abusive or hostile to the individual. In these situations, work is performed as a type of malicious compliance by the workforce. People will work, but there is no sense of ownership, resulting in a nominal work product: no more, no less, just the bare minimum to get by. This often results in mediocrity as the norm within these organizations. This sense of impotency over any aspect of the work environment is where apathy spawns, grows, and ultimately is passed on to others. Wow! The authoritarian model does not sound like much fun. Maybe our buddies the hippies have the right idea: peace, love, and no child left behind.

The Communal Model and Apathy

When we refer to communal living we are actually discussing communism. We chose not to call it communism because we felt that most of our readers are old enough to mistake the old Soviet Union as an example of communism. Though it had aspects of communism, the Soviet Union was a socialist government (a fairly twisted variety at that). For our conversation, we are strictly addressing the organization where everyone is an equal, with equal power in determining the goals and direction of the entity. Boy that sounds great, doesn't it? In theory, this may sound like a swell idea. But, the reality of these entities is very different. As we discussed above, this model relies on consensus governance. One of the traits of this approach is speed or lack of speed.

The communal model within an organization is generally as graceful and agile as an aircraft carrier attempting to make a 180-degree course change (it takes miles). This slowness can easily be perceived by the participants as an inability on their part to meet objectives or make a difference. Their work and environment takes on the air of a futile exercise. After all, in order to effect real change in these types of entities, it takes the blessing of many individuals that have their own agendas and views. Prolonged exposure to the perceived futility of these situations is the breeding ground for apathy.

Now your organization probably has elements of both an authoritarian and communal model and falls somewhere in the middle demonstrating traits from both sides. However, in order to address the potential causes of apathy within your own environment, it is necessary to identify which associated traits are applicable for your organization. We will leave this section with a couple of common symptoms that each model produces to help you with the identification of your own situation.

Symptoms of an Authoritarian Model in Organizations

The symptoms are as follows:

- Very few people within the organization can actually make a decision.
- The few that can make decisions are treated with reverence and fear.
- People are viewed as successful within an organization based on their relationship or proximity to the decision makers.
- The culture promotes a "go along to get along" attitude.
- There are understood and implied penalties for any contrary attitudes.
- All communication is politically correct; dissenting and contrary ideas are silenced.
- There are negative consequences for those unwilling to conform.

Symptoms of a Communal Model in Organizations

The symptoms are as follows:

- Everything is done by a committee.
- Everything takes a very long time to get done.
- The majority of your schedule is allocated to attending meetings.
- You can never find an available conference room.
- The focus of meetings is more on who is invited to it versus actual content.
- A large portion of time is spent consensus building or "politicking."
- Dissenting or contrary views are encouraged but often ignored.

Additional Factors That Promote Apathy within Organizations

We introduced the organizational continuum to provide a frame of reference for discussing the primary contributors to apathy. The culture of your organization can be one of the most powerful generators of apathy, but it is not the only one. Any environment, practices, or events that marginalize the individual or impact communication creates an atmosphere that is ripe for the proliferation of apathy.

With that said, we will leave you with some other contributing factors that can lead to apathetic behavior.

■ Rapid change in the success or failure of an organization
■ Constant reorganization
■ Lack of recognition (tangible and intangible)
■ A lack of understanding the "why" surrounding circumstances or direction
■ Monotony
■ Lack of challenge or stimulation; boredom
■ Lack of cognitive complexity in understanding the mission of the organization
■ Too many tasks; not enough time, or unequal workload (perceived or real)
■ Lack of resources or budget cuts
■ Ineffective leadership styles

Causes of Apathy within a Security Program

Whew! We made it. We know that we took time discussing the various causes of apathy. We apologize, but this is complicated stuff that we are trying to present in a simple, understandable format. First, we looked at the causes of apathy in humans, then systems, and finally organizations. We did this because any security program is a system, it is populated by humans, and it operates within some type of organization. As a result, any such security program or effort will be susceptible to falling victim to apathy—and all of the negative consequences therein—that we have discussed thus far.

Of course, we still haven't forgotten that this is a security book, so we would be remiss if we did not identify some other specific causes of apathy that are produced directly by the actions of the security program itself. These items do not only contribute to overall organizational apathy, but they can also cause apathetic reactions specific to the implementation, compliance, and support of your security efforts. The most common cause of apathy within an organization is when the members of the security program fail to consider the powerful effect that the culture of the organization has on the success or failure of their efforts.

Methods or behaviors that are deemed as acceptable or tolerable within one organization may be viewed as oppressive or excessive within another. For example, the culture at a defense contracting firm is often going to be different than that of an ice cream maker. In fact, even between two organizations in the same industry, there is likely to be two distinctly different cultures. Perhaps this is easier for us to see because we work in many different organizations throughout a given year. This variance is a source of continuing fascination for us. It has almost become a hobby (we really need to get a life!). But the variances in the cultural elements of an organization, and how they are demonstrated, can be the difference between success and failure for a security program.

To give you an example, we once worked in a very powerful organization where we could not ride the elevator with the company founder. In most situations, even direct eye contact was discouraged. Actually, only a select few could get anywhere near this guy. He was always surrounded by bodyguards and barely visible. We used to joke (yes, consultants do make jokes) that he had actually been dead for several years. It was actually a corporate version of *Weekend at Bernie's*. In the grand scheme of things, this was not a big deal, but it spoke volumes about the culture of this organization (hint: authoritarian as they come). Though it is fairly obvious that a security program should heavily consider the culture of the organization during design and development, this crucial step is often missed. In the prior example of the highly authoritarian model, the security program was never built to support such an archetype by any of the security managers that led it. As a result, each subsequent security officer—and there were many—failed to significantly manage the security risk of the organization and win the hearts of the employees, not from a lack of skill or through implementing any flawed models, but instead by addressing security issues in a manner that is not acceptable in that environment.

The effects of this missing step often include the development of a security program that is misunderstood by the rest of the organization. For example, implementing a police-force style approach in an organization that is very communal will often lead to confusion and communication difficulties by those outside of security. This occurs because the employees outside of the security program are conditioned to use consensus to find solutions, while a police-force style approach by security is often just a "no" without any further dialog. In a real-world example, it is like trying to provide a long explanation about why you were speeding after you have been pulled over by a police officer. In our experience, the police officer is often not very interested in going through a consensus building exercise to work through the speeding issue. It is more, "Do you know how fast you were going?", your quick response, and then "Here is your ticket, have a nice day." The way in which you feel in that situation (powerless) after you are driving away with that ticket in your hand is the same way that employees in a communal model feel when you use a police-force style approach in your security efforts. It just does not feel very good at all. These situations are direct contributors to our good old friend, apathy. This seems like an appropriate segue for discussing the perceived personality of your security efforts.

Security Personality Model

You see, every security program has a personality. It is usually determined by the mission and mandate (M&M) of the organization, combined with the security experience of the security officer and other team members, and lastly their individual definitions of security.

The reason we raise this concept here is because we have learned over the years that the personality of a security program can be summed up by others outside of security in a couple of words. In fact, we have tested this idea on many occasions. When you ask people for their perceptions of a specific security program, you often get answers like "big brother," "department of no," "dead men walking" (this one is usually used right before a security reorganization by the business), or the "hack force." People can be quite inventive and we highly recommend that you find out the terms that have been bestowed upon your security program; they are generally worth a good laugh and can teach you volumes about how you are viewed. We also should mention that there are times when the perception or terms used are positive, but in our experience they are generally not as exciting. We guess the positives are just not as funny, so they do not get as much attention. By the way, if you have no idea what yours is, it is most likely a really good one. As you can see, there are positives and negatives to the perceptions that are created by each personality type. This is important to recognize because once an overall perception is formed by those outside of a security program, it will often influence your security efforts and the production of apathy. In addition, this perception is not limited to one person. It is often spread and assigned to everyone associated within the security program, regardless of their true individual personalities. Essentially, perception becomes a self-fulfilling prophecy. More importantly, those within the security program often do not take the time to understand their own personality, which can make the problem even worse.

In order to package this concept, we have come up with ... drum roll, please ... that's right, another range of archetypes. It begins with a look at where most security professionals come from, since this often highly influences the personality of the program that will be perceived by those outside of it. We have found that most security professionals come from one of five backgrounds:

- Military or paramilitary—Individuals with a background in the military or police.
- Technology—Individuals with a background in information technologies, generally network engineering.
- Audit—Individuals with a background in compliance or review.
- The businessperson—Individuals who often have limited experience in security, but are experts within the actual business of the organization. For example, in a hospital, a doctor who becomes the chief information security officer (CISO) or someone in an accounting firm who is actually an accountant.

- ■ The randoms—Individuals who were given some type of security responsibility that have no experience within the discipline and are not experts in the business, usually with a horizontal move from another position within the organization. (These are usually the same guys or gals who were working on Y2K projects in the 1990s.)

As we mentioned, each person will come to the security program with his or her own ideas, feelings, and most importantly, a definition of security. Generally speaking, individuals with a military or law enforcement background tend to focus on compliance, while individuals from the audit world will focus on verification. These ideas and practices are what your security program demonstrates to the rest of the organization, forming the overall perception or personality. With that understanding, let us take a closer look at the different types of professionals who inhabit a security program and the different ways by which they contribute to security apathy.

The Architect

This is generally a person who has gone up through the ranks as an information technology engineer. He or she tends to be solutions oriented in the approach to security. Each new issue is nothing more than a puzzle for which an answer must be found. This group has the potential for generating apathy due to the types and amount of change that it generates for an organization. The architect is there to architect, as a result the majority of what he or she touches will produce change to either something that exists and needs a retrofit or a new item being created from scratch that will change an existing environment.

The Cop

This is generally an individual who has a background in some type of law enforcement or comes from a highly controlled and structured environment. The cop tends to be compliance oriented focusing on conformity issues. An example is the self-proclaimed "security hall monitors" who pride themselves on their intolerance or inflexibility when addressing security matters. This group can produce apathy by making those outside of security feel powerless.

The Auditor

This is generally a person whose roots began in the world of accounting or the Big-X consultancies. The auditor's interest and focus tend to be on detective control sets that allow him or her to verify compliance or lack of compliance to security policies and protocols. Similar to the cop, these folks make people feel powerless.

The Hacker

Don't let the name fool you, we are not talking about software hackers. We are talking about the ultimate devil's advocate, capable of providing details on how to break any design. These are the folks that can find fault with anything. This is not necessarily a bad thing, but it does pose a limitation when the objective is to develop a solution. The manner in which this group generates apathy is through perceived negativism. Without a countering influence, these individuals can create feelings of futility or aggravation which are precursors to apathy.

The Policy-Wog

The moniker is not very flattering, but this is an incredibly valuable role. These are the folks who are capable of developing, interpreting, and articulating the security policies of the organization. Though this group can be incredibly helpful to most areas of the organization, its focus on policy development and interpretation can be incredibly dull to others. Lack of interest equals apathy.

The Businessperson

This person generally helps reduce apathy in those outside of the security program, but often generates it in those within the security program. Apathy is reduced within the business because these people have the same skills as most of the people for which they are engaging, so they become someone with which the business can relate. At the same time, the businessperson may struggle to gain credibility with those inside the security program due to an often limited security expertise and ability to speak the same language as the team, thus leading to apathy.

The Random

This person does not have a background in security, yet has been given the helm for commanding security efforts. These folks struggle for credibility within the organization due to their lack of security experience. The perception may or may not be legitimate, but regardless of the truth the damage is already done. The failure to inspire others and establish credibility in the security space can have a detrimental effect in motivating people within the organization, resulting in apathy toward security.

Before you jump on your computer and start composing your "flame mail" about these categories, please keep in mind that they are stereotypes; most people will be a composite of these various types. However, where the individuals will generally be composites, the security organization will not be. It will be viewed as one distinct type.

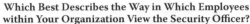

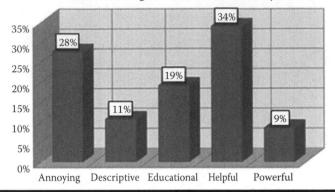

Figure 3.3

Figure 3.3 is great. Just as many people within an organization who hate us as security professionals think we add value. Even more depressing, almost no one believes we are powerful even though security affects most of what goes on within an organization. Weak and hated … awesome!

Exercise 8

The following exercise can also be found within the Appendix.

Objective

The objective of this exercise is to evaluate how the actions of the security team are contributing to apathy within your environment.

Exercise

Ask at least ten people for their perceptions of your security office. Present the question in a format that allows for open-ended answers versus closed questions.

Considerations

- Informal settings work best for "off-the-record" conversations.
- Always make the answers anonymous (do not e-mail them out) and without repercussion. In other words, make it safe to tell the truth.
- Be creative in your presentation, such as asking for a metaphor that best describes perceptions of the security office.

■ Honesty breeds honesty. Be up-front with them and you will have a greater chance of getting honest useful feedback.

Examples

■ When you think of security, what is the first thing that comes to mind?
■ When you think of the security team at our organization, what is the first thing that you think of?

In conclusion, there are positives and negatives to the perceptions that are created by each personality type. This is important to recognize because once an overall perception is formed by those outside of your security program, it will often influence your security efforts and the production of apathy. Even worse, this perception is often assigned to everyone associated within the security program, regardless of their true individual personalities. This can be dangerous, particularly when this perception is negative.

Now that we have taken a look at the security personality model, we will move on to another generator of apathy: the imbalance of accountability and authority. Never a dull moment in these security books, huh?

Equilibrium of Accountability and Authority

One of the other factors that can cause apathy toward security is an imbalance between the security program's authority and accountability. This is a simple concept that states that the authority of the security program should be commensurate with that for which it is accountable. On many occasions we have worked with organizations where the CISO reports at a supervisor or manager level within the management hierarchy, but has been tasked with the security posture for the entire enterprise. Well, we hate to say it, but chances are that the CISO's level of authority is not nearly sufficient to accomplish, let alone influence, a mission of that magnitude. In this case, the feelings of impotence take hold and produce a level of apathetic behavior within the security organization. Now there are instances where the authority exceeds responsibility; they are rare, but they do exist.

Imagine if you had the authority to mandate the means by which security would be undertaken throughout the organization without any responsibility for the outcome. Ah! If life was only so simple. But, even this "idyllic" situation has a catch and it comes in the form of apathy. The natural tendency is to exercise authority when it is given, especially if your task is as daunting as security for the entire organization. The exercising of that power, without the corresponding level of accountability, often creates a big-brother environment. In this situation, the security program is not a partner with "some skin in the game," instead it has now become "the man!" This simple maneuver has just

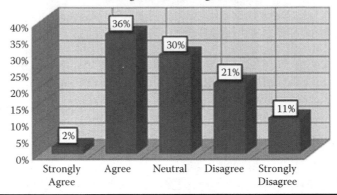

The Members of the Security Team Are Viewed as Authority
Figures in Our Organization

Figure 3.4 **The most popular answer in Figure 3.4 is that security is viewed as an authority figure (36 percent). This is interesting considering that in earlier questions respondents also suggested that most security programs are not viewed as powerful. No wonder why we are having problems, we are viewed as police officers that do not have enough power to make an arrest.**

created an authoritarian model within the organization with all of its pitfalls and sociological implications.

As a result of both of these extremes, we always strive to achieve equilibrium between authority and accountability when designing a security program. Another correlation that is important when addressing apathy for your security program is the balance between the security professional's skills and the position of interaction with the organization.

The most popular answer in Figure 3.4 is that security is viewed as an authority figure (36 percent). This is interesting considering that in earlier questions respondents also suggested that most security programs are not viewed as powerful. No wonder why we are having problems, we are viewed as police officers that do not have enough power to make an arrest.

Security Interaction Points within an Organization

In our first book, *The CISO Handbook*, we discussed a model known as the "security pipeline." This security model described the various points of interaction in which a security program can engage within an organization. It is simply the various places and times that provide an opportunity to secure an element within the organization. To further simplify this idea, we will use the concept of an event. For our purposes, this event is neither positive nor negative, just a thing that happened.

Think of the timeline associated with this event. If you wanted to influence the event, there are three opportunities:

1. Proactive: before the event occurs
2. Adaptive: while the event is happening
3. Reactive: after the event is over

This concept is also applicable when discussing the security efforts for the organization, regardless of whether the solution is technical, sociological, or physical. The security program can influence the solution before, during, or after it is deployed.

Figure 3.5 illustrates the components of the "security pipeline" and the various tools available at each stage. The risk over time curve is considered to be exponential, meaning that the risk becomes increasingly greater once an element is introduced into the production environment. This corresponds with the increasing difficulty to reduce risk after the introduction of a new element. This enforces the idea that a proactive approach to addressing risk is preferable and more efficient.

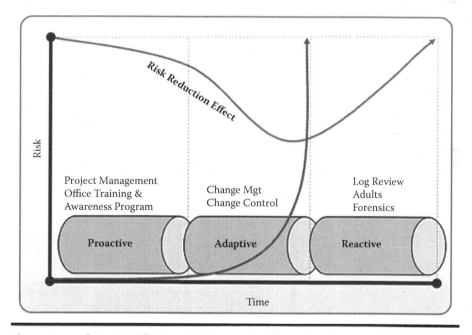

Figure 3.5   Figure 3.5 illustrates the components of the "security pipeline" and the various tools available at each stage. The risk over time curve is considered to be exponential, meaning that the risk becomes increasingly greater once an element is introduced into the production environment. This corresponds with the increasing difficulty to reduce risk after the introduction of a new element. This enforces the idea that a proactive approach to addressing risk is preferable and more efficient.

The area that the program chooses to engage needs to correspond to the mission, skills, and aptitudes of the members of the security program. For example, if your security program has chosen a proactive approach where it will participate in the design and development of "new stuff" in order to deploy secure solutions for the organization, then it will be necessary to have some architects in the group. Conversely, if the approach is to address security from a compliance standpoint, then it will be necessary for the team to have an auditor's skill set.

We raise this issue in order to illustrate a point. The approach that your security program uses must be considered when analyzing the creation of apathy. This is because the pipeline provides an opportunity for creating change, and more importantly, a sense of futility.

The model itself is meant to describe where and how security tries to influence changes within an organization. Since we have established that change is a precursor for apathy, the places in which your security program participates should be managed carefully. If it is not applied in a manner that is deemed acceptable by the organization, apathy is bound to follow. The next issue that the pipeline exposes is the need to have the proper skills and experience for the segment of the pipeline in which the security program operates.

Engaging security professionals in an area that does not match their skills, attributes, training, and temperament will lead to a frustrating experience for the individual performing the task and those attempting to utilize the service. The continued inability to meet the expectations of the function can lead to a sense of futility toward the activity; for example, asking an individual to derive a set of compensating security controls for an identity management system when his or her skills, experience, and capabilities revolve around policy development. This is likely to be a frustrating exercise for the security professionals, as well as the consumer of the security product (the engineering teams). We learned earlier that futility is one of the other precursors that trigger apathy. So, treating security resources as a generic product will lead to apathy within the team when they are put in situations for which they do not possess adequate skill. Further, it has the potential for creating apathetic behavior in individuals and groups outside of the security program through frustration and a lack of confidence.

Eating the Elephant in One Bite

We love the old adage "my eyes are bigger than my stomach" when describing someone in line at an all-you-can-eat buffet. But, it is also applicable to executive management and their ambitions for security. In many cases, the mission, associated schedules, and available resources create an impossible situation for the security program. We saw this in 2002 when the Health Insurance Portability and Accountability Act (HIPAA) started to become a reality that organizations around the United States had to address. Since the law was vague, no one was sure what constituted sufficient controls, but the projects that were initiated to achieve this mysterious unknown target bordered on the insane. We would walk into these organizations and there would be these massive initiatives and a HIPAA countdown to compliance clock on the wall. These projects were on par with the boss asking you to build and launch the space shuttle in the next five days. We mean truly unrealistic stuff. For those of you who have been around security for a long time now, nothing breaks the morale of a team faster than the "Death March" project. Why?

It is the same story as before. This type of situation creates a feeling of futility on the part of the participants. No matter how dedicated they were to the effort, unrealistic goals and objectives are crushing to the individual sense of accomplishment. Unfortunately, that seems to conflict with current management dogma: set big goals … "stretch" goals! After all, that is the mark of a leader … a visionary! We say, bah! (big raspberry at current management dogma!) It crushes the poor souls who are going to be tasked with the initiative. Pull this trick enough times and you will have a demoralized, apathetic team. By the way, you can probably sense our personal pain with this one; we have all been part of a "Death March" or two during our careers. For those of you who have not, you should count yourselves fortunate.

Missing Tangible Items of a Security Program

We know that the focus of this book is targeted on the intangible elements of your security effort, but we will take a moment to talk about the impacts that missing tangible items can play in generating apathy. It is fairly simple. If you do not have a documented M&M, security policies, project portfolio, etc., it often leads to confusion by those within the organization regarding the role of security. This confusion often manifests itself in the form of misunderstanding and miscommunication. The resulting agitation and frustration is another form of futility—futility that is felt by both your security program and the organization. Told you it was simple! Of course, correcting the situation takes a little bit more work, but that is discussed in our first book.

Communication—The "Why"

As we mentioned earlier, the majority of people within an organization seldom understand the "why" of security related procedures. This lack of understanding on their part creates an environment of malicious compliance. For example, one of our wives had come home from work and was irritated by the fact that her company had required her to change her network user credentials, again. Her irritation was compounded by the fact that the company had increased the complexity of the password and now required passwords that eliminated words found in the dictionary. Though this may seem like an obvious security measure, it created a state of malicious compliance on her part. In her eyes, she was not participating in the company's security effort, rather she was having security inflicted upon her. What was eye-opening about the whole event was when the reasoning behind this change was explained to her, her reaction changed. Her attitude went from one of frustration and irritation to "Oh, that makes sense! Why didn't they just tell us that?" We have all seen these types of turnarounds, but what was astonishing was the complete and utter acceptance and support for something that, just moments earlier, had been on par to having a root canal performed without any Novocain.

Security is a very confusing and complex subject. As such, even people within a security program struggle with how to communicate the whys, and as a result often do not even bother. One of the exercises that we do regularly within organizations is something we call policy mapping (you may have a different name for it). We accumulate every single security policy and associated statement that the organization has and begin to map it to the business requirement that is supporting it. The requirement must be associated with a need of the organization, whether it is derived from the industry, regulations, contracts, or unique attributes of the business.

For example, the statement that says "the organization must encrypt confidential data over public networks" is then associated with the business requirement that necessitated the statement. In this particular case, the requirement may have come from a federal regulation that is applicable to the organization. The objective is to determine the degree to which the policies address the needs of the organization.

All of a sudden, the why becomes very clear, reducing the resistance and hence the associated apathy toward the security measure. Where organizations run into trouble with this exercise, which is a frequent occurrence, is when they have orphan statements. These statements have often been implemented within the environment, but do not have clear business reasons to which they can be associated. We find that in these situations these environments are generally riddled with employee apathy toward security.

Causes of Apathy Section Summary

As long as there are humans and complex interrelated systems such as a security program operating within an organization (another system), some form of apathy is bound to be produced. The positive thing is that half of the battle is just recognizing the relationship between your actions and apathy. With an idea of these relationships, many mines and pitfalls associated with it can be avoided.

So, now that we have all of the causes of apathy, it seems logical that we will go ahead and start to look at some of the effects of all this apathetic behavior. We presented this material in order to aid you in the detection and diagnosis of the early symptoms associated with apathy. Now, we will direct our attention to the cause and effect relationship of apathy specific to the True Security Model. This is where we really start to peel back the onion.

Figure 3.6 is a graphical depiction of the human, system, organizational, and security program causes of apathy.

Cause and Effect of Apathy on the True Security Model

Well, we are excited because it is far easier to write about a cause and effect relationship than solely about the causes, especially when addressing all of this intangible

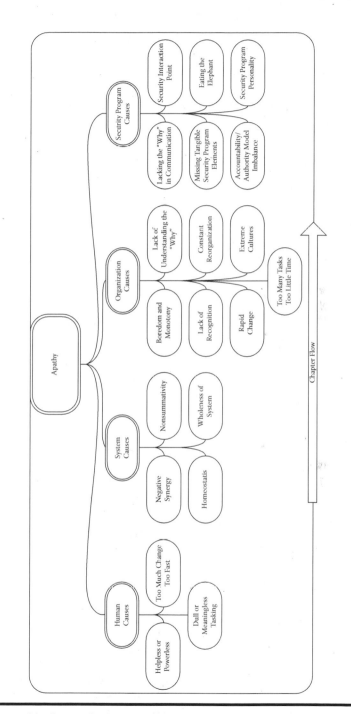

Figure 3.6   This figure depicts the human, system, organizational, and security program causes of apathy.

stuff. In fact, we have been providing various effects of the security constraints throughout this book, so you have already developed some of the context necessary for developing a deeper understanding. This stuff can still be complex though, so in this section we have made a couple of changes to the structure in order to aid you. The first modification is in our focus and approach.

We are going to direct our efforts in this section more specifically to the cause and effect of apathy on your security efforts. As a result, you are not going to see much on the overall effects of apathy on humans and systems in general. Of course, as we mentioned earlier, your security program is a system that is comprised of humans; so much of what is presented will be blended between effects that occur from apathy in humans, systems, and your security efforts. It is not intentional, but is unavoidable.

The other modification that we will be making in this section is the employment of the True Security Model that was introduced in Chapter 2. We do not introduce models merely to appear intelligent; we failed to accomplish that task many years ago. We do it in an effort to make intangible and difficult concepts easier to grasp. The effects of apathy in attaining true security are definitely intangible, so the True Security Model should serve very nicely.

Within this section, you will also see us revisit the concept of the security con. This seems to make sense since the con is the manner in which security professionals are compensating for the effects of apathy. So with these items in mind, let us get going.

Apathy and the True Security Model

In Chapter 2, we identified the various groups commonly found within an organization and the associated desired actions that we need to obtain from these groups in order to achieve true security.

As a quick refresher on the True Security Model, refer to the target groups and desired behavior table below:

Organizational Group	Desired Action or Behavior
Board of directors	Endorsement
Executive management	Priority
Middle management	Resources
Supervisory management	Support
Employees	Diligence
Consumers	Trust
Security program	Execution

For each group, we are now going to explore the cause and effect relationship that apathy can have on the desired action we need to obtain from that group. We will begin by providing some common symptoms that are displayed when apathy is present, and then we will look at some of the more intangible effects. We will also discuss the ways in which CISOs and others are compensating (security con) for the effects of apathy within the group. Of course, we will start at the top of the food chain with our pals on the board of directors.

Apathy and the Board of Directors

Apathy is often caused at the board level by either fear or a lack of interest. From a fear perspective, board members usually do not like to address the subject of security because they often do not possess an understanding of it, not even at a high level. There is nothing like fear to create anxiety and unpredictability in an executive. After all, they are in charge because of their extensive knowledge; they are smart folks. These people are experts in many other aspects of their lives. As a result, they are often most interested in items and issues which they comprehend and to which they can contribute. The result is that their level of interest, engagement, and participation in security is whatever constitutes minimal acceptable levels for that organization.

Apathy at the board level is a little bit more subtle and less pronounced than with some of the other security constraints and groups within the organization. This is the case because of the visibility and accountability that has been bestowed upon board members as of late. They are scrutinized by stockholders and just about anyone else who has an interest in the associated organization. Given some of the shenanigans that have appeared in the news recently (can you say Enron?), it is no wonder. This issue coupled with the structure and reporting mechanisms that are outlined for board meetings can make apathy a little less obvious. But don't despair, apathy is still present, alive, and thriving.

This behavior has both its pros and cons. The pro is that members of the board are unlikely to try and micromanage the security efforts for the organization. The con is that obtaining a meaningful endorsement from the board is much harder to attain.

Board members are generally unwilling to mandate or wholeheartedly endorse something unless they fully understand the subject or understand the organization's need for it. Apathy toward security creates a barrier to developing an understanding of either the subject matter or the importance for the organization. Now, it is possible to be apathetic toward security, but still understand the need or the relevance of security.

These situations present some rather strange behavior on the part of the board. It generally takes on the appearance of due diligence without the diligence. They will go along for the ride with security by doing things like setting up a security committee and other associated diligence items required of their board member-ship. But their lack of interest or understanding in security raises an issue that we consistently observe. This problem has to do with the accuracy of the information that is presented regarding security. Since they often do not understand or care about the security information that is presented, they fail to recognize the inac-curacy or absurdity in the representation of the security posture that is offered. We have been in organizations, household names, where the security committee at the board level has been presented or is managing a portfolio of security projects that is completely different from that which is managed by the security program. Stop and think about that for a moment:

> The portfolio of security projects that is represented to the highest levels of management for the organiza-tion is nothing more than fiction designed to present an appearance of politically desirable activity.

Sadly, this is not a rarity in our experience, more the norm. Now, you may be asking yourself: how can this be the case with all of the security regulations and the involvement of the security program?

Regulations ... ha! What part of any existing security regulation states that you can't have two sets of security projects? Dang, as sad as it may sound, with the right auditor, you might even score higher. OK, so if the regulations do not catch it, of course the CISO will say something. Enter the security con.

CISOs are often forced to be very careful about what they disclose at the board level. This is for obvious reasons. If they raise an issue such as the existence of two separate security risk project portfolios, they better have a really good reason for this practice or ensure that their resumés are up-to-date. The disclosure of this information is going to make a lot of people look like fools or, worse, conspirators. Plus, if they are still doing the right thing at the security program level, does it really matter what is being reported at the board to people who are not interested in the first place? We guess it depends on who you ask. Though we cannot speak for every situation, it would appear logical that shareholders and consumers probably want accurate full disclosure regarding these types of issues. Either way, this is still a form of a con.

Apathy and the Executive Team

On "Mahogany Row," apathy is often much more obvious than with the board of directors. It is also generated for different reasons. Executives are often apa-thetic regarding security because it is generally not one of their priorities, when considering everything else vying for their attention. After all, how many times a day do you think about your life insurance policy? No one will say it is not important, but few will say that it is urgent. That is unless you have just been diagnosed with a terminal illness. The correlation between your health and the importance of your life insurance policy is similar to the priority given to security by executive management in relation to changes in current circumstances. They will be far more attentive to security after a security event than prior, when all else is deemed well. As a result, they tend to be apathetic toward security during quiet times in order to enable them to spend their energy somewhere else.

Example

We worked in an organization once where the CEO detested security and considered it a waste of time, especially when compared with all of the other initiatives that required his attention. Therefore, he assigned a "security official" who had no background in security and a limited understanding of the domain. In fact, it was an unwritten rule in executive meetings to not bring up the "S word" unless you wanted to be BBQ'd or lynched in that session. The topic literally made this person go crazy. In order to create an appearance of diligence, he instructed his team to focus on a couple of the easier security projects that would enable the appearance of momentum that he could use when addressing the board (security con). Other than these token initiatives, not much else was sanctioned. Security was definitely not a priority for this CEO in this organization, more a hindrance.

Generally, the apathetic behavior of this CEO and most of the executives that we observe leads to a security effort that works very hard at providing the appearance of effectiveness, but is really not accomplishing anything of substance. The other means by which apathy is demonstrated by this group is through extreme delegation. By this we mean assigning the responsibility so far down the organization structure that one never has to hear about it. By having security report at a very low level, apathetic executives are able to further insulate themselves from the security message. Further, it provides plausible deniability that they were ever aware of a potential risk. Sweet ... go apathy go!

The security con in all this is propagated by anyone who goes along when there is an apathetic executive in a power position—from other executives who turn a blind eye and keep their mouths shut to other employees who know that there is security work that needs to be done.

Apathy and Middle Management

Within the True Security Model, we are in need of resources from middle management. Apathy in middle management stems from two different sources. The first is the cascade effect from executive management. If executive management does not prioritize security, chances are that middle management will reflect that indifference. It then becomes a game of risk.

As long as nothing is going wrong, it is easy to de-prioritize security. There is very little direction or scrutiny toward these activities. Once again, if you consider the burden placed on management to do more with less in a shorter period of time, security is an easy place to cut corners. This behavior presents itself as apathy toward security.

The effects of apathetic middle management generally result in two things. The first is the inability to get adequate resources for security initiatives. Symptoms of this behavior include responses that are slow in coming and minimal in content. The general lack of interest is a very obvious reminder that you and your work are not a priority. Their response is out of courtesy or the need to provide the appearance of support. The second thing that often happens is when resources are provided, they are not the level or caliber that will be effective in meeting your need. Rather, they are the most expendable to the manager who has assigned them. Once again, this behavior is designed to provide the bare minimum in order to demonstrate support, without inconveniencing the resource manager. Both of these items are made easier, and in some cases promoted, if the executive who oversees the area is also apathetic toward security.

We have given you clues as to how the security con is presented during this section. The con is the false representation that security is important and properly addressed within the organization while achieving an alternative agenda. Every time that a resource manager has given the perception of support, he or she is perpetuating the con. As a quick side note, we always love when this situation plays out in an organization and the security team is able to make what are thought to be ineffective resources, effective.

Apathy and the Supervisory Team

Apathy within this group is often caused by a resistance to change. Supervisors are often much closer to processes and procedures within an organization. When security comes around, it is usually trying to change something for which the supervisor has become accustomed. This often generates apathy in bulk.

When supervisors are apathetic toward security, it can be disastrous. At this level, you are deep into the tactics and implementation of everything within an organization. If this group is apathetic toward security, the effects are that your security efforts, even if supported by other higher-level groups, will simply not happen. We have seen this many times where the security program has gained support from all of the groups above the supervisors, but then wonder why nothing is getting done. This is usually the case because the supervisors are the individuals who understand the nuances of the environment that will enable delivery, and are responsible for guiding the resources that will be used during the process.

The security con within this group can be performed by both the supervisors and the security team. The supervisor's participation is similar to that of middle management. He or she offers token support in order to present the proper appearances for political correctness. The security professionals respond to the lack of progress by misrepresenting the level of success that is achieved by their initiative. This is particularly the case if the security effort has received support for the initiatives from the other groups of management. In those cases, upper management is expecting results, and the security team either has to come clean or perpetuate an illusion of success. Any way you look at it, both of these groups are knee deep in the con. This is a well-recognized concept in psychology and communication known as "self-serving bias."

Self-Serving Bias

Self-serving bias is the tendency for humans to take credit for success, even if their role was minor. Conversely humans also tend to deny or obfuscate responsibility for failures, in an attempt to protect their ego.

Apathy and Employees

This one is easy, especially since we have used other examples to this point about apathy within employees. Employees are similar to supervisors in that their response to change can induce stress, create a sense of powerlessness, and ultimately become or give the impression of being apathetic.

When employees are apathetic regarding security they are less likely to adhere to security processes and procedures. As a matter of fact, they are likely to attempt to circumvent such controls if they are considered to be arduous or inconvenient. This often leads to situations that create increased security risk for the organization.

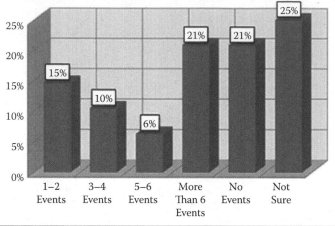

We Have Had a Security Event at Our Organization That Can Be Directly Attributed to Employee Non-Compliance with Documented Procedures

Figure 3.7   More than half of the respondents in Figure 3.7 claimed that they had at least one event that can be attributed to noncompliance with documented procedures. So now, who is going to say that apathy does not affect our security efforts?

The probability of high risk security items such as employees writing down their passwords on a yellow sticky, failing to shred sensitive documents, or leaving information sitting on a photocopier become common practice in an environment populated by apathetic employees.

The security con at this level is usually solely performed by employees through their job performance. When employees are apathetic, chances are they are masking the true diligence of their compliance to security protocols.

More than half of the respondents in Figure 3.7 claimed that they had at least one event that can be attributed to noncompliance with documented procedures. So now, who is going to say that apathy does not affect our security efforts?

Apathy and Consumers

Ah, consumers, the orphans of organizational security. Consumers become apathetic for a couple of reasons. This primarily happens because the consumers *want* to believe that the product or service in question is secure. This is true for everything from getting on a plane to online banking; it is just easier to believe than question. After all, if it looks secure, then it must be secure, right?

The second reason that consumers become apathetic is because they get swept up in the monotony of the security controls. Whether it is waiting in line at the security checkpoints in the airport or the requirement to log in three distinct times and answer a personal security question before accessing their bank account online. The focus is on the inconvenience of the circumstances, not on reasons that prompted the security controls. The effort is redirected toward evading the controls versus contemplating the risk of the situation. Lastly, consumers or humans have a tendency to defer to those that they believe to have a superior understanding or power to their own.

When individuals are placed in circumstances that they feel are beyond their control or outside of their scope of expertise, the tendency is to defer to the prevailing wisdom. In other words, just go along; smarter people than you have already made the decision. This is a common scenario when interacting with specialized experts such as doctors, police, government officials, etc.

This apathy creates a situation where consumers fail to question the security of the products and services that they are utilizing. If after performing a cursory security review consumers are satisfied, they will often continue to use the service blindly from that point forward. This is particularly the case if the product or service is produced by a recognized brand. As a result, the effect of apathy at this level is that the consumer does not engage often enough to have the necessary information to make accurate decisions regarding the situation.

The security con within all of this is performed by everyone within organizations that are providing insecure goods and services to consumers. Within these environments, organizations take advantage of the fact that consumers are not highly involved from a security perspective. They use that blind acceptance to enable the consumption of insecure products and services.

Effects Summary

As you can see, the specific causes of apathy within humans, systems, and organizations are highly applicable to these groups. Of course they are; these groups are comprised of humans and are members of many systems. This makes the effects that we have described highly predictable. The usual places are anywhere change, monotony, futility, or failed communications exist, so, almost everywhere you look in most organizations today. That is why you got this book.

We will now move on to the final section within this chapter. Hopefully, you are starting to see some of the relationships between the causes and effects of apathy, leading to the development of some of your own solutions. Well, we will not keep you waiting any longer; let's give some ideas on how to solve this problem.

Solutions to Apathy

Within this section, we will examine some solutions and considerations for addressing apathy. First, Skye will provide some considerations from systems theory that can aid in combating general apathy. There is some great research in this area that should add value in strengthening your organization, as well as your security efforts.

From there, we will get even more touchy-feely and explore some of the emotional responses that are related to apathy. Skye will illustrate how understanding and thoughtfulness—empathy—can aid in the reduction of apathetic behavior.

We will conclude this section by looking at some actions that can be taken by CISOs to reduce apathy toward their program. First, we will provide some techniques that can be applied by anyone within an organization, whether they are affiliated with the security program or not. Lastly, we will discuss techniques that can be applied by members of a security program to reduce apathy toward security.

Through the use of this information, we hope to end this chapter with readers possessing a solid set of tools to further their ability to attain true security. We will begin by letting Skye elaborate on the first two topics: systems theory considerations and touchy-feely considerations.

Systems Theory Considerations

One of the most powerful items you must recognize when considering apathy from a systems theory perspective is that as a security professional, you are part of a greater system (the organization) and you affect and are affected by all the parts within that system. When considering how apathy can be contagious in an organization and promote negative synergy, you should use your system view to constantly be looking for ways to reduce apathy whether you are the cause or simply a witness. More importantly, you should make these efforts even if this behavior is not directly related to security. Perhaps that is just lending an ear to someone in finance who had a bad day or showing compassion to another employee who is scared about losing his or her job. These efforts, though they may seem small, are crucial to the overall health of a system and in developing an environment that is ready for security success.

Touchy-Feely Considerations

Since we just mentioned that your interactions with others within a system or organization are crucial to your security success, we will now provide a couple of other human emotions–based ideas that can help. The first item is to understand your response or the response by others when apathy is experienced. It is crucial to focus your efforts on the situation that is causing the problem, versus blaming the person. Often, many within an organization view apathy (attribute) in an employee as a dispositional characteristic of that person, rather than a response to a situation that is difficult, unpleasant, or challenging. It is easier to deem someone as cynical or apathetic from the inside out, versus considering what elements in the organizational culture or climate are causing an apathetic response. One view represents the person as the problem, and the other is representative of the person responding to the situation.

However, if humans are not innately dispositional to become apathetic, then let's explore more effective communication behaviors that are effective. A good place to start is in the juxtaposition emotion of apathy, which is empathy.

em•pa•thy–noun

1. The intellectual identification with or vicarious experiencing of the feelings, thoughts, or attitudes of another.
2. The imaginative ascribing to an object, as a natural object or work of art, feelings or attitudes present in oneself: By means of empathy, a great painting becomes a mirror of the self.

Random House Unabridged Dictionary© **Random House, Inc. 2006.**

In his book, *Emotional Intelligence*, Daniel Goldman (1995) argues that humans are not born with the disposition of apathy or empathy. Both are learned behaviors that can be traced back to infancy. Children (and adults) learn this skill as it is modeled by their caretakers. This is both troubling and comforting because there is hope for humans to learn the skill of empathy if coaching is employed. Empathy is the ability to take in what another person is feeling via reading the verbal and nonverbal cues that are represented in the behavior presented before you. Considering that about 90 percent of our communication is established nonverbally, that leaves only 10 left for the vocal code or words spoken. So, as you wax eloquently, realize that often it is the unspoken word that speaks volumes to employees. Pay close attention to the messages you are sending to your colleagues and the messages they are sending to you. Take an interest in these messages, particularly those that are nonverbal, and try to understand, appreciate, and empathize with the thoughts, emotions, and attitudes that they reflect.

Security Solutions

The first solution that we propose for combating apathy toward security is to acknowledge that apathy can have a significant effect on your security efforts. Hopefully, we have amply demonstrated that through this chapter. Once you recognize that there is a correlation between apathy and a diminished ability to achieve true security, the next step is to attempt to measure it within your environment. Hey, wait a second, apathy is invisible, isn't it?

Whenever we start an engagement with a new organization, the first thing we do is start measuring the security constraints. When you know what they look like, it is actually very easy, particularly since we have been doing it for years now. (Do not worry; you should have this ability too, if you don't already after reading this book.) When it comes to apathy, you can almost taste it when it is highly resident in an organization. Though it might sound silly, one of the most effective tests for its measurement is to compare your environment to the *Dilbert* comic strip. Give it a shot, if you haven't already. We have found that the greater the correlation of your environment to that of the comic strip, the higher the prominence of the security constraints will often be. Now, we understand that this is hardly a scientific method for identifying these issues but, after using this method for a number of years, we can attest to its validity.

In summary, the most effective way to measure apathy is to simply open your eyes and look for it. Your newfound awareness and knowledge of its triggers—such as change, monotony, or futility within a situation—should aid you in its identification. To assist you with this process we have created this exercise.

Exercise 9

This exercise can also be found in the Appendix with a worksheet.

Objective

The objective of this exercise is to evaluate the level of apathy within your environment.

Exercise

List all areas within your environment where you have witnessed apathy. When engaging in this type of self-reflective activity, be mindful not to pinpoint particular individuals as apathetic—as a character flaw versus a situational response. Be specific or as general as you deem appropriate for your situation. For each area where you identify apathetic behavior, attempt to identify the why, as well as the effects this will have on your security efforts. Remember, there are no wrong answers.

Example

Situation	Why	Impact on Security Efforts
Apathetic employees	Organization was just purchased by a new organization creating a feeling of powerlessness at the staff level	Employee activities when influenced by apathy lack diligence in applying necessary security processes and procedures

After completing this list, you should begin to see trends where you can focus your attention. Often, the same issue will continue to manifest itself many times in different areas. Though the symptoms may be slightly different, you will find the root cause is similar if not identical. Once this exercise is complete you should have a better idea of where to focus your efforts. Further assessment should be conducted to see if, first, you are focusing your attention meaningfully and, second, if you are making effective progress.

Organizational or Security Approach

There are two distinct ways in which you can try to reduce apathy in your environment as a CISO or security professional in general. The first one is to do it from an organizational perspective, while the other is to work solely from a level within the security program. First, we will look at the organizational approach.

Trying to reduce apathy from an organizational perspective often proves to be difficult because of the sphere of influence that is normally associated with a CISO or really any member of a security program. But there are a couple of things that you can do. The most important of these is to focus more on increasing empathy, rather than reducing apathy. This is a typical sales technique that is very affective for establishing a positive relationship.

Think about the people within your organization with which you have a good working relationship and ask yourself why. Chances are that the answer is that you share something in common. Whether it is experience, philosophy, or objectives, chances are that there is something. That is your objective when battling apathy. Building a bond with that individual that is forged in commonality. Something that tells the other person that you understand his or her pain and issues and that you will help wherever you can. The trick is that you cannot merely walk up to people and say: "I understand your pain and issues, and would like to help." If only it were that simple. You actually need to convey to them through shared experiences or ideas that you *get* their situation.

Showing an interest in the fellow humans around you can be very powerful and can often have an effect that snowballs (positive synergy). There is no reason that you or anyone else in an organization for that matter cannot be a catalyst for this type of behavior. With that, let's move on to some stuff that is more within a CISO's sphere of influence: the security program.

There are six areas to focus on within your security program if you are trying to reduce the impacts of apathy. None of these items should be a surprise since we have been weaving them in throughout the chapter. We have already given you the single most important item, which is to acknowledge, identify, and measure apathy. Here are the others.

The Culture of Your Organization

Take time to understand your organization's culture and ensure that your security program works within it, not against it. Also, be aware that the farther to the left or right that your culture resides on the continuum, the more sensitive you will need to be in your efforts. Further, understanding the culture will aid you in understanding the power structure and the proper way to approach it.

The Security Program Personality

The perception that your security program exhibits is the reality with which outsiders must work. The first step is, once again, to accurately identify the personality of your security program and determine if that is beneficial or detrimental given the corporate culture. Next, create a marketing plan that can be used to adjust the perceptions of those outside of the program. Keep in mind that this can be accomplished whether you are the CISO or a security engineer. If you are a CISO, you can generally make direct changes to your security program. If you are simply a member of the security program, you should direct your efforts at first convincing others within the program that change is needed, and then with a group effort making external changes. Of course, while you wait for group change, you can make changes in your personal daily interactions that can impact the opinion of the security group as a whole.

Review Authority and Responsibility of Your Job Role

In a perfect world, this is always in equilibrium: authority equals responsibility. In cases where it is not, make adjustments as quickly as possible. We make it sound so easy. Merely adjust your authority ... ha! In this equation it is far more realistic to adjust your responsibility. For example, if you have too little authority, begin making your case for giving up some of the responsibility. Chances are that no one will actually want it, creating a case for an increase in authority.

Choose Carefully Where You Interact with Security Events

As we mentioned earlier, you have a choice where you make critical changes within the environment, either during construction of solutions, changes within the environment, or once already in production. Choose areas in which your security program will operate and assess the impact in terms of change to the environment and perception of changes by associated employees.

Lastly, make sure that your team has the aptitude, experience, and interest to function in those areas. Failing to take this into account can result in apathy within your security program, as well as outside of it.

Train People on the "Why" of Security

Any time you or your team take action, whether implementing a new security policy or performing a risk assessment, ensure that anyone in the organization that is touched by the action understands why it is important. Your objective is to gain enthusiastic support, not malicious compliance. This one item can be the most powerful tool on your apathy reduction tool-belt.

Figure 3.8 is the same old story. We cannot figure out why the discipline of security is not using training more effectively as a tool.

Make Security Sexy

This one may sound stupid, but it is possible to make security sexy. This is one of the few places within an organization where an employee gets to play "cops and

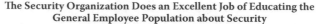

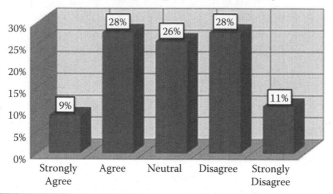

Figure 3.8 Figure 3.8 is the same old story. We cannot figure out why the discipline of security is not using training more effectively as a tool.

robbers." The profession of security still carries an air of James Bond with all of the fancy technologies, intrigue, and intricacies. The only downside is we just do not seem to have the sexy villainous … bummer. Anyway, this mythology can be used to your advantage to create interest in the topic. Generating interest in the topic of security reduces the monotony surrounding some of the procedures that can generate apathy. The best place to implement this item is within your security awareness campaign. Have fun with it; we are one of the few organizational groups that get a free pass to build a marketing effort. You do not see finance building an awareness campaign, do you? Take advantage of this opportunity.

Take Away the Places Where Apathy Likes to Hide

Nothing eliminates the "It's not my job" mentality faster than clarity of definitions, roles, responsibilities, and milestones. Successfully applying structure to a situation eliminates the "wiggle room," instilling a sense of accountability and responsibility. This is absolute kryptonite for apathy.

Chapter Summary

Hopefully, this chapter has increased your awareness and provided some understanding of many of the causes, effects, and solutions to apathy. With this understanding, we are sure that you will be in a better position to measure apathy in your own environment and curb its impact on your quest for true security. With that, our work is done here for now. We will now move on to the next security constraint on the list: myopia.

Chapter 4

Myopia

"We do not wish to see the entire forest; this one tree is just fine!"

Overview

It is often uttered by many a security professional, in fact ad nauseam, that "security touches everything." Every time that we look to secure something, whether an organization, technical system, or building, we must consider the people, process, technology, and facility elements in order to provide a secure solution. The unfortunate thing though is that, in reality, achieving this comprehensive perspective by those both inside and outside of a security program is usually one of the biggest challenges for our security efforts.

We once were called into work with an organization right after it had an important server stolen from its environment. In our first meeting, the executive team was totally frustrated. They explained how they had spent all of this money on security and really tried to integrate security into the development process and other critical elements of this solution. How could this server, which was a major component of this recent project, simply disappear? During this project, they made certain that the server was appropriately hardened, was protected by all the right types of firewalls, and was overall technically sound (technology). They assured that the people who were using this system were adequately trained on security concepts (people). They were confident that all of the process elements such as system backup and patch management were all in place and securely implemented (process). With all of this hard work, they were simply in awe when they got the call that this server had been stolen shortly after deployment and the data on it was now missing. What happened? Myopia, my friends. Though, they secured the server from a people, process, and technology perspective, no one ever considered that after the server was configured at the headquarters it was shipped off to a break room in a small field office way out in the middle of nowhere. In the middle of the night, a couple of months later, the office was burglarized, and the server was stolen along with the refrigerator and the coffee maker. In fact, the thieves probably did not even know what they were getting, which was a ton of personal information about this organization's customers.

Now, we wish that this example was a unique incident, but it is not. The bummer about security is that it is the one thing that you miss that always gets you. This is significantly different than other disciplines where you can build something and if 90 percent of it works, you can deem it a success. Heck, for home improvement projects, we deem a project a success if 60 percent of it works. Security, not so much. This is why myopia is an absolute killer at derailing your efforts and achieving true security.

If any of this sounds familiar, you are in luck. This chapter is focused on the causes, effects, and some solutions for being successful in the midst of organizational myopia. Our approach to this chapter may also sound familiar. We plan on following a very similar format to the one we used in the last chapter.

We will begin by looking at the causes of myopia in humans. Are we genetically predisposed to have tunnel vision? Hope not! From there, we will explore the causes of myopia in systems. Our friend, systems theory, always is a wealth of knowledge on this kind of stuff. After looking at myopia in humans and systems, the next stop is the organizational causes.

There is a ton of stuff occurring in organizations that produce significant amounts of myopia. From extreme specialization of job roles to a migration of the workforce from permanent to contingent employees, myopia is spreading like a virus.

Last but not least in the "Causes" section, we will look at the causes of myopia in security. We hope you have some time on your hands because there is a long list of contributors.

After causes, we will then return to the cause and effect relationship of myopia within our True Security Model. This is where we identify some tangible demonstrations of myopia within each of the various groups from the board to common employees.

With a clear picture of the problem through the exploration of the causes and effects, we will end this chapter with some tangible solutions. Do not worry; we promise there are some things that you can do to combat myopia. We will let Skye get us going by explaining some of the human causes of myopia.

Causes of Myopia in Humans

When looking at myopia in humans, we have to start with how humans use items in their environment to create structure and progress. One of these items, which is very applicable in our discussion of myopia, is the human ability to use tools. Recent research published in the article "Humans Have Evolved Specialized Skills of Social Cognition: The Cultural Intelligence Hypothesis," by Herrmann, Call, Hernàndez-Lloreda, Hare, and Tomasello (2007), presents that the heavy reliance on tools by humans is a precursor for specialized training and on the formation of roles within an environment. Further, the way in which humans learn to use tools is significantly different than other species. Humans have developed the ability to learn the use of tools from a social perspective, meaning that they are able to absorb information and formulate how to use and why to use particular tools in particular situations. This is very important to recognize in today's modern organization, where groups are divided by the tools or technologies that they utilize on a daily basis. This may explain why database programmers who use databases as their tool have difficulty associating with, say, the finance group who uses a calculator as their tool. Both of these groups use their tools as not only something that helps them to perform their job, but also as a relational element from a social perspective that binds the group together. As a result, this makes interaction with other groups that do not use that specific tool more difficult. This ability to learn specialized skills by itself is not the only item that can lend itself to a myopic view of the world. There are other areas of study we will now look at that teach us more about why and how humans fall victim to myopia.

In her book, *Mindfulness and Mindful Learning*, Ellen Langer (1989) coined the term "mindlessness" as one potential effect of the human ability to be highly specialized, focused, and categorical in our thinking. According to Langer, mindless behaviors are rooted in (1) an inability entrapment in rigid categories, (2) functioning on automatic pilot, and (3) operating from our own single perspective (Langer, 1989). Let us take a look at each of these ideas.

Entrapment in rigid categories prohibits humans from taking in new information, thus we are trapped in a set of nonnegotiable categories that serve as a way for us to manage our surroundings (Langer, 1989). It is natural that humans create categories to make sense of their world. We use these categories to serve as a method for organizing stimuli or information from our environment.

The next cause of mindlessness as illustrated by Langer is operating under automatic pilot. We are all guilty of engaging in automatic pilot. Have you ever been driving and suddenly realize that you took an exit that you would normally have taken if you were driving to work and yet you did not intend to go to work? Maybe you were meeting a friend for coffee and the car, seeming to have a mind of its own, took you toward your daily, obligatory path that leads you to your office.

Langer's final cause of mindlessness is the manner in which humans tend to engage in life operating from one single perspective, usually one that orchestrates around our own needs and desires. This is very similar to the self-serving bias we discussed in the last chapter. It is not a stretch to believe that humans will highly focus on items that are closely aligned with their needs and wants. How many times have you wanted ice cream and all of a sudden you cannot focus on anything else except the closest ice cream parlor?

As we dig further in our quest to better understand myopia in humans, another concept we should review is presented in the book *Inattentional Blindness*, by Arien Mack and Irvin Rock (1992).

One of the most well-known studies for demonstrating inattentional blindness is one that I often conduct with my students in the classroom. The study was originated by Daniel Simons of the University of Illinois and Christopher Chabris of Harvard. Students are asked to watch a short video of two groups of people playing basketball. One team is wearing black t-shirts and the other group is wearing white t-shirts. Just like the subjects of the original experiment, the students are instructed to either count the number of passes made by one of the teams, the number of aerial passes, or the number of times the ball bounces on the ground before being passed to another player. There are multiple variations of the experiment where an unexpected event (UE) happens. For example, a woman with an umbrella walks right through the middle of the game. Another UE is a person dressed in a gorilla outfit that walks through the game and actually pounds on his chest while facing the camera dead on! After the subjects watch the video, they are asked if they noticed anything that seems out of the ordinary. In the majority of the experiments (both in the original research and in my classes) 50 percent of the subjects do not see the UE! They are prepared with answers for the original task—such as the number of passes for the team wearing black or white t-shirts—but they miss the umbrella lady and gorilla about half of the time!

The results exemplify how we consciously or unconsciously ignore information that we perceptually deem as unimportant for us to finish our task.

In summary, myopia in humans again has some innate and learned qualities and is primarily caused by the constructs and categories that we create at a young age, coupled with specialized training, repetitive behaviors, unchallenged perspectives, and rote memory versus thinking critically or creatively. We also want to again mention that what was presented here will serve us as we move forward for our needs of myopia specific to security, but there is much more research available on this subject that has all kinds of interesting applications. We highly recommend that if interested, you continue to learn more about these concepts. A great place to start is with the books and research that have been mentioned in this section. Below is a summary of what we have covered.

- A precondition for humans to quickly learn the use of tools within their social groups, leading to development of specialized skills
- Susceptibility to mindlessness
- Susceptibility to inattentional blindness

Well, we do not believe it is much of a stretch to take some of these human-level concepts and identify their applicability within an organization. You only have to sit through one meeting in a common information technologies group in just about any organization to see demonstrations of mindlessness (Langer, 1989) and inattentional blindness (Mack and Rock, 1992). This is particularly the case if you have members of different technical disciplines and specializations within the session. You might as well have brick walls in between each member in the meeting, and you can almost taste how aloof, mindless (Langer, 1989), or inattentionally blind (Mack and Rock, 1992) one member with a certain specialization, such as application development, will be to another, with say network skills. By the way, this is if you can ever get these types of people with different skill sets to meet. Let's move on to some system specific causes of myopia by Skye.

Causes of Myopia within a System

Because the basic qualities of a system rest in the interrelated nature of all of its parts, myopia can be detrimental to a system, especially as a system grows and becomes larger.

The major cause of myopia in systems is a result of the system being populated with humans. Human relationships between employees are what tie a system or organization as a whole together. You can imagine as you increase the number of employees within an organization, the number of potential relationships multiplies exponentially. Why is this important? Well, if the components (employees) of your system (organization) are acting from a single perspective, or are so specialized in their specific task that they do not see how it effects the entire system, then this further increases myopic behavior as the communication channels deteriorate between these employees. This leads to a system itself that becomes highly vulnerable.

On the continuum of open and closed systems, a myopic perspective inherently moves the system toward exclusion of information and thus closes the system. A closed system can function pathologically for a while, but generally spirals toward chaos and death of the system, or in our case, an organization. Another outcome could be that the high-functioning part of the system leaves the dysfunctional part and becomes a new system or merges with another system, leaving both systems vulnerable.

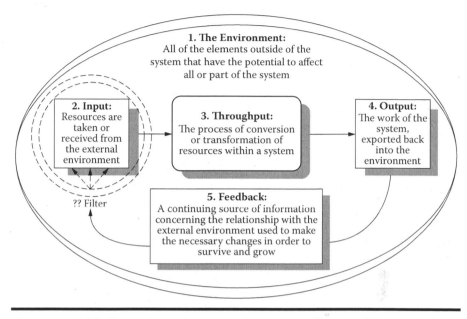

Figure 4.1 This figure shows how myopia acts as a filter to all inputs, limiting the quantity, quality, and focus of the information that reaches the system for processing.

Figure 4.1 illustrates how myopia acts as a filter to all inputs, limiting the quantity, quality, and focus of the information that reaches the system for processing.

It is amazing how applicable some of the human behaviors and systems theory are when applying them to situations found in a common organization on a normal day. For example, just as a system tries to cleanse itself of negative elements when they exist, so does the common organization. Just look at mergers and acquisitions within an industry that is performing either very poorly or very well. The poorly performing organizations look to get absorbed into new organizations in order to survive while the strong organizations look to merge with weaker organizations in order to enable additional processing and capability. We will now move on to some other causes of myopia that occur specifically within organizations. It should be starting to become clear how many generators of myopia exist.

Causes of Myopia within an Organization

The good news about the causes of myopia within organizations is that it does not require a Ph.D. degree to understand. In fact, most of it is just common sense. The current manifestation begins by taking a brief look at the history of the modern organization.

History and Myopia

> "Life moves pretty fast. If you don't stop and look around once in a while, you could miss it."
>
> **Ferris Bueller**

The point in history where we will begin this conversation is the Industrial Revolution. It is this period from the late eighteenth century that marked the transition from an agrarian society to one based on industry. To be more specific, it began the age of automation. It was the beginning of assembly lines and machine tools that were capable of creating other machines. This also marked the point in history where we humans started looking at the workforce in a very different manner. We began to view people as another cog in a larger machine or system. This view prompted a change in the workforce that we still see today—an emphasis on specialization to achieve efficiency.

An early example of this change in philosophy was Henry Ford. He hired individuals to learn the specific skills that his mass production system required and paid what was then a very high wage in order to retain them. He also changed the duration of a workday from nine hours to eight hours and shortened the work week to five days. All of these things were done to convince individuals to take a rather mundane job, perform it well, and stay. He came to this conclusion to combat employee turnover that occurred because of the repetition of rather monotonous work. He created an environment that leveraged the efficiencies of specialization while at the same time limiting the inefficiencies caused by turnover.

At this point, you are probably wondering why we discuss good old Henry Ford and his ilk in this book. The answer is that organizations still use the basic concept of specialization today. The fact is that as long as a worker is performing predictable, repetitive tasks the specialist will ultimately be more efficient than a generalist. However, that efficiency comes at a price. That price is (trumpet sound) myopia!

Well, let us think about it. If you are a specialist, how often are you asked to step outside your field of expertise? This type of behavior produces a limited perspective for a large majority of individuals within modern organizations. A limited perspective will produce individuals with a restricted ability to explain or resolve the issues associated with anything outside of their specialization. It will also probably support compartmentalized thinking, conditioning for running on autopilot, or an emphasis on a single perspective. Hey, wait a second, haven't we heard those concepts before? Oh no, now there may be a reason why everyone is kind of zoned out and unfocused at work. Oh yea, and with organizations shifting more and more to a specialized work environment, the problem is only going to get worse. To demonstrate, let us take a second and conduct a short exercise.

Exercise 10

This exercise can also be found in the Appendix with worksheets.

Objective

The objective of this exercise is to evaluate the level of myopia in your environment.

Exercise

Within your own organization, take a moment and think about your last two weeks on the job. How many demonstrations of myopia did you observe during your interactions with co-workers? By the way, it is OK to count yourself as a demonstrator as well. We will not tell anyone.

We could go on for a while about the transition to industrial and again into the information revolution, but suffice to say that these changes have a real effect on the workforce. Myopia is a natural progression of the Industrial Revolution and the quest for organizations to optimize efficiency. Now that is a reasonable explanation, but history only explains a piece of the puzzle.

It is no surprise that most survey participants feel that their organization is heavily compartmentalized (Figure 4.2), but it is a reality that needs to be factored into our security efforts.

Complexity of Systems

Oh no, systems theory! Yep, good old systems theory! You can't get away from the fact that organizations are systems. Sure there were systems 200 years ago, but they

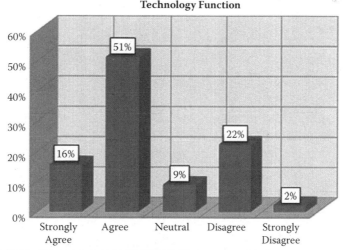

Our Organization is Highly Compartmentalized by Business or Technology Function

Figure 4.2 It is no surprise that most survey participants feel that their organization is heavily compartmentalized (Figure 4.2), but it is a reality that needs to be factored into our security efforts.

weren't the multinational, 24/7, Web-enabled organizations of today. Any attempt to suggest a similarity of the nature and complexity of the Ford Motor Company (circa 1925) and a multinational conglomerate such as Exxon Mobil is ludicrous. Today's organizations have become terribly complex. Take this fact and combine the prevalence of roles requiring highly specialized skills along with the pace of everyday life; you are beginning to ask a great deal from the average person. In the book *Future Shock*, Alvin Toffler (1970) illustrates how the complexity of our society and its creations is vastly outpacing human evolution. The result is a phenomenon that he coined as "future shock" or "too much change in too short a period of time" (Toffler, 1970). You see, as much as technology, techniques, and knowledge have evolved, the ability of the basic component, or humans, to address the changes has not kept pace with the increase in complexity of all the related systems.

That is where myopia comes in. Myopia represents a safe haven from all of the moving parts within a system, especially if the complexity or pace of all the moving parts is overwhelming. It represents a place to focus and attempt to make sense of all the chaos and noise that is part of modern organizations and society. To a certain extent, it is a reflex mechanism by the individual to provide context and understanding to a very dynamic environment. Everyone has experienced a period of overload where issues and events are just moving too fast to absorb and address. However, the vast majority of individuals establish that comfort zone, an operating boundary, and stay where it is safe and understood.

So far so good? OK, we have addressed a little bit of history and the complexity of systems. Is that all there is? Nope, we also need to look at the composition of modern organizations. Who are they hiring to address the desire for workforce specialization?

Those Who Perform the Work

In his book, *Age of Discontinuity*, Drucker (1992) presents how the past couple of decades have seen a shift from the industrial economy of the late twentieth century to the "knowledge economy" (Drucker, 1992). We know, just as you were getting used to the idea of specialization and the industrial economy, we change things up again. Our apologies, but the world moves awfully fast.

The definition of the "knowledge economy" (Drucker, 1992) in its simplest form is that knowledge is used directly to produce economic benefit. This single change produced workers that were completely self-contained. They brought their skills and knowledge to work, applied them to achieve specific tasks for their organization, and promptly took them to the next job. These workers did not need the infrastructure and support mechanisms that an organization used to provide in the days of Henry Ford. The skills and expertise that they developed were based on their knowledge, making it highly portable.

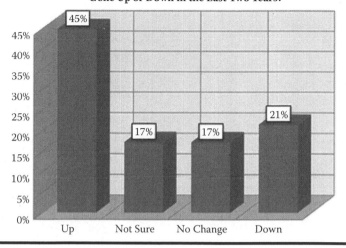

Figure 4.3

As the relative size of the contingent, contract workforce continues to increase (Figure 4.3) we will have ever-increasing levels of myopia to address in security.

Look at the example of a programmer in 1970. In order to perform his or her craft, that person required a multimillion dollar mainframe the size of Rhode Island. It was unlikely that he or she had such a computer at home. Compare and contrast that situation to modern programmers. Most of the tools and accoutrement necessary to exercise their craft can be purchased at Circuit City. In his book, *Managing in the Next Society*, Drucker (2003) presents that this situation has spawned a different kind of worker, one which has been labeled appropriately enough as a "knowledge worker" (Drucker, 2003).

This shift in individual workforce freedom has not gone unnoticed by the hiring organizations. Directly hiring specialists who are highly skilled has become, in many cases, cost prohibitive. These same individuals can make far more money on the open market "renting" their unique skills for short periods of time. Though the lack of available, qualified candidates was initially viewed as a hardship—ask any recruiter during the late 1990s who were hiring Web developers—the benefits have become apparent to many organizations.

From the perspective of the organization, consultants represent a ready pool of experts within a specific domain of knowledge. In some cases, it is the concept of the "hired gun" or someone who is an undisputed expert with the exact knowledge and experience required by the organization to achieve a specific objective. In other cases, it may be the ability to obtain the needed resource, or in many cases a large quantity of resources, quickly. Whatever the motivation, the use of a contract or flexible workforce is on the rise. Unfortunately, using this flexible workforce does not come without consequences, one of the largest being an unusual form of myopia.

Consultants often report to multiple management structures, the one within their consultancy and at least one within the client organization for which they are performing services. This duality often creates complexities and bureaucracies that make it difficult to truly understand any of the specifics within either of these systems. This lack of perspective, regarding the big picture, results in a "just-complete-the-assigned-task" mentality, a type of tunnel vision that is driven to complete the assigned task. This behavior is usually encouraged by all the management groups because consultants or staff augmentation is considered to be relatively expensive. This results in a mindset to keep the consultant focused on his or her scope of work and nothing else. This highly focused emphasis on scope, schedule, and budget is becoming more commonplace in organizations and not solely due to the need to manage consultants.

The emphasis on the delivery and measurement of objectives within modern organizations has led to the adoption of project management principles and techniques—a move we highly applaud. This approach allows organizations to single out specific objectives and allow for the assignment of specialists to achieve the goal. Within these organizations, the work year is divided into a series of initiatives or projects. The projects are used by the organization, divisions, or departments as a means to plot progress usually toward a much larger goal. This mindset is perfect for the use of consultants. In most cases, consultants are engaged to complete a specific initiative within a specific timeframe. Good fit. However, intensive immersion in the initiative creates myopia on the part of the consultants and the project team, since the incentive system purely focuses on the delivery of just one initiative. As with most things in life, one man's pro is another man's con. We are not stating that consulting is either good or bad, merely that it is a reality of the modern work world. Be aware that one of the intrinsic aspects of this arrangement is that it can and does create various forms of myopia within organizations. As we said, a pretty easy set of ideas, no Ph.D. required. The next cause of myopia is something that every person who holds a job commits, or feels like he or she commits, everyday. The topic is professional fraud.

Professional Fraud

The reaction to the term "professional fraud" is always very interesting. We do not mean in it in a malicious sense, but as a way to describe the discrepancy between how we portray our professional selves and the reality of our capabilities. Think of it in terms of your resumé. Is your resumé 100 percent accurate? Does it address all of your limitations and shortcomings? Of course not! It is your personal marketing brochure that was developed to sell the most fabulous product ever conceived: namely you!

Now, take the metaphor and insert it into your daily work life. The fraud is the difference between what you present yourself as capable of and the reality of your capabilities. The high quantity of specialization within most organizations today has led to a brain drain of available resources to perform all the specific and very specialized types of work. As a result, many of the people who get jobs today, particularly specializations, are simply not qualified to perform the functions for which they have been hired. Individuals who find themselves in this situation work very hard to avoid situations where their little secret may be exposed. Do not forget, these folks were hired because they are experts; they are supposed to know everything related to the problem space of the initiative. This self-limitation or unwillingness to engage in areas that may expose their secret can create a form of myopia.

So far in this section, we have focused on the resource element, but organizations are also struggling with the management elements. In fact, organizations are struggling so much with this element that we saved it for last.

Knowledge Management

We want to reiterate that there is nothing wrong with building a system or organization that requires specialization. In fact, if it is built properly, the output of that system will be highly optimized and normalized. For highly specialized organizations, there are two critical components that will afford success. The first is a resource or set of resources with the knowledge, experience, and skill to perform the required tasks. The second component is the proper elements of management to guide their effort. Management elements such as a functional—rather than dysfunctional—communications mechanism, clearly defined objectives, roles and responsibilities, governance, and chain-of-command are all necessary to properly manage a workforce, especially a flexible workforce. This is where we see many organizations fall. The mindset is that these resources are highly compensated experts who can manage themselves. We would argue that a U.S. Navy Seal team is also a highly skilled group of experts, but the Navy does not let the team operate autonomously. They are generally used as part of a larger operation in coordination with the other assets that have been deployed to achieve the objective.

Very rarely in organizations do we see adequate processes and procedures in place for the communication and workflow between various organizational groups and specialties. These same organizations always identify this as an issue, but are generally myopic in their approach to correct it. Ironic isn't it? It should be obvious that this situation is a major contributor of myopia. If you look at each specialization in an organization as an island, then you should look at the management and communication structure within the organization as the boat that ferries information between each different island. No boat = No communication = Myopia. That was easy.

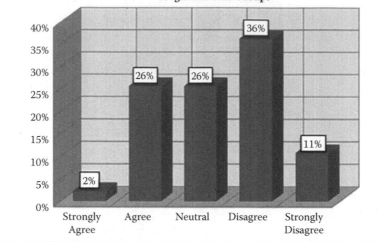

The Communication is Sufficient in Our Organization across Organizational Groups

Figure 4.4

Lack of strong communication, combined with heavily compartmentalized contract workforces, will continue to increase organizational myopia (Figure 4.4). This is without a doubt a rising trend that will require additional levels of effort to overcome.

Summary

It is clear that the organizations of today are forced to survive in an environment that is highly challenging. From the rapid changes in technology to how tasks are completed, organizations must adapt or die. One man's problem is another man's opportunity. An organization that allows this type of dysfunctional behavior will eventually pay in the form of lost business or bankruptcy. However, organizations that develop mechanisms to acquire specialized resources and effectively manage them will grow and flourish.

We have only skimmed the surface of the causes of myopia within an organization and could probably write an entire book on the subject, with more help from Skye, but we must bid adieu to this topic and move on to myopia within a security program.

Causes of Myopia within a Security Program

Regardless of the line of business, most modern organizations are producing one thing in mass: myopia. Because this is typically an institutional issue, myopia will find its way into most security programs. However, before you begin to feel sorry for yourself and assume the mantle of victimhood, we are here to tell you that you are part of the problem. To quote an ex-coach: "Before you point the fingers, pull the thumbs." In other words, look at yourself and what you are doing before looking for blame in others. That is exactly what we plan on doing. We are going to look at the elements and factors within our security efforts that facilitate the proliferation of myopia.

What is Security?

Do not panic, we have not manipulated the space and time continuum and hurdled you back to Chapter 1. But, we did spend time discussing this issue for a reason. It is the root cause for a number of security program woes. We won't beat the dead horse for too long, but it is worth reiterating the need and how the lack of a functioning definition will produce myopia.

A lack of a functional, appropriate institutional security definition allows for individuals to insert their own version. If you refer to any section in this chapter, prior to this one, you will find information demonstrating that the definition that individuals develop will have substantial boundaries that keep them within the comfort zone. A failure to define security is an acceptance of each individual's personal view of the topic and an accessory to the development of myopia. This definition should be defined for whatever situation it is needed, whether it is to promote understanding within a project or for the entire security program. Short and sweet … you're welcome!

Figure 4.5 illustrates the need for a tailored approach to information distribution from the security organization. It is not unrealistic to think that each group within the organization has a different level of comprehension, but it is unrealistic to furnish only one flavor of information and expect everyone to understand it.

Techno-Centric Security

Attend a security conference and you will hear that modern security efforts place too high a premium and emphasis on technology, sounding like a broken record that is endlessly skipping to the same part. What is not addressed is why this occurs, merely that it does, and to stop the behavior. Great, if we do not understand the cause, how can we adjust the behavior or the motivating factors behind the behavior? All we have to do is crank up the Mr. Peabody's Wayback Machine and return to Chapter 1 for our answer.

The relevant point in time is the discussion regarding security as an idea or a concept. Techno-centric security is a result of the human need to make nebulous concepts concrete. In this case, technology functions as an anchor to aid us in the visualization and discussion of the concept of security. People need to have something with which they can relate. The result of this is that security becomes the firewall, the antivirus product, or the intrusion detection system. That makes it a neat package that they can wrap their brains around. Now if they had something

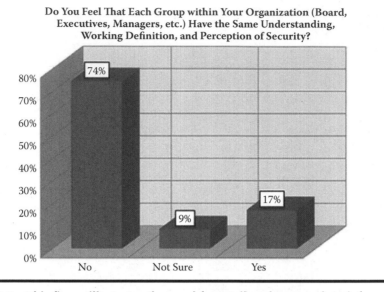

Do You Feel That Each Group within Your Organization (Board, Executives, Managers, etc.) Have the Same Understanding, Working Definition, and Perception of Security?

Figure 4.5 This figure illustrates the need for a tailored approach to information distribution from the security organization. It is not unrealistic to think that each group within the organization has a different level of comprehension, but it is unrealistic to furnish only one flavor of information and expect everyone to understand it.

else as an anchor like, oh, maybe a functional definition of security, that would aid in reducing the myopia toward techno-centric security.

It's a Game of Inches

Security is a "game of inches." If we may use a sporting analogy, it is very much analogous to playing goalie on a soccer team: your performance is generally measured by how many scores you allow, rather than the number of shots that were turned away. Security is no different in that we can secure 99 percent of an organization, but it will always be the 1 percent that nags us and eventually beats us. Our response to this situation has been to increase the level of specialization, particularly in the areas that involve technology. For example, it has been determined that the public-facing network interfaces are a source of risk for organizations. Now, we have individuals who work, live, and think almost exclusively in that specific domain of security. These disciplines generally take a great deal of energy and concentration in order to stay ahead of all the trends and changes. Sometimes there just is not any bandwidth left over for security issues outside of their specific area. The result is one of the toughest forms of myopia to conquer, that which is self-imposed. This is not an indictment of our profession, we are merely stating a fact that leads to myopia within our own ranks.

Pedigree Matters

Because security is a multifacetted, multidisciplinary domain of knowledge, it is unlikely to find one person who can act as an expert for all of it. As such, the knowledge and expertise that a professional brings to a security effort will be a product of his or her education and experience. Are you still with us? If the security program is stocked with individuals with the same background and education, there is a strong likelihood of creating a myopic view of security. For example, if your security program is staffed with former military police from the Marine Corps, the program would likely have a specific view of security. This view may or may not be appropriate depending on the organization and the mission of your security program. Remember that variety is the spice of life and a good recipe for a balanced healthy security effort.

The Generalist versus The Specialist

Our profession loves specialists. We create very specific roles like penetration tester or network security engineer and on and on. We can give story after story of how the inability of specialists to look at security comprehensively becomes a breeding ground for myopic behavior.

The ironic thing for us is we have been preaching that security programs should have been using more generalists for years. We wrote this in articles and illustrated in our presentations that most security programs were primarily struggling because (1) they did not use generalists enough and (2) the generalists they did use did not possess strong enough communication skills to act as the communication bridge that they should be. We are used to getting our fair share of criticism, which is often justified, but what always surprised us was the amount on this specific issue, at times leading to straight out hostility. Many argued with us that communication skills should take a back seat to strong specialized security skills in most if not all situations.

Figure 4.6 indicates that the security profession is split between the idea of using generalists and specialists. Where does your security program fall and why?

Of course, we like to believe that the recent rise in the use of generalist roles such as the security architect (just check any job board these days to see their popularity) as an acknowledgement that (1) we were right for once and (2) putting a heavy emphasis on specialists for most security efforts does not work in most organizations. Further, we believe it is the myopia that is generated by specialists that is fueling this need for change and the new popularity of roles like the security architect.

Though there has been more acceptance of generalist roles, the security profession still hasn't arrived at a consensus that generalist skills are needed badly when addressing security in most organizations. We are still stuck in the "Henry

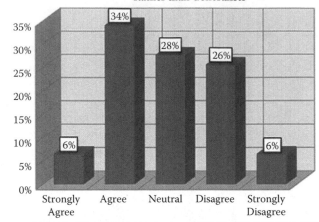

The Majority of Our Security Team Are Specialists Rather than Generalists

Figure 4.6 This figure indicates that the security profession is split between the idea of using generalists and specialists. Where does your security program fall and why?

Ford" mode, choosing to focus on specialists to staff our security organizations. This may be an effective means of building a Model-T Ford, but it certainly is not the way to build a balanced and effective security organization. This factor, combined with the scarcity of generalist resources, has fueled the growth of myopia within our field.

No Hablas Security

Security has its own language. Terms such as "compensating controls," "risk profile," "threat profile," "access control lists (ACLs)," "man trap," and "dry pipe" do little to foster communication to individuals outside of the security arena. As a matter of fact, they produce the opposite effect by turning people off. No one likes to feel stupid or left out of a topic or conversation. Security professionals who use this type of nomenclature when discussing security outside of their peer group will create a form of myopia through a failure to communicate. Essentially, this leaves people to work with their own definition and understanding of security.

Life is a Wheel

Myopia will breed myopia. Whether we are discussing tangible security elements, such as security policies, or intangible items, such as philosophy, what we sow is what we reap. These items will propagate themselves and continue to return in another form. From that respect they are like a weed. For example, if your security policies only address physical issues, then the perspective of those who read them will similarly be influenced to view physical security as the dominant issue of concern. This is specialization by process, where your security program is directing the organization to specialize on one factor of security. We know what comes with specialization; that's right, it's myopia.

Buyer Beware

Many organizations rely on vendors as a form of educational institution. They will invite vendors in a certain security discipline, to educate them on that specific area of knowledge, but often on over-arching security concepts as well. This is not necessarily a bad practice, but you must take it in context. Understand that vendors are also observing the trends and demand within the market space. Many organizations are asking for a comprehensive view of security and a good vendor is always looking to match a need with a solution.

The issue arises specifically in that vendors, specifically product vendors, are always organized by specialization (they read the Henry Ford Story too). The larger the organization and the broader the product offering, the higher the degree of stratification and specialization will be. The mission and mandate (M&M) of such organizations demands the use of specialists in each product space domain. Let us prove this little postulate with an exercise.

Exercise 11

This exercise can also be found in the Appendix with worksheets.

Objective

Many organizations trust their vendors to provide them with detailed knowledge and understanding for many complex security issues. The objective of this exercise is to evaluate whether your vendors have a comprehensive view of security or one that is fairly narrow within their specialty. This is important in determining the level of credibility that you bestow in the vendors on a given topic, specifically if they claim to have a heuristic view of security.

Exercise

The next time you find yourself in need of a security product, try this approach. Invite several product vendors to your company, preferably market leaders in that specific area who offer multiple products that could meet several of your organizational security needs. This probably is not very different from your current process. Where we would like you to alter your tactics is in asking each vendor to come prepared with a sales pitch, as well as the ability to provide:

1. One person who can speak knowledgeably about how all of his or her products interoperate or leverage the features of each other
2. A high-level, one-page diagram that illustrates the idea to facilitate the conversation

Product companies, in general, whether focused on security or not, will always assign a product manager per product. They seldom assign a role for working across product lines. As a result, these organizations rarely employ generalists, let alone a security generalist. Where this is detrimental to a security effort is when the sales organization represents itself as a generalist and presents a specialist or myopic view of a security topic. Keep in mind that this will only create myopia if the organization's security professionals blindly accept what they are told by the vendor.

Security Training

General user security training is a double-edged sword. On one hand, it expands the perspective and knowledge of the end-user population and on the other hand it can breed a form of myopia. Since security is a vast topic, it must be subdivided into consumable bite-sized chunks that can be spoon-fed to the security neophyte, with each little chunk taught within a single class.

The myopia comes from the misconception on the part of the student that the class represents the universe of security. Once completed, the student now knows about security. This is relatively easy to circumvent by discussing the vastness of the subject up-front with the class. It takes less than five minutes and will prevent the potential for this brand of myopia. Oh, if life was only so easy! This is seldom done because the folks teaching the classes are generally specialists or academics who only understand the universe of their teaching guide.

Causes of Myopia Section Summary

As you can see, there are many different causes of myopia within an environment. It should also be interesting to note that whereas apathy is often something that people choose to do, myopic behavior in many cases is still a choice, but more a direct effect of our level of focus on a particular task or function. As a result, we believe that this makes it more dangerous. We will continue our discussion now with a look at the cause and effect of myopia on our True Security Model.

Figure 4.7 represents a graphical depiction of the human, system, organizational, and security program causes of myopia.

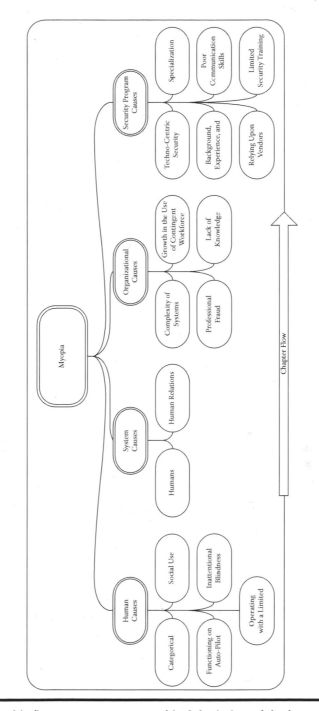

Figure 4.7   This figure represents a graphical depiction of the human, system, organizational, and security program causes of myopia.

Cause and Effect of Myopia on the True Security Model

This section will highly resemble the approach that we used in the last chapter on apathy. As we mentioned above, be aware of how easy it is for each of the groups discussed to both produce and fall victim to myopia. This constraint is truly nefarious in that its very nature prevents its correction. People who are myopic tend to truly believe in their perspective, making it difficult to correct. The other troubling aspect of this constraint is both the prevalence and frequency of occurrence. These two factors make it one of the more influential of the constraints outlined in this book.

Within this section, we will again direct our efforts more specifically to the cause and effect of myopia on your security efforts. As a result, we will not focus on the overall effects of myopia on humans and systems in general. Of course, as we mentioned earlier, your security program is a system that is comprised of humans, so much of what is presented will be blended between effects that occur from myopia in humans, systems, and your security efforts; it is not intentional, rather unavoidable.

The True Security Model will also again be utilized in the same manner as the last chapter on apathy. The goal is to provide a tangible framework to provide support and reference as we deal with intangible concepts.

We will also close out each section with a look at the security con. The con associated with myopia is far more subtle, but present nonetheless. We believe that this can be attributed to the fact that many of the people who suffer from myopia, including those that are security professionals, simply do not realize that they have this affliction. We will have more on this topic later on in the chapter. First, we will present a quick review of the True Security Model.

Myopia and the True Security Model

Below are the various groups commonly found within an organization and the desired actions that we hope to obtain from each group in order to achieve true security.

As a quick refresher on the True Security Model, refer to the target groups and desired behavior table below:

Organizational Group	Desired Action or Behavior
Board of directors	Endorsement
Executive management	Priority
Middle management	Resources
Supervisory management	Support
Employees	Diligence
Consumers	Trust
Security program	Execution

For each group, we will explore the cause and effect relationship that myopia can have on the desired action we need to obtain. We will begin by providing some common symptoms that are displayed when myopia is present, and then we will look at some of the more intangible effects. We will also discuss the ways in which chief information security officers (CISOs) and others are compensating (security con) for the effects of myopia within each group. Of course, we will start at the top of the food chain with our pals on the board of directors.

Myopia and the Board of Directors

Myopia at the board level and most executive positions within an organization, which we will get to next, is usually the result of the groups around them possessing more, and usually better, information about security than the board members themselves. In the world of economics, this is known as "information asymmetry."

Information asymmetry describes a condition where the relevant information regarding an issue is known to some, but not all, parties conducting a transaction. This phenomenon is most often ascribed to the manipulation of others within financial transactions such as real estate and purchasing a car or a computer. This condition often leads to the accumulation of wealth by the individual with the best information.

Because board members are generally not security experts, they can only make decisions based on the information that is provided to them by others. If that information is limited or insular, then naturally their decisions regarding security will also reflect that limitation. In short, their perspective and associated decision will reflect the myopic information with which they were furnished. In many cases, the only people qualified to provide a comprehensive view of security are the members of the security office within an organization. In our experience though, these people seem to have difficulty getting into board meetings, or at least getting active participation in the sessions when they are invited. Instead, the security office often leverages the access afforded to another group, generally always present in board meetings, with significant influence in these meetings: internal audit. As a result, more times than not, security piggybacks on audit to carry many of its messages to the board. On a positive note, this enables security to borrow some of the influence and credibility of audit and also provides board members with information in an audit format, which is something that board members are generally accustomed to receiving. The downside to this approach is that the information that makes its way to the board is based on audit findings or other detective controls.

The bottom line is that board members seldom get enough of the right information to form an accurate picture of the security posture for an organization. This is because the perspective of an auditor is based on tools and techniques that are often reactionary in nature. The audit process is a form of detective control that is initiated post facto; it does not function as a preventative control. Though this view of security is valid, it is also limited. The emphasis evaluating the effectiveness of something that has already transpired is a form of myopia.

As we mentioned in the introduction of this section, the security con at this level is far more subtle than with other security constraints. It occurs when members of the security office recognize that the information presented to the board is an incomplete view of security for the organization. If they remain silent, which many often do, this is a demonstration of the con. What makes it subtle is that there was no action required by the perpetrators; just remain silent and let the information, or lack of information, do its work.

Myopia and the Executive Team

Myopia at the executive team level is often caused, again, through a manipulated message based on the types of security information presented to the group. You would think that the origin of such messages and information would be the security program, but this is not always the case. In most organizations, the executive team is actually fairly well insulated from the security team. All of this security mumbo jumbo apparently gives the executive team a headache. Not to say that there is an absolute void between the two groups, but when communication does occur, it is generally at such a high level that it really does not provide enough context to allow a comprehensive, big-picture view of security. That's the paradox which security professionals must address. Executive management likes to operate at 50,000 feet. That mode of operation acts as a distillation process that allows for the simplification of complex issues. However, security does not distill into a model that is consumable by executives. It takes background and education to work with the "50,000-foot" model; the kind of time that most executives are not willing to spend individually. The result is that they turn to other sources that claim to have created the big picture that requires little context or education. As a result, the perception of security at the executive level is often formed by other means.

The first of these is through what executives read in the news. We have been in at least ten different organizations where a directive is issued by an executive based on a story related to security that they read in the newspaper or saw on the news. The difficulty with this approach is that often these messages are based purely on fear of issues such as terrorism or the loss of customer credit card information by a large company. The other way in which executives get their messages and information about security is through high-level vendors, such as large consultancies.

The message from these groups is often based on the needs of a vendor, not necessarily that of the client organization. This approach is also appealing because executives like to meet with other executives. The results of these meetings can be tragic because the partner or high-level manager at the vendor will often be just as myopic in his or her view of security as the executives within the client organization, even if this vendor specifically sells security widgets or services. Another related area from which executives love to get their security information is research firms.

Organizations such as Gartner and Forrester are the executive's best friend. They perform their industry "research" and present the issues in bite-sized chunks that are ideally suited for the executive palate. This information is then consumed and interpreted in a vacuum, resulting in direction or some edict that many times has nothing to do with the client organization. You know what they say about work that is performed in a vacuum: "It sucks!" However, the saving grace in this situation is that the executives in question did not have to interface with those pesky security people in their own organization, thank goodness!

Another powerful means by which executives receive information about security is through audits. This group loves audits and often believes that audit reports are the final word when it comes to security. This is another element that can be associated with the regulatory effect and it is important to recognize this overemphasis that executive management places on audits. Finally, the last way in which executives learn about security is, just like everyone else, through personal experience with items such as securing their home computers.

These experiences, often technical in nature, are things we all deal with in our lives. Examples include items such as addressing when their antivirus software is stealing 50 percent of their central processing unit (CPU) cycles, a crashed home machine, or a virus infection caused by their children downloading software from the Internet.

The result of these types of exposure for this group is that it often leads to the formation a myopic perspective that is based on fear (from the news and security vendors), is highly reactionary (from the auditors), and is highly technical (from their own experiences with personal computing equipment). If the security effort at the organization does not have a strong communication channel to this group, which we mentioned is often the case, then the effect of these other influences will dominate their decision making regarding security.

The perpetrators of the security con at this level are potentially anyone that is part of the channels that provide security information to this group: from news organizations who represent their messages as comprehensive while they are actually just messages of fear designed to sell newspapers or boost television ratings, to security vendors who teach with the motive to sell more widgets or services. Last but not least, as security professionals we also participate in this behavior when we stand by and let it occur, or actively participate in it ourselves.

Myopia and Middle Management

Hopefully, we made it clear that most of the myopic thinking caused above middle managers is based on a lack of information leading to a limited perspective. As we work down the food chain in an organization, this begins to change. When it comes to middle managers, they are just what their name suggests, in the middle. On one hand, they are the individuals who have to deal with the myopic perspective of their superior management. On the other hand, middle managers generally live outside the gates of "Mahogany Row" with the commoners of the realm. This happens to be the same neighbors occupied by most security programs. As a result, middle management often has much more exposure to the security program, providing a powerful education vehicle. This presents an interesting predicament for middle management: go with your education and experience or the perspective of your boss. Myopia at this level occurs when middle management does not properly balance the influence of a myopic perspective from its boss with its own educated views on security. This variable makes it difficult to consistently get the support from middle management that is required for the attainment of true security.

In some cases, this group is made up of good soldiers who strictly follow the guidance and direction of their superiors, which can lead to difficulty if their management has a limited perspective of security. If the security effort is able to properly educate the middle manager or the middle manager already understands security, then you are in good shape, but you are not out of the woods yet. The unpredictability of the middle management will generally deny you an automatic win.

The con at this level is usually performed by middle management. After all, they are placed in a tough spot. Sitting in the middle, they often have to play politics in order to achieve larger objectives. This means sacrificing some issues in order to support others. Security is generally an afterthought for this group, which makes it easy to overlook or sacrifice.

Myopia and the Supervisory Team

At this level, the causes of myopia begin to shift even further away from a lack of information and more toward compartmentalized thinking. Supervisors are the noncommissioned officers of the organization. They are the sergeants and corporals who live directly in the trenches with the troops. This close proximity to the work and its associated details produces an individual with far more specialized skills and views. This level of specialization leads to the weaknesses that we discussed earlier in this chapter, including compartmentalized thinking or lack of focus outside the supervisors' specific tasks. Unless a concerted effort is made to educate the supervisory group it is not uncommon for security to be left out of their narrow perspective or focus.

The impacts of myopia on this group can be significant, especially if there is a great deal of myopic thinking at higher levels of management. In these situations, many of the processes and procedures that this group employs have been designed by those who do not, or choose not to, understand security at higher levels of management. This results in the continued proliferation of myopia, unless the supervisory group has the ability to modify the existing processes and procedures to reduce the effect, and has the awareness to understand the need to make changes.

This situation, coupled with the tendency for this group to be highly compartmentalized in its thinking, leads to trouble in receiving the support that you will need from this group in order to achieve true security.

The security con at this level is virtually nonexistent. This is due to the fact that the actions that could be considered as negative are generally unintentional. This is the nefarious nature of myopia: you don't know what you don't know. The danger comes when this behavior or belief set is so firmly entrenched that there is an unwillingness to learn new things or challenge the status quo. Then you are really stuck.

Myopia and Employees

The largest portion of the population within organizations is generally represented by employees who do not possess any management responsibilities. If executive management is operating at 50,000 feet, this group is living its professional life at sea level. At this level, in today's world, specialized skills are required in order to perform virtually any job function. This level of specialization produces compartmentalized thinking yielding a high probability of developing a myopic perspective regarding security.

Since this group comprises the bulk of the organization, the effects of myopia can again be significant. The difficulty stems from the item that we hope to obtain from this group: diligence. But, how can we expect diligence toward issues outside of the group's area of specialty, e.g., security? The answer is that we shouldn't.

The con is really not present at this level. Each individual within this group simply does not possess the power or influence to affect or benefit from a misstatement of security. As a result, the actions taken by individuals at this level seldom lack the political or self-serving motives that we attribute to the con. Generally speaking, most employees want to do the right thing, if they are made aware of what constitutes the right thing.

Myopia and Consumers

Consumers are also victims of specialized thinking leading to a myopic perspective, but the causes are different than that of an organization's employees. Consumers live up to their name; they consume with little regard to anything other than their own fulfillment. There is nothing wrong with this behavior. They provide utility to the organization, in the form of currency, and the organization provides goods or services that are consumed. It is the great capitalist way! However, a closer look at this common exchange yields some interesting findings. The first is the self-centered nature of the consumer.

Consumers care little about other consumers. As long as one gets the goods or services at an acceptable price, life is good. As long as bad things do not happen to me, life is good. For example, you decide to purchase a brand new computer from the Internet. The computer arrives without incident and operates perfectly. About a week later, you read about how this company had 25 percent of its credit card records stolen by hackers. Further, you determine that your credit card information was not part of the group stolen. Though you may be interested in how they will safeguard your information in the future, your interest in the individuals who were victimized is minimal. We are not saying that you are uncaring, selfish, or a narcissist. What we are saying is that you are human, and humans tend to be far more concerned with their own concerns and issues than those of others. This type of behavior is myopic. The other way in which myopia can develop within consumers is with a product-centric focus.

In this case, consumers become fixated on the product or service they are acquiring, and not on any of the security surrounding the service, delivery, or transaction elements of the product or service. This leads to the same result: compartmentalized thinking and a lack of interest in security.

The effects of this behavior are again a myopic perspective that leads to a blind trust. Trusting blindly is not the same thing as the pure informed trust that we want from this group. This is because the uninformed nature of a blind trust can lead to random results and behaviors in the future.

There are two groups that take center stage for the security con at this level. The first group is the sales and marketing team within an organization. We add the group to the list because it generally controls all of the information that is presented to the customer. After all, if information is unlikely to increase sales or improve the image of the organization, then why would it be distributed? That is not an unreasonable question, but it does take advantage of the implied or blind trust of the consumer.

The next group that is involved in the con is the security program within an organization. This occurs in any situation where the security of the consumer is placed in jeopardy and the security organization fails to correct the problem or make it known allowing consumers to make an informed decision. In that case, they are flexing their asymmetrical information muscles and taking advantage of the blind trust of the consumer.

Lastly, we believe the consumer is participating in the con. This is not participation by direct action, but participation by inaction. We are not saying that everyone should become a security nerd, but it should not be unreasonable to ask some basic questions about how an organization handles your confidential information prior to handing it over.

Effects Summary

What we find interesting about myopia is the different ways in which it is caused, manifested, and propagated within and amongst each group differently. Of all the groups, the most ironic sufferer of myopia is executives. How many times have you heard an executive mutter the words, "I want a high-level view of this issue" or "Let's not get down in the weeds on this stuff"? This approach to thinking requires high levels of abstraction for every subject. This process does not work well in security because of its all encompassing nature. When details are removed, it cascades into the removal of interrelated items and nuances. The end result is a myopic, oversimplified version of the issues. No wonder executives don't like security, their primary tools for developing big-picture views do not work, often making them the most myopic in the organization. We find the idea of the big picture thinker as the most myopic very fascinating. Now let's move on to some solutions for myopia.

Solutions

Before we get going, one thing we want to make very clear when addressing the issue of myopia is to remember that it almost always boils down to a limited perspective. This perspective may be the intent of the individual or group, but the cause is usually the same: limited information. No one wants to make decisions without the right information, but hopefully we have made it clear how the types of information that people receive can be filtered by either the person or the surrounding environment. As a result, the majority of solutions that you will see in this section focus on the best way to get the right information about security to the right people in order to enable the right decisions. We understand that this can be an undertaking, but it is by no means impossible; just remember to be patient.

Alright, now that we have a better understanding of our enemy, it is time to see what can be done to deal with this troublesome little gremlin called myopia. To begin this section, we will ask Skye to chime in on some considerations that support the creation and maintenance of a healthy system and then she will describe some of the human-focused soft skills that are helpful in combating this menace.

System Theory Considerations

Always remember that a healthy system is constantly adapting to new information as part of its normal life-cycle. However, without clear and useful communication channels, this function can be severely impaired and unable to perform efficiently. Therefore, we must always be aware of the means by which information is collected, processed, and distributed. In addition, care must be taken to ensure the proper operation and availability of these mechanisms. Just as a car requires scheduled tune-ups, communication channels require periodic review and adjustment. Do not take these items for granted as they are the life blood of any system.

Touchy Feely Considerations

The key to reducing myopia is to first recognize that there is often far more information available in every situation than what your current state of mind may be allowing you to absorb. In your day-to-day activities, constantly look for new information that will bring a more enlightened view of the world. This can be achieved through being present in every moment, being open to new ways of thinking and the perspectives of others, and through recognition that there is always more out there to learn.

What is most important is that the only person who needs to change anything to achieve a more comprehensive view of the world is you. With some effort, it is amazing the doors in your mind that can be opened.

Security Solutions

OK, this is starting to get scary. We actually understood everything that Skye said and it made sense. So, let's see how we can apply some of our newfound knowledge to our primitive world of security. We will begin by looking in the mirror and evaluating ourselves, as security practitioners, and then looking at how we can affect the behavior of others.

Look in the Mirror

As we stated earlier, the nefarious aspect of myopia is that you may suffer from this ailment and not even recognize the condition. After all, you can't know what you don't know ... or something like that. So, our first prescription is to take a look at yourself, your background, and your environment. Though every situation is unique, we have developed a quick exercise to aid you in determining your level of myopia.

Exercise 12

This exercise can also be found in the Appendix with worksheets.

Objective

The objective of this exercise is to evaluate your own level of myopia as it pertains to security.

Exercise

- Brainstorm all of your security issues on a piece of paper.
- Reflect on your security issues by writing down what issues fall into the following categories: people, process, technology, facilities, and miscellaneous.
- Now place your findings in the above categories or categories that you came up with that we did not address.
- Is there one particular category that disproportionately outweighs the others?
- Assess your level of comfort for the following categories: listed below or use your own self-created categories.
- Honestly assess your findings. Do you find your ability to address security questions highly polarized or lacking breadth and depth in one or more areas?

Example

Category	Description	Level of Comfort (circle one)
People	This area represents the sociological controls that can be put into place to modify the behavior of individuals regarding security issues	High, medium, low
Process	This area represents the ability to integrate secure processes into the organization's business practices	High, medium, low

Category	Description	*Level of Comfort* *(circle one)*
Technology	This area represents the ability to apply technical solutions to meet the security requirements of the organization	High, medium, low
Facilities	This area represents the ability to evaluate and safeguard the physical components of an organization	High, medium, low

Measuring Your Own Gap

If you felt unsure about some of these categories, it's cool. We are not stating that you need to be *UberSecuriteeGeek* and know everything about each category. After all, each of these categories gets pretty deep. However, if you find that your level of comfort is limited to one or two of these areas, it may be an indicator of a myopic perspective, at least specific to security of course. Even if your job does not require an understanding of some of these areas, we feel that a well-balanced security professional still will understand the fundamentals. Our fundamental message is that you need to open yourself up to the possibility that there are important items that may be just beyond your current focus. Once you take that step, you will be amazed at how many of these overlooked items become clear and relevant. We know what you are thinking, "OK guys, this isn't the *secret* where I wish something into happening … give me something tangible!"

This is where conventional wisdom and tools become useful. The first place to begin is with the industry standard frameworks. Things such as National Institute of Standards and Technology (NIST) Series and ISO27001-2 are very useful for identifying gaps in your perspective or fundamental knowledge. If you find that you get the basics but are looking for a little more depth in one subject or another, professional organizations generally have their own best practices. For example, in the area of facilities, the IESNA Guideline for Security Lighting and Crime Prevention Through Environmental Design (CPTED) practices represent two well-accepted practices from which you may learn a great deal.

Measuring Others

There is no doubt that a myriad of sources exist for expanding *your* perspective on security. However, making yourself smarter is only half the battle. If we only had to worry about ourselves, the organization would likely be secure. Unfortunately, or in actuality, fortunately, for all of you team players, we also have to consider the level of myopia that exists outside of our security program. The means by which we prefer to measure myopia for those individuals is through the use of information mapping. It is a relatively easy process where we break the organization down into groups and determine the sources of information that influence their view and comprehension of security. If you recall, earlier in the chapter, we cited a number of examples where the information received by a particular group directly influenced its perspective on security. Therefore, it is necessary to discover these channels to determine if the information is myopic itself or if it can be used to deliver a more balanced message. We understand that tracking down every source of information for every group would be a daunting task. So, in the name of expediency, we always begin by determining who is receiving security information from the security program. Of course, this assumes that the security program itself or you directly are not delivering a myopic message, but hopefully that will not be the case in your situation. This should reduce the analysis set to a reasonable number of groups. If you are unable to answer this first question, it just became your homework assignment: find out who is getting their decision-making information from your security program. If you can answer this question, then start with the groups in the True Security Model. It would look something like the following:

Group	What Information Is Your Security Program Providing to This Group? (e.g., regular interaction, training, awareness campaigns, presentations, studies, risk reports)	What Other Sources of Security Information Are Received by This Group?(e.g., audit reports, personal experience, sales material, news outlets, vendors)	Is the Level and Quantity of Information Sufficient for the Group to Develop a Comprehensive View of Security?(yes or no)
Board of directors			
Executives			
Middle management			
Supervisors			
Employees			
Consumers			

This table would be the beginning of a mapping process. After completing this mini-map, if you find that there are a large number of gaps, it is best to conduct further investigation to identify whether a myopic perspective exists on the part of each group where there is a deficiency. We can tell you from experience, usually where there is smoke, there is fire. The next step would be to drill down into each group, building a more focused information map, and begin developing a plan for providing better information to each group. This may sound like a lot of work, but in a medium-sized organization it can be done in about a week. The maps do not require a large amount of detail, just enough to point you in the right direction.

Now that you have a better idea of your level of myopia and that of the organization, it is time to take some corrective action. Myopia is like fungus; it grows and spreads in the darkness of ignorance. It is time to expose the mold to a little sunshine.

Sunshine = Communication

If communication is the lifeblood of a system, then it is safe to assume that it is the lifeblood of your security program. It is also not just the quality of the information that is communicated, but the means by which it is communicated. This means that we need to focus on the mechanisms that are available and the different ways in which they can be used. Though this is not a book on communications, it is wildly important that we create a baseline in which you can move forward. Therefore, here are some considerations.

Rule 1: Using security specific nomenclature does not make you look smart, it makes you look like a nerd. People, in general, do not like to feel stupid or be made to feel like an outsider. Know your audience and speak with them—not above their level or below their level—but at their level. This shows respect, creates community, and enhances interchange of ideas. Our fancy security-speak manages to do both. In our experience, security-speak actually acts as a trigger that provides a person with permission to be ignorant and turn off the conversation. Save your security-speak for discussion with your fellow security nerds. Choosing your words carefully is certainly sage advice, but which words do you choose?

Rule 2: Know thy target audience. Once again, we will return to Communications 101: always know your target audience. We will not belabor this point because we covered this topic at length in our first book, but this is the second most common mistake that we see our security brethren commit. For example, we doubt that the board of directors would be terribly enthralled with the logs from your brand new intrusion detection system. Determine your audience in advance and provide the information in a form that is understandable, interesting, relevant, and consumable to them, not to you.

Rule 3: Pick a theme for your messages. Because security is so large and difficult to get your arms or head around, do not try to circle the globe every time you communicate a message. For example, do not provide a 900-page report to a group and expect them to remember even ten pages of it. Instead, before submitting any type of security communication to a group, identify the overarching theme to be delivered, then make your message short, sweet, and to the point.

Rule 4: Limit the use of security vendors or consultants for delivering your security messages. We understand that there are times when a consultant's voice carries more influence with your management. But, turning the delivery of your message over to another party is risky. There are many great vendors in the realm of security, but it is natural that because a vendor is not officially a part of your organization, his or her agenda may be slightly different than yours and that of your program. After all, vendors are trying to sell a product or service, or prove that the one you just purchased works properly. The even bigger risk, however, with vendors delivering your messages is that in many situations they will create their own rating systems or nomenclature for common security issues or practices. Because these vendors become so focused on their own products or services, this new language is usually a side effect of their own myopia within their organization. What is comical is that it is usually worse in the larger security vendors, yet all of these vendors have recently been trying to pitch a comprehensive view of security through a complete line of security products or services. The result is that they are often flying completely blind, and allowing them to deliver your messages in these situations will make your job more difficult by severely confusing the target audience with a language that only the vendors themselves understand.

Rule 5: Fear is a poor salesman. Remember that the use of fear, uncertainty, and doubt (FUD) is a turnoff for most people. It is far too easy for them to dismiss you and your message as nothing more than alarmist rhetoric. Just remember the story of "The Boy Who Cried Wolf" or "Chicken Little"; there is a lot of wisdom in those stories.

Rule 6: Utilize your view. One of the coolest things about security within most organizations is the perspective or "view" that is available. This view is one that is attainable by few others within the organization. Ask yourself: is there really any meeting, short of board or executive meetings, to which security professionals cannot gain admittance? In most cases, you can go to any meeting, sit down, and just participate. When the other meeting-goers ask why you are there, simply reply that you are attending for security. In most cases, the meeting will then just roll right along. In the name of full disclosure, we have actually done this before, though we do not recommend that you start doing this tomorrow at work. The point is that because security touches everything, it is not beyond the realm of possibility that you would need to attend that meeting. Of course, the other participants will usually not understand why you are attending the meeting, nor would they care (myopia). They will be fine just having you sit, listen, and learn. Oh, what a powerful tool this is!

The other potent item associated with the global view provided to security, and specifically CISOs, is the fact that you have access to both a horizontal view, across management levels, and a vertical view, from the board down to the regular employees, of the organization. This capability is easily the most overlooked and underutilized weapon in the CISO arsenal. This view allows access to the majority of available communication channels within the organization. It also enables one to create custom information channels to accommodate one's needs that might not exist otherwise. CISOs and their teams have the opportunity to be like an airline that travels to every destination, carrying messages to far off locals that are starving for attention. In essence, this capability enables any security professional, within just about any security role, to act as an information broker. This capability becomes even more useful when you consider the state of most formal and informal corporate or government communication channels.

Rule 7: Team meetings are training gold. If possible, inviting individuals to attend selected meetings within your security program can go a long way to helping them understand the scope and breadth of security. Make them an honorary member of the team. We have done this on numerous occasions to break through the myopia barrier. In addition, if other groups will let you attend a team meeting or two, go for it. This seems very simple, and is, but can be unbelievably powerful. Give it a try.

Rule 8: Utilize generalists in your security program. Generalists in security programs usually are categorized as security architects. In today's myopic world, security architects are crucial at bridging the gap of communication across disciplines. Of course, in every security program you will also need specialists, but we have yet to encounter even one security program that is not better off with at least one generalist or security architect. If your program does not have one, evaluate if this is leading to a myopic perspective within the group. If you are not in a role on the security team where you are in charge of hiring, try to work with the others on your team that are. Hopefully this book has given some information to help in making a good case.

Rule 9: Be patient. If you are successful at getting people to achieve a more broadened view, this will often lead to more questions and considerations from this audience. Be patient when this occurs and take the time to feed an inquisitive mind when you find one.

Rule 10: Do not confuse a broadened view with having to be responsible for everything. Just because you should be aware of the security considerations of physical security does not mean that you need to be responsible for the physical security of the organization. Your view or understanding of items does not need to translate to owning accountability for them within your job role. Conversely, if physical security is not one of your job responsibilities, you should not simply forget about it. Remember how we opened the chapter with a story about how a server was stolen because of a myopic perspective? In every situation it has been caused by a myopic view due to people that did not follow this rule.

Affect the Behavior of Others

So far, all of the solutions have been targeted at you. These are things that you can do to aid the cause of security. However, to combat myopia, we need to be able to positively affect others within the organization.

The first recommendation is direct and relatively simple. Make aspects of security relevant to everyone in the organization by making security everyone's responsibility. This can be powerful because most people are conditioned to focus on things more closely when they are made directly accountable for them. Here are some tips for doing this, you know, the tangible stuff.

The easiest way to do this is, when possible, get the powers that be to add security-specific responsibilities to every job description within the organization. It does not have to be terribly egregious. It could be as simple as requiring all employees to secure all working papers prior to completing the work day by not leaving anything on their desk when they leave work. In addition, combine statements with an explanation of why they need to perform these tasks. You may remember that providing the "why" was a solution to combating apathy from the last chapter. When you combine the "why" element with the "responsibility" element in job descriptions, you essentially can kill two birds with one stone. You address apathy by enhancing the understanding of your security approach and myopia by expanding the perspective of your fellow employees. The best way to get these changes implemented is through meetings with the hiring folks, usually located in human resources. Our experience is that these people are usually open to making these changes to job descriptions, but you have to focus on the "why" with them as well. Be patient and they will usually get there and understand the benefits this can bring to the organization as a whole. While you are waiting for the windfall of those efforts, there are other things that you can do right now.

Since people will usually forget about their job descriptions fairly quickly after beginning a job, you will also want to continue to remind people of their security responsibilities. This can be achieved through security training and awareness campaigns that target employee responsibility. This does not need to be a monumental task, just a few frequent reminders to let them know that someone is paying attention to their conduct.

If you look back on the section that discussed communication, we elaborated on your ability to become an information broker within the organization. Now is the time that this little secret pays off. Take that information and start using it to aid others in accomplishing their own goals. That's right, go out and commit a few good deeds for someone else. This act of charity will come back to you and your security effort tenfold. From that point forward, you will have their attention. Further, they will want to be part of your team; after all, you are one of the people who makes them successful. Lastly, they will want more of that global perspective once they have had a taste of it. All of these factors combined allow you, over time, to deliver messages and themes that can break through the typical myopia of today's workforce.

Chapter Summary

We have tried to provide some practical techniques and considerations that you can do to combat myopia within your environment. Remember to begin by focusing on expanding and measuring your own view of security, and then look to influence others. Also, keep in mind that this is a never-ending process. As long as you choose to work in this field, it will be a continuous cycle of learning and relearning. We are not merely pundits of this philosophy, but as security practitioners, we are also going through this exercise in our own lives. The key is to be aware that any time you work in a group, there is going to be a perspective out there from which you can learn something new. Take the time to broaden your own horizons and build communication bridges to new sources of information. It will pay in the end.

Chapter 5

Primacy

"I'm actually very easy to deal with ... just as long as we do everything my way!"

Overview

So far, we have discussed two constraints that are the sleepers of the four. What we mean is that they are fairly innocuous with no blazing trumpets to announce their arrival. The myopic person does not realize he or she is myopic and the apathetic person does not care enough to announce his or her apathy. Hence, we use the designation of passive constraints. Of course, that does not make them any less powerful, just a little more difficult to diagnose. The next constraint does not suffer from shyness, in fact, quite the contrary. The security constraint of primacy is a true extrovert who frequently takes center stage in a variety of forms.

What is primacy? If we look in the dictionary, it is defined as:

> Primacy: "the state of being first (as in importance, order, or rank)."
> *The American Heritage® Dictionary of the English Language, Fourth Edition*

This is something that we all see every day in the workplace. It generally takes the form of corporate politics or individual ego. This can be something as simple as working harder than your fellow employees to get a promotion, to actively manipulating a report to move your career ahead. Sometimes it is just someone's competitive nature. So what makes primacy so difficult for our security efforts?

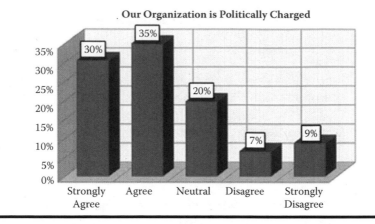

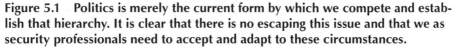

Figure 5.1 Politics is merely the current form by which we compete and establish that hierarchy. It is clear that there is no escaping this issue and that we as security professionals need to accept and adapt to these circumstances.

The results in Figure 5.1 shouldn't surprise anyone. History has demonstrated that most human interaction will develop aspects of competition and hierarchy. Politics is merely the current form by which we compete and establish that hierarchy. It is clear that there is no escaping this issue and that we as security professionals need to accept and adapt to these circumstances.

The answer to this is simple: unpredictability. Due to its close alignment with the good old human ego, the manner in which primacy is demonstrated can vary heavily from person to person. Making things more confusing, these demonstrations are not always a bad thing. Establishing an order of precedence or a chain of command is actually very healthy. Of course, for every person demonstrating acts of primacy for the greater good there is someone else who is clearly working only with his or her own interests in mind. It is the latter that can keep even the sanest of chief information security officers (CISOs) awake at night.

To start things off and get your mind lubricated for the work ahead, we have provided an example from one of our recent encounters with corporate America. This is a classic example of how even a simple company celebration can lead to countless demonstrations of primacy.

Primacy Tune-Up

We were working in one of the larger organizations in North America. This company is a household name and was definitely the type of company that many people dream of working for. It just so happened, while we were there, they were celebrating the successful achievement of a critical milestone. To celebrate this achievement, they scheduled a very large party and invited all of the employees and even vendors to participate in the celebration. At first glance, the event looked like it would be a lot of fun. There were bands playing and food stations everywhere.

Everything seemed like a normal event, except for one thing. As people arrived, it became very clear that the caterers either did not anticipate the number of attendees or were not given accurate estimates. As people started to filter into the event, the lines for food immediately swelled to absurd lengths. At most stations the food lines were up to 45 minutes long. The effect on the crowd was pure agony. The effect on nerds like us was pure ecstasy. You see, we had already formulated our true security model and this debacle was furnishing us with a laboratory of about 7,000 rats; we mean people to analyze. Nothing demonstrates the elements of primacy in humans like primal needs, which for most of the attendees were about to go into overdrive. In this case, the need to eat was clearly the issue driving the decision making of the attendees. Here is some of what we saw.

Some used strategy to try and get food quicker. They devised a plan to systematically review the line length of each station, waiting for any break in a line that would give them an advantage. We like to think of these folks as the "scientist rats"; we mean people. They were using their opposable appendages, hyper-evolved primate brains, and any other advantage at their disposal to work the statistics in their favor. Regardless of the mechanism, they were attempting to assert primacy over others through logic.

Others would gamble. They would walk around the event once, measure the length of each line, and pick the one that they believed was the best. What was interesting in this is that when they chose incorrectly and were in a very long line, they would either succumb to the mistake and continue waiting, or start the process all over again. In these situations, this led to some people having to wait even longer to eat than if they simply chose a line at random in the beginning.

As the event progressed and the food issue became more and more apparent, the event organizers began to try to guide people from one station to another. In these instances, there were some who followed the guidance of the organizers and went to the stations in which they were directed. This was also interesting because the organizers had difficulty recognizing which stations had which type of food. As a result, some were directed to long lines only to find once they got to the food stations that this particular station was only comprised of desserts. This is a bummer if you have not eaten anything else yet.

Because of these directional difficulties, others attempted to use their influence as managers within the organization to either help themselves or help their team get food faster. These folks would assert their authority to guide people to one station or another, based on who they wanted to get food to quicker. Other managers took over the role of directing traffic for a different reason; they felt they could do it better than the event organizers. As such, they began to direct traffic accordingly. What was interesting about this is that the direction of the managers often was conducted regardless of its effects on the plans of the event organizer.

The next group on our little tour of primacy was the ethically challenged. These individuals had no issue with cheating, whether it was cutting into line ahead of people or wandering backstage where the food was prepared to obtain their prize, just as long as they got their food sooner.

Another interesting reaction was observed in most of the vendors. Their behavior was fascinating in that they were guests at the event, and as such lacked the same sense of competition or entitlement as the employees. Rather, they acclimated to the chaos and acted as if there was nothing wrong. Great party!

Lastly, there were also those, either managers or employees, who chose to do nothing. They simply waited in line in the hot sun for food that really was not that good, especially by the time they finally got to it.

The point of this story is that we are all driven by needs, and we all react to these needs differently. Whether we are slitting the throats of our co-workers for the last burger at a company event or jockeying for the corner office, primacy is a factor in every aspect of our work life. Therefore, we felt that we could not achieve true security within an organization without combating this creature head on. Stay tuned, the fun is about to start.

This chapter will focus on the constraint of primacy within organizations. As has been the case in each constraint chapter, we will again begin this chapter with the human causes of primacy. In this section, Skye will explore some of our needs as humans and that which motivates us to fulfill them. From there, we will delve into the causes of primacy within systems. Following primacy in humans and systems, the next stop is the organizational causes.

This one should be fun because we are sure that everyone has experienced the anguish of primacy in the workplace. This section will try to identify some root causes of this type of behavior.

To close out the section on causes we will look at the reasons for primacy in security. Oh yes, as long as CISOs remain security professionals and security professionals remain human, we too play in the primacy game.

Once we have established a baseline understanding of the causes of primacy, we will redirect our energy toward the cause and effect relationship of primacy within our true security model. The intent, once again, is to take this abstract concept and make it tangible and addressable during your security efforts.

Finally, we will end the chapter without any solutions since we firmly believe that solutions are overrated. We were just checking to see if you were paying attention. We promised you solutions and we are going to deliver them. As we were saying, the final portion of this chapter will present some tangible solutions to address the issue of primacy in organizations. With that said, let us begin. Skye will get us going with some of the human causes of primacy.

Causes of Primacy in Humans

As humans, we have innate characteristics that make us prime for demonstrating primacy. The first is that as a species, humans are pack animals. Thus we like to live, interact, and achieve goals within groups. Throughout history, we have worked in groups to perform necessary tasks such as hunting, gathering, child rearing, and for means of security. Nowadays, the goals may have changed, but our participation and dynamics within groups holds strong.

Most of us still work in a group setting, an organization or company of some sort, and we generally live as part of one or more relationship and family groups. As a result, we are accustomed to the hierarchy and social positioning that comes within a group dynamic. The issue of course is an individual's position of rank or importance within the group. Historically, the leader of a group would reap the benefit of this social structure, whether it was in food, shelter, or choice of mating partners. Though circumstances may have changed, the basic premise of our "pack" or "tribal" nature remains unchanged with the leaders receiving more than the followers. This basic innate aspect of human social structure drives us to establish working groups, with a defined hierarchy, to achieve the goals of the group.

A great example of this type of behavior for those of us in the United States is observed during jury duty. A group of random individuals is selected from a pool, placed in a room without a predefined social structure, and asked to operate in a collective. When you are on jury duty, there are always those who try to establish their dominance and control, while others wait to see who will be designated as the group leader. The faster the leader is established, the faster due process is achieved and deliberations commence. The reason is simple: the competition is over and there is nothing to fight over other than the case itself.

You may be asking yourself, why would anyone want to be a leader in a jury pool? Good question. Considering what drives the goals of individuals, we must first look at basic human needs.

Needs and Drives

Humans behave in many ways to satisfy the needs or perceived needs that they may have. A need is a condition that exists when humans are or believe themselves to be lacking or deprived of something that has been deemed as necessary. For example, food, water, and sex are basic human needs. Our need for food will determine our behavior to achieve the goal of satisfying hunger. If you found yourself hungry and driving by a fast-food outlet, you may stop and have a meal. If you have ever made the mistake of grocery shopping while hungry, you find you make irrational purchases that satisfy your momentary state of hunger. Regardless, when a need exists, it can create a drive that "motivates" us to find a means of satisfying the need. However, until the need is satisfied, the individual is existing in a state of tension that increases as the perceived need increases. That may describe the state of human needs, but what about things that we *want*? Won't that lead to goal directed actions?

A want can lead to similar behavior as that created by a *need* because a *want* can be considered a conscious recognition of a need. The only difference between the two is that individuals can generally rationalize a want as something that is optional, whereas a need is mandatory. The two can become indistinguishable when dealing with an individual that has an inflated ego combined with the means and drive to achieve the want. This is the case when examining some of the odd or eccentric behavior of the super rich.

Though mankind has evolved somewhat over the years, our needs remain the same; we merely demonstrate them differently. In the past, perhaps the need for shelter was demonstrated by a hut or cave, whereas today it is demonstrated by the five-bedroom house on the beach.

The means by which we attempt to fulfill these needs is ultimately at the source of our motivations. In the work environment, these motivations often lead to demonstrations of primacy.

Let us continue exploring the drivers of primacy with a look at how primacy is caused within any system.

Causes of Primacy within a System

The way humans respond to information is a valuable assessment of how a system is functioning. When you have individuals responding to information of messages sent and received within the system, a communication climate is formed—much like the culture of the corporation. The climate of the system can either be supportive or defensive. Supportive communication creates an air of open communication and honest feedback and moves the system in a way that encourages growth—creating an open system. When the climate of the system inspires defensiveness, which is often the case within an organization or system that is ripe with primacy, then honest communication is smothered or covered up in an attempt for employees to defend themselves in most situations. Thus information is secretive, strategic, and not freely exchanged. More importantly, this environment accelerates and encourages primacy-related demonstrations, as members of the system are forced to participate in order to survive. From a system's perspective, in most situations, this moves the system toward the closed end of the spectrum, where growth is limited and chaos ensues.

Causes of Primacy within an Organization

As we mentioned earlier, organizations are nothing more than groups of people with a common goal. As such, they are also highly suitable for demonstrations of primacy. The first way that primacy is caused within organizations is through the organizational culture.

Organizational Culture

Because we already provided an overview of organizational culture in the chapter on apathy, we will proceed directly to the discussion on organizational culture as it relates to primacy. Let us start by looking at primacy in a vertical organization.

Vertical Organizations and Primacy

It was typical for primitive man to compete for the "alpha" position within the tribe so as to secure the best food, shelter, and choice of mates. These tribes were a form of vertical organization where power was aggregated and concentrated at the top of the structure. Think of them as the prototype of a modern vertical organization.

As is the case in these types of organizations, the rewards are usually disproportionately aggregated along the same lines as power. Though the employees of vertical organizations may not be competing for food, shelter, or mates, they are competing for the power that provides the utility (cash and status) to obtain those very items and more. As evolved as we may claim to be, in the modern vertical organization it is all about power, baby, and those things that power can bring you.

Highly vertical organizations create an environment where competition is fierce to gain power where you either get it or you do not. Those that are highly skilled in the behaviors associated with primacy will often be successful in these environments at getting close to those that are in power and eventually at acquiring some of that power for themselves. Think of it as a sweepstakes where the fittest and most aggressive of the human animals will survive and claim the prize. Because demonstrations of primacy are often a requirement for survival, you can imagine how infested these organizations are with this type of behavior. This is certainly a good example of a "dog-eat-dog" atmosphere.

Well, doesn't that sound awful? People competing against one another to gain the attention of those in power … tsk … tsk … tsk. Meanwhile, what about the folks who actually have the power in highly vertical organizations?

From the perspective of those who are powerful in a vertical organization, the name of the game is to keep the power. This activity is likely to promote displays of primacy in order to establish or maintain territorial boundaries. This is no different than any other animal.

Horizontal Organizations and Primacy

Boy, vertical organizations sound like a jungle when reviewing them from the perspective of primacy. Thank goodness, we are out of there and into the safety and sanctity of the horizontal organization. Wrong! The same motivators are present within a highly horizontal organization as in one that is vertical. Individuals will still seek positions that will return the greatest amount of utility (money and status). The difference lies in the activities that one undertakes to achieve this goal. In horizontal organizations, power is derived by your immediate network of cronies and the ability to accomplish objectives. The network of cronies is comprised of like-minded individuals that find value in cooperating with you and your agenda. Because horizontal organizations distribute power throughout the organization, their support and compliance allows for that which is highly valued: the ability to execute. Primacy in these types of environments generally

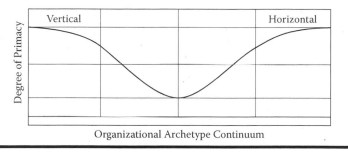

Figure 5.2 **Figure 5.2 illustrates that the closer an organization gets to an extreme, at either end of the archetype continuum, the higher the degree of primacy that shall be demonstrated and accepted by the population.**

takes the form of withholding needed support or worse the active campaigning against an initiative. The individual who is able to inflict his or her will through this display of primacy is the winner of the desired gain in power.

Though culture is an important factor in determining the type and degree of primacy that is used within organizations, it is by no means the only factor. When the day ends, primacy is a means to an end and the fulfillment of a real or perceived need. In the following section we will discuss situations and circumstances within organizations that often lead to demonstrations of primacy.

Figure 5.2 illustrates that the closer an organization gets to an extreme, at either end of the archetype continuum, the higher the degree of primacy that shall be demonstrated and accepted by the population.

Organizations That Reward Based on Job Title, Not Performance

In many organizations, significant increases in salary can generally be associated with a promotion rather than as a result of job performance. We are sure that you have seen this before: the good-old-boy network where who you know or the length of employment entitles an individual to a promotion or salary increase. We know this is a rather harsh statement; it was intended to be. The reason is that there are a number of unintended results of this practice, foremost of which is the message that primacy is good. In other words, the message is that primacy results in promotions and salary increases and all of the other positive aspects associated with the modern workplace.

We can name countless organizations that solely promote based on tenure rather than performance, or give promotions based on an ability to get along and not make waves. In these organizations, primacy is often rampant as employees focus on what it takes to move up the food chain versus actually performing their job.

Organizations That Believe in Protecting the Sacred Cow

Every organization has at least one: the sacred cow. The sacred cow is the individual or group of individuals who shall never be fired for any reason. It could be the best friend of the chief executive officer (CEO) who is about as bright as a door stop, but holds the position of vice president, or, based on a true story, the woman who had sued the company for sexual misconduct, won the case, and was now considered untouchable. She only came to work a couple of days a week! Whatever the case, these folks are catalysts for primacy.

First, those who enjoy the untouchable status generally know it, and will use their advantage to get away with demonstrations of primacy. Second, those around the sacred cow will use primacy to try to closer align themselves with those of untouchable status. These situations exist in just about any organization that we have done work for.

Highly Segregated Organizations

Earlier in the book, specifically in the chapter on myopia, we described the increase in the use of employees with highly specialized skills and how that has led to organizations that are compartmentalized by job function. We further discussed how communication across these groups generally lacked formality and was seldom well organized. In other words, there are too many groups divided along their specific specialization. For example, the human resources team does not talk to the network team, which does not talk to the security team. This sounds like something we have experienced before, but where? Oh yea, high school! And just like the cliques and groups that were formed at the average high school, organizations that are highly divided will be more prone to acts of primacy as employees compete internally, within each group, to attain more power and as leaders of groups compete with the leaders of other groups for a more prominent position in the organization. And we thought we were finally done with high school.

If you think about it, organizations really work in the same way as any other type of group during any point in human history. The only thing that has really changed over time is the prize for which we compete. In ancient history, it was the cave and in an organizational setting it has become the corner office (a nicer, bigger cave). The final cause of primacy within the workplace we will discuss is a dark little secret that everyone knows about, but few are willing to discuss.

Organizations That Only Focus on the Content during Communications

In the chapter on apathy, we explained that every communication between humans consists of two parts: the message itself and the relational component that represents the relationship of the parties participating in the communication. Within most organizations, the elephant in the room is the relationship component of communications. We feel this is the case because the relationship elements of a communication have nothing to do with the business of the organization, but everything to do with the individual agendas and goals of those participating in the discussion. As a result, the only elements that are legitimate points of discussion are often the message content, not the role and authority of the participants. However, it is these relationship factors that provide the opportunity for acts of primacy. Let us illustrate this idea with a real-life example. The names and locations have been altered to protect the innocent.

Once upon a time a CISO had a meeting with the organization's CEO to provide some elementary training on concepts surrounding security, specifically regarding business continuity planning. Before proceeding, it should be noted that there were a number of factors that affected the relationship component of this dialog:

1. The CISO was only operating at a manager level within the organization, leaving five full levels of management between the two participants.
2. The CISO was in his mid-30s, while the CEO was in her mid-50s, easily a 20-year discrepancy.
3. The culture of the organization was highly vertical.

With that information, let us return to their conversation. The CEO asked the CISO a rudimentary question to which he provided a reasonable answer (content). The CEO gave him a "squirreled" face and repeated the same question (relationship). Puzzled by why the same question was posed in exactly the same manner, the CISO answered it the same way using a different metaphor (content). He simply felt that his explanation had failed to communicate the message. The CEO then asked the same question a third time in a rather irritated manner (relationship). The CISO, dredging up everything he could remember about dealing with difficult people, responded with the same answer (content), however presenting it in a different, softer, manner. The CEO stopped him in mid-sentence and asked: "Don't you get it? I am going to keep asking the same question until you tell me what I want to hear!" Game over, end of story.

This is a true story and sadly not isolated to this particular organization. We use it here because it is a pure example of the relationship dominating the content component of the message. It is also an example of the inability to even discuss the relationship component. What was the CISO to do? Stop the CEO from talking and request that she refrain from pulling a power play so that they could do what was best for the organization instead of the CEO? You see, it doesn't sound very politically correct.

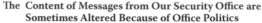

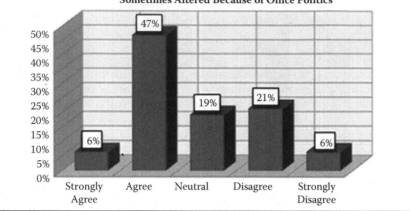

Figure 5.3

If you weren't convinced that politics impacts the quality of security, the data illustrated in Figure 5.3 should make it clear. More than half of the respondents feel that the content of messages is altered due to political pressure. Ouch!

It should be obvious from the example that primacy uses the relationship component of human communication as the medium of facilitation. The fact that it is an organizational taboo makes the relationship component the autobahn for primacy—a place without speed limits or restrictions.

Primal Leadership

Daniel Goleman is a leading researcher in the area of emotional intelligence, research on the brain, and application of principles across multiple contexts such as business, healthcare, and education, to name a few. In his book, *Primal Leadership*, he discusses "dissonant styles of leadership" (Goleman, 2002). Many of the styles he discusses are apropos for our conversation on primacy in humans. One such style Goleman discusses is "leading by command" or "do it because I say so" (p. 75). Often, when things feel out of control, a leader—usually a CEO or person in upper management—pulls rank to rectify the problems by creating a reign of terror. This coercive style of leading might create a false sense of reality by making it seem that operations are functioning and status quo is acceptable. The effect that this has on employees is a fear-based response that inhibits the employees of speaking freely and changing what is wrong in the first place. Silencing employees does not empower them to want to make positive, long-lasting changes in their work environment.

Another style Goleman discusses is the "SOB paradox." A great example that he offers, which most can relate to (or plausibly maybe you are one) is the "rude, hard-hitting CEO who by all appearances epitomizes the antithesis of resonance, yet seems to reap great business results" (p. 80). People with this temperament typically have a myopic fixation on financial goals and ignore the organizational and emotional toll and human costs because longevity is not a reward that strokes their ego and pocket.

In addition to these communicative styles at work, Goleman identifies another important concept that he calls the "CEO disease" (pp. 92–94). The CEO disease encapsulates the information that remains in a vacuum around a leader. In other words, employees withhold important information or unpleasant assessments of the way things are working to these leaders at alarming rates because of the intense and often negative responses that will come as a result of sharing the information. A kind of shoot-the-messenger response calls for silence to keep the peace.

Figure 5.4 demonstrates the most dangerous type of dysfunctional communication where the relationship component of the communication is dictating what constitutes acceptable content. This is censorship at its finest. If this were to occur in the press, it would be a major First Amendment violation, but we allow it within interpersonal communications on a regular basis.

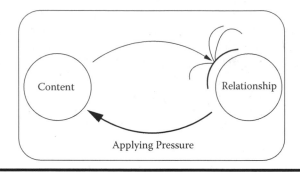

Figure 5.4 **Figure 5.4 demonstrates the most dangerous type of dysfunctional communication where the relationship component of the communication is dictating what constitutes acceptable content. This is censorship at its finest. If this were to occur in the press, it would be a major First Amendment violation, but we allow it within interpersonal communications on a regular basis.**

Summary

It is obvious that we could continue providing examples on this topic for a very long time and, at this point, we bet you could as well. When evaluating what causes primacy in most organizations, it really boils down to this: primacy will flourish within any organization that:

1. Is either highly vertical or horizontal
2. Provides rewards based on moving up the food chain, not performance
3. Protects sacred cows
4. Is highly segregated by specialization
5. Makes it taboo to focus on the relationship component of communications

Hopefully, we have provided you with the mindset to look at your organization a little differently. With this awareness at your disposal, we are now going to apply it to your security efforts. What causes primacy within a security program?

Causes of Primacy within a Security Program

When discussing security with our peers, it is common for them to unknowingly discuss the impacts of primacy on their daily activities. We hear about the need to alter reports so as not to embarrass someone powerful or the sheer frustration that they feel at constantly being excluded from critical meetings. What is often missing from these conversations is a degree of self-actualization as to how they may be contributing to the primacy that is so adversely affecting their own security efforts. This is where we are going to spend our energy in this section.

Getting Ahead Using Security

As we mentioned in the prior section, when considering primacy from a security program perspective, there are two areas that one must focus his or her attention. The first is the quest for utility by those within the security program. The second is the predominantly negative and Draconian means by which many security organizations execute their function.

Some may argue the point, but the fact of the matter is that as a CISO you are still human, and as a result you will be driven by the same needs as any other person. Most CISOs are also driven individuals like anyone else. As a result, most of you reading this book will want to progress within an organization in an attempt to fulfill your personal needs and wants and there is nothing wrong with that. However, security is often a poor mechanism when used as a tool for personal advancement.

Power within an organization is based on an individual's proximity and contribution to the revenue stream or control over the reporting of information regarding it. Security often possesses neither of these elements unless your organization sells security as a product. Hence, security is not, has never been, and shall never be a business enabler. With that basic understanding of power structure within an organization, let us look at the other factors that make security a bad tool for personal advancement.

First, security in most organizations is a rather new concept. Only recently have we begun to see security gain prominence and recognition on the executive organizational chart. As a result of this, highly motivated individuals not only have to sell themselves when they want to move up the food chain, they also need to sell the whole concept of security, which is no small task. This additional energy and potential frustration may lead to demonstrations of primacy that are more frequent than in other executives. This behavior is generally deemed uncivil at the executive ranks unless it is done with guile and a great deal of subterfuge—activities that require even more energy.

The net result is that we have seen a great deal of turnover in the field of security, particularly in leadership roles. We believe that primacy and the resulting demonstrations are a prime contributor to this revolving door syndrome.

Figures 5.5 and 5.6 have got to be our favorite metrics within the book. If you consider that the majority of respondents for this survey were security professionals, the data is somewhat ironic. On one hand, it is believed that those outside of security are acting in their own best interest. On the other hand, we security professionals appear to be altruistic, only working in the best interest of the organization. Perception truly is reality.

What You Say and How You Say It Matters

Security is a game of constant review and analysis. We try to determine what an optimal state of security should be and then perform evaluations of our environment to determine which areas are deficient against that optimal state. The

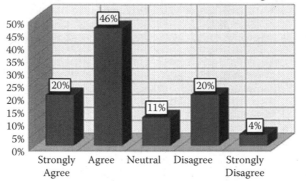

There are People in Our Organization Who Make Decisions That
Serve Themselves Rather Than What is Best for the Organization

Figure 5.5 Figure 5.5 has got to be our favorite metrics within the book.
If you consider that the majority of respondents for this survey were security
professionals, the data is somewhat ironic. On one hand, it is believed that
those outside of security are acting in their own best interest. On the other
hand, we security professionals appear to be altruistic, only working in the best
interest of the organization. Perception truly is reality.

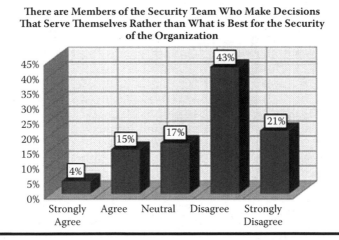

There are Members of the Security Team Who Make Decisions
That Serve Themselves Rather than What is Best for the Security
of the Organization

Figure 5.6 Figure 5.6 has got to be our favorite metrics within the book.
If you consider that the majority of respondents for this survey were security
professionals, the data is somewhat ironic. On one hand, it is believed that
those outside of security are acting in their own best interest. On the other
hand, we security professionals appear to be altruistic, only working in the best
interest of the organization. Perception truly is reality.

key to that statement is the word "deficient"; our job is to emphasize that which needs improvement. By its very nature we dwell on the negative. As a result, our communications and messages tend to focus on the deficiencies of the environment and indirectly of those who are responsible for those areas.

This fundamental aspect of security works in direct opposition to what we know about human beings. First, bringing attention to the deficiencies of another area within the organization is no way to make friends and influence people. The other issue is that negative messages tend to evoke an emotional response on the part of those receiving them. This makes the response toward messages unpredictable and leads to potentially combative situations. Security is basically inviting acts of primacy by others, with greater power than security, with the information and messages that it distributes. Let us take the time to demonstrate this concept with a story: Scooby Doo Fade Out.

Once upon a time there was a CISO who was looking to make a big splash in the organization. Up to this point, the CISO had been unable to truly capture the attention and priority from the rest of executive management. So, one day this person decided to conduct a covert security penetration study of the entire organization. Furthermore, the test was guided with insider knowledge of what to attack. With this sensitive Intel, the penetration team was able to exploit the weaknesses in the organization and to obtain some of the most confidential information of the business.

Once the CISO had concluded the test, the report was presented to the board of directors, bypassing executive management. This study embarrassed every executive from every business unit in the company. You would think that the findings of the report would be of paramount issue, but no. The issue—though never discussed out loud—was the embarrassment inflicted on those in power. They had been blindsided by this test and thoroughly humiliated. This was the retribution that entailed:

1. Signature authority for the CISO was revoked. This person could not authorize the distribution of funds for any purpose. An executive without signing authority, that's a classic.
2. The security office was moved under a different executive manager who would micromanage the function with no knowledge of security.
3. The security office was restructured into a consultancy without any oversight or participation in design, development, or implementation of security controls. The security office also could only consult on projects it was invited to, and of course all of the business units stopped inviting it.

The bottom line is that the executives within the organization restructured and reduced the security function to nothing more than a point on the organization chart. The speed at which all of this occurred, by those in power, was truly mind-boggling.

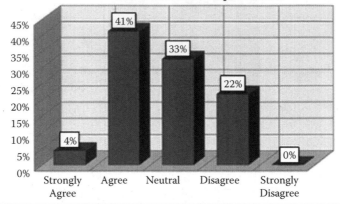

Reports Have Been Produced by the Security Program That Make Other Groups Look Bad

Figure 5.7   Figure 5.7 demonstrates that security has been used as a means of embarrassing or getting others in trouble. It is important to keep in mind the ramifications of this practice with inciting primacy.

Within five weeks of the report, the entire security apparatus for the organization had been neutered to a point of ineffectiveness. This is probably the finest example of primacy that we have ever, or ever will, witness. It had nothing to do with security and everything to do with the tone and tenor of the message and the approach of delivery.

Figure 5.7 demonstrates that security has been used as a means of embarrassing or getting others in trouble. It is important to keep in mind the ramifications of this practice with inciting primacy.

Exercise 13

This exercise can also be found in the Appendix with worksheets.

Objective

The objective of this exercise is to review how the actions of the security team may provoke demonstrations of primacy by others.

Exercise

Look at the last six months of communiqués to areas outside of your security organization and determine if the tone of the message was positive or negative. Next, review the means by which they were delivered. Was there a positive or negative response to the delivery mechanism?

Walk Softly in the Land of the Giants

Primacy is actually a fairly primitive reaction. It is a legacy of our history that is part of who we are as human beings. It is usually an unconscious or reactionary response to events or stimulus provided by our environment. Once again, the nature of security is to limit our exposure to risk by controlling aspects of the environment that are most likely to develop into vulnerabilities. We do this through the introduction of security controls.

The name alone, security controls, should provide insights as to how security evokes displays of primacy. Controls change the nature and dynamics of the environment of the organization. They are generally not voluntary, rather inflicted on the population. Further, they represent change to the population. Both of these factors will evoke feelings of powerlessness on the population of an organization. The place where powerlessness is truly dangerous for a security program is that it directly challenges those with power or those seeking additional power or utility within the organization.

Individuals who hold the power within an organization have most likely achieved it through domination over their competitors (primacy). You may not agree with this statement, but it has overwhelmingly been our experience to be true. These individuals tend to view power as currency to be spent and lent at their discretion for their causes. When security introduces a new control, it can be thought of as a bill for goods or services that they did not authorize. This perceived usurping of power is seen as a direct challenge to their authority and power, presenting any CISO or any security professional for that matter as another opponent to be dominated and controlled.

Summary

It is clear that some of the fundamental aspects of security will provoke demonstrations of primacy in others. The very nature of what we do and the typical means by which we share our information is a breeding ground for this type of behavior. However, there are ways of addressing this issue—discussed in the Solutions section—and learning to adapt to it. After all, unless we can change human behavior, primacy is here to stay. Before moving on, Figure 5.8 represents a graphical depiction of all of the causes of primacy to this point. We will now move on to the cause and effect of primacy on our true security model.

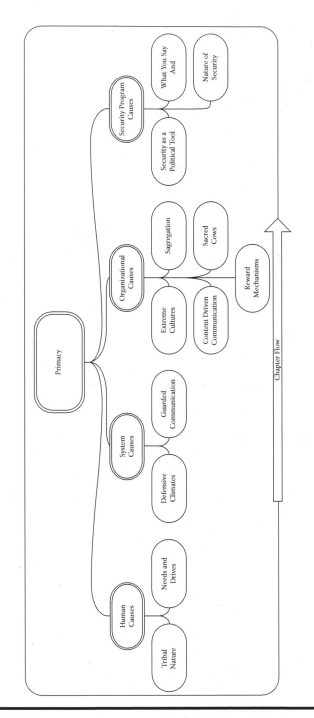

Figure 5.8 **This figure represents a graphical depiction of the human, system, organizational, and security program causes of Primacy.**

Cause and Effect of Primacy on the True Security Model

Now that we have provided some of the causes of primacy, we will move the discussion to its impact within our true security model. The advantage of this constraint versus some of the others we have discussed is that primacy is much more apparent than the others. Unless you work in a one-person organization, almost everyone should be able to identify at least one demonstration of primacy that has affected their lives. The other item to remember with primacy is that it is caused by different reasons and has different effects on different groups within our true security model. As a result, though it is easier to identify, it can be more difficult to grasp than some of the other constraints. In order to provide some structure to this conversation, we will again return to the use of the true security model to demonstrate the cause and effect relationship of primacy. This should help us focus on various organizational groups in isolation as well as provide us something tangible to help us explore a very intangible subject.

We will also close out each section with a look at the security con. The con associated with primacy is much more pronounced than with some of the other groups, so hang on and enjoy the show. First, we will present a quick review of the true security model.

Effects of Primacy

Below are the various groups commonly found within an organization and the desired actions that we hope to obtain from each group in order to achieve true security.

Organizational Group	Desired Action or Behavior
Board of directors	Endorsement
Executive management	Priority
Middle management	Resources
Supervisory management	Support
Employees	Diligence
Consumers	Trust
Security program	Execution

For each group, we will explore the cause and effect relationship that primacy can have on the desired action we need to obtain. We will begin by providing some common symptoms that are displayed when primacy is present, and then we will look at some of the more intangible effects. We will also discuss the ways in which security professionals and others are compensating (security con) for the effects of primacy within each group. Of course, we will start at the top of the food chain with our pals on the board of directors.

Primacy and the Board of Directors

Primacy at the board of directors' level is very different than with any other group. The reason for that is that this group represents the pinnacle of power and control within an organization. Demonstrations of primacy are usually a result of the need to exert authority in order to maintain their existing level of control or as a result of pure ego. The latter of the two is rare because board members can be replaced by other board members, so they tend to play nicely. However, in cases where the authority and control of the group is in jeopardy, they will band together to squash that attempt. In these situations, their ammunition is information.

As a result, when operating from purely a primacy perspective, board members will always be hungry for as much detailed information as they can acquire. This need for information is the ticket for obtaining the endorsement that you desire from this group. It is an implied quid pro quo, where they get the information that they desire and you get the endorsement that you desire from them. This will be the case whether their focus is security or any other function within the organization. Now, whether they get the right information is another story.

The security con at this level is often performed by those around the board that are still in search of acquiring more power. These people will often attempt to manipulate or synthesize information in order to present the information in a light that best suits their own interests and agendas. Generally, the members of the executive team are the guiltiest of this practice because they are the ones who most commonly interface with this group.

Primacy and the Executive Team

Ah, the executive team. No primacy there. Yea, right! Primacy and executives is like bread and butter or peanut butter and jelly. In many cases, these folks have often worked their whole lives to achieve the power position that they currently hold. Because these individuals, like the board members, have attained power, primacy is often utilized to maintain their power and control. As a result, every move they make will be measured and weighed against its negative impact to their power situation. Everything becomes a risk:reward ratio or a cost:benefit analysis ... everything. And it generally is measured in terms of power and control. As was stated above, knowledge truly is power in most organizations.

The manner in which information is used will be the primary tool of the executive. When dealing in the world of politics, the use of information is a tricky game. On one hand, executives need enough information to use for their own purposes as well as to present the proper image of competency and diligence. On the other hand, too much information reduces their ability for "plausible deniability" if something goes wrong within their chain of command. As we stated, it is a risk and reward game.

Where this impacts your ability to achieve true security is twofold. If the security efforts of the organization are in bad shape, it may be difficult to get the priority needed by executives to correct the problem. We know this seems counterintuitive, but reducing the priority on a problem area also serves to reduce its profile to those higher up the food chain within the organization. It keeps these types of issues where they cannot hurt anyone or their agendas. This behavior is often enabled by the poor measurement capabilities of security we discussed in Chapter 1.

The other impact to security is how primacy at this level impacts upstream information. When possible, executives will synthesize and sanitize the information that can flow upstream to the board of directors if it can negatively impact them. Yes, we know this is a harsh statement. Again, poor measurement practices, coupled with a limited or complete lack of understanding (myopia) and limited interest (apathy) by the board, makes this situation possible.

This is without doubt the heart and soul of the security con. We see the con at this level running rampant in most organizations. Obviously, executives that operate in this manner—and it is not all of them—are the key perpetrators. In addition, others around these situations, generally security practitioners, are also to blame when they know it is occurring and stand idly by watching or when they are even contributing.

Primacy and Middle Management

As you start to move down the management chain in an organization, you get more competition for power simply because of the increase in the number of competitors. There are obviously going to be more middle managers than those at the executive level, and they will tend to be at earlier points in their own careers. These are the prime candidates competing in the power lottery, continuing in their quest for more power, having been fueled by the attainment of their current management position.

Primacy at this level of management is difficult to categorize because many of these people have attained their management position as a result of skill and hard work. This group is truly a mixed bag of primacy and the related demonstrations. For those who are looking to move up the ladder, primarily for the power and control that it promises, primacy is often displayed in the form of proxy-power from their executive.

These people are the storm troopers for their current executive and wield that power by proxy. They mimic the agenda of their executive: if the executive provides priority to security, they will give it their support. Conversely, they will withhold resources if their executive deems it unworthy. The other area that provides pressure when addressing primacy is among their peer group.

These people are competing with other managers to try and become more powerful or retain their existing power or status. Because of this, they are often resistant to security coming and shining a light on their area, especially if they have some skeletons in the closet.

Due to the pressures on this group associated with primacy from both a vertical and horizontal perspective, there will often be significant variance in responses to security from this group. Your ability to get resources for security initiatives will often come down to what value you can provide the middle manager in assisting them with their quest for additional power. In most cases, there is often not much to gain from allying with security, particularly if executive priority is lacking. As a result, these managers will often be very defensive about the support they provide to security. That is, unless you can provide them some type of competitive advantage over their peers; for example, security performs a penetration test on their environment and they know they will look better than other groups. If not, then you are likely to be treated as another competitor from another team on the organizational playing field.

The security con at this level is often demonstrated by the middle managers through the perception of support. No one is going to come out and say they do not support security. Therefore, if the manager is truly not on board with security he or she will create a perception of support that costs him or her the least amount in terms of time, energy, political capital, or resources. This attitude is generally reflected through reactive fulfillment of resource requests by security and the presentation of subpar resources.

Primacy and the Supervisory Team

The supervisory team is also trying to move up the corporate ladder. This group shares two common traits: first, they are generally overallocated and, second, they are the closest to the people who are actually performing the majority of work. As a result, they will want to appear diligent to their management, but will also need to maintain order with their subordinates. These folks usually gain credibility and essentially power over their teams by shielding them from distractions and unnecessary detours from their primary objective. This ability to maintain the focus and, theoretically, the productivity of their team is also what upper management is looking for. These two barriers create strong incentives for supervisors to pay marginal attention to security—just enough to appear interested and diligent, but not enough to impact their true objective.

Think of it as the engine room on a ship. This is where the majority of work gets done, a place where the ship officers do not like to visit for fear of soiling their uniforms. Supervisors and their teams live here and, for the most part, are responsible for keeping the ship moving. In these areas, something like security, a concept that is often misunderstood (myopia and apathy), will be omitted since it is not perceived as contributing to the continued operation of the ship. So, when security comes along and opens up the hatch to the engine room to take a look, shining a flashlight into every aspect of engine room operations, you can imagine how excited these people are to see security coming.

The security con at this level is usually performed by both the security team and the supervisors. Supervisors will often remain silent about security issues in order to avoid attention and protect their teams. When they know that there is a security issue that should be raised and addressed, yet fail to do so, they are perpetuating the con. CISOs and their team often aid in perpetuating this form of the con by turning a blind eye to issues they know do exist. They do this for the same reasons as other groups; they do not want to get dirty with things such as how the organization actually functions (this of course does not pertain to all CISOs). The result is a false sense of well-being. After all, because no one has raised any issues, everything must be fine.

Primacy and Employees

Primacy is not necessarily a behavior that is demonstrated by the average employee, at least not in the terms with which we have described it. Employees will not be playing politics and generally will not be in a position with which to exert authority or power over your security efforts. However, they can and will demonstrate their discontent with overt demonstrations of primacy on the part of others. It will usually take the form of reluctance or silent defiance.

Because our requirement from this group is diligence, reluctance or silent defiance do not aid us in our effort to attain true security. When looking at the effects of primacy on security from employees, the key point to remember is that the perception of one will often be shared by many. This group exerts power through sheer numbers and leveraging its access to information. If employees believe that the security effort makes sense, they will follow it diligently. If they do not feel that it makes sense, then they won't. This opinion is often formed early and will spread quickly through the ranks of employees.

The con at this level is generally perpetuated by the employees when they have deemed the security effort as bogus, yet project the image of acceptance and diligence. In these situations, they will smile as the security team walks by and remove the sticky with the password to the finance system into a drawer, only to move it back out once security is gone.

Primacy and Consumers

Consumers are another group that does not actively demonstrate primacy. Though they are humans and driven by their needs, they do not exhibit primacy in the context that we have described. In fact, this passive behavior actually contributes to the severe acts of primacy by others.

For the most part, consumers take a very passive role in the security of products and services that they consume. They do not ask many questions either because they do not know what to ask (myopia) or are simply not interested (apathy) in the subject to begin with. This certainly is unfortunate because consumer pressure can easily translate into the necessary elements (support, priority, resources, etc.) from the various levels of management within an organization.

The sad fact of the matter is that consumers are often used as pawns in battles of primacy, cited as the primary factor in decisions when it is convenient and overlooked the rest of the time. Though many would argue when asked that they are looking out for the consumer, the actions of most organizations would suggest that they are a secondary thought at best.

The con is perpetuated by those that make self-serving decisions that exploit the blind trust of consumers within an organization. That can range from the CEO to those on your security team.

Lawmakers also take advantage of this blind trust. Many consumers believe it is the role of the government to enforce security within organizations through security regulation. Regulators take advantage of this blind trust by creating laws that are confusing, vague, and contain little or no enforcement for noncompliance (e.g., Health Insurance Portability and Accountability Act or HIPAA). We know this statement is harsh; it was meant to be.

Effects Summary

Primacy in modern organizations is analogous to gladiatorial combat in many instances. The tactics can be just as ruthless and the carnage can be just as severe. Primacy is a weapon most often used in a quest for power and authority. Though we described instances where primacy can be used to protect one's territory or established power and authority, it is an offensive tool that is generally used for the acquisition of these two items in modern organizations. Just remember, primacy can take many different forms, affect individuals in different ways, and influence behavior in ways that can be highly unpredictable. For this reason, it is the single most difficult of the constraints to address and manage. However, that is exactly where we are going next: solutions to dealing with primacy.

Solutions

As we stated earlier, primacy is the most unpredictable of the four constraints. It is closely aligned with the human ego and as such will manifest itself in different ways by different individuals. However, merely because the displays of primacy differ, the fingerprint is unmistakable. It is obvious when an act of primacy has occurred and we all have our personal war stories on this topic. The fact that it is easily identified is an advantage for us though and gives us a toehold for addressing the issue and its negative impact on the ability to achieve true security.

As always, we will turn to Skye to give us the considerations for systems theory and human considerations to lead off our Solutions section.

System Theory Considerations

When considering systems theory, the primary consideration is recognizing the cyclical nature of communication within systems. When inputs are tainted with primacy, the output warrants defensive communication in nature. Defensive outputs will be interpreted by the receiver, who in turn will generate defensive outputs (inputs to the next cycle of the system), thus creating circularity and feedback that is important. Defensive communication breeds more defensive responses and, thus, the negative cycle continues. This cycle will continue to spiral moving the organization toward the closed end of the spectrum thereby limiting communication feedback and resources until the system closes, which ultimately limits the free exchange of ideas.

When we can identify and grapple with how systems depend on environmental stimuli or never-ending cycle of information input, processing, and output, it becomes imperative to identify when inputs have been tainted. This is the point where outputs are perpetuating a negative spiral as a result of the negative climate—the circularity aspect. Intervention in the processing portion, hence modifying the output, is the correct course of action when addressing this issue from a theoretical perspective.

Human Considerations

As we discussed earlier in the chapter, the primary motivation for humans is the fulfillment of their needs. This drive to fulfill a need does not just affect behavior, but also influences how humans perceive information and their environment. Taking the time to evaluate situations from the perspective of the people with which you are dealing is key in these situations. It sounds simple, but that does not mean it is any less powerful.

Human Responses to Information

J.R. Gibb said, "A supportive communication climate encourages open, constructive, honest, and effective interaction. A defensive climate, on the other hand, leads to competitive and destructive conflict. The competent communicator strives to maintain a supportive communication climate."

In his article, "Defensive Communication," J.R. Gibb, *The Journal of Communication*, 1961, 11(3), 141–148, illustrates that human responses to information generally fall into two categories: defensive or supportive. Defensive responses try to exhibit fun stuff like control, superiority, conviction, judgment, or a lack of interest. Supportive messages, on the other hand, focus on problem solving, genuine interest in the subject, empathy, honesty, openness, and engagement.

The difference between the two types of responses is night and day. When you are providing the content of your messages, be aware of which type of response is provided by your audience. Because primacy often manifests itself in defensive responses, the ability to recognize the response of your audience can provide valuable information about how you may be triggering the primacy button with the content of your messages. Use this information to make adjustments with the way in which you are presenting the content of your message. It is crucial to remember that we are not saying to alter the content of your message, just focus on the way in which you are distributing it in order to create a more positive atmosphere.

Another important consideration from a human perspective is to recognize the tendency of humans to process negative information in more of a personal manner. This personal response to these types of messages makes them more likely to impact the ego of the receiver, an overriding component of primacy. This issue makes it imperative that the target for any security communications needs to be understood prior to the delivery of messages. This is particularly important for initial communications.

> Finally, the most important human consideration is the duality of human communication: relationship and content. Within most work environments, though both communication channels are recognized (either consciously or subconsciously) when people are communicating, it is only the content of messages that tends to be the focus. It is imperative to find a balance in your communications—relationship and content— that is healthy for both you and those you communicate with.

Security Solutions

This is where the rubber meets the road. We are going to attempt to address the constraint of primacy for security solutions. We have to admit that we burned extra brain juice attempting to figure out an approach for you—a dangerous proposition when you consider that we do not have that much to begin with. Seriously, our entire team worked overtime in an attempt to find some useful research to apply in the area of primacy specific to security. Unfortunately, there is very little published on this subject. (Note to self, this is the second time we have selected a book where there is limited research on the subject. Don't do it again!) The difficulties of addressing this subject are compounded by the fact that the manifestations and mechanisms of primacy are as unique as the individuals practicing them. Oh no, the boys from So Cal are in trouble this time.

As a result, from our perspective (myopia) we are breaking new ground with this section of the book. Our approach was to review several years of engagements, peer review, and craft knowledge in an attempt to distill the means and manner we have either used or seen others use to overcome these issues and achieve success in these situations. The following is our recommended approach for dealing with primacy and the various manifestations that can hinder your attempt at true security.

Step #1: Assess Your Own Situation

Before doctors attempt to treat a patient, they must evaluate the symptoms to make a diagnosis. The only difference when dealing with primacy is that you are both the doctor and the patient: "physician heal thyself." That is right, we start by looking in the mirror and asking ourselves some tough questions about what drives us and how this can impact primacy within the organization.

Exercise 14

This exercise can also be found in the Appendix with worksheets.

Objective

The objective of this exercise is to evaluate how your own motivations may contribute to primacy within your environment.

Exercise

What is the fundamental motivation that drives you as a security professional?

Priority	Item	Primacy Index
	Notoriety	Increase
	Family happiness	Neutral
	Improved organizational security	Increase
	Larger budget (if you have one)	Increase
	Increased status	Increase
	Teaching others about security	Decrease
	Getting paid	Increase
	Other	N/A

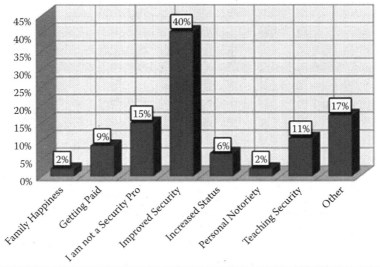

What is the Fundamental Motivation That Drives You as a Security Professional?

Figure 5.9 In figure 5.9, though improved security is the top answer, notice all of the other answers that received votes. There are no wrong answers to this question, but it is interesting to consider how your actions may vary depending on your specific answer.

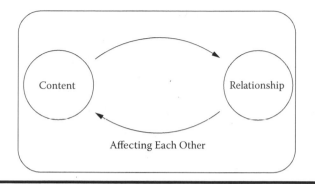

Figure 5.10 A healthy communication, as illustrated in Figure 5.10, is a balance between the relationship and content component where both affect each other.

As you may have noted, there are more issues that will generate primacy then neutralize it. Reflect on the impact that your motivations may have on producing demonstrations of primacy.

Was "improved organizational security" your first response? How about "getting paid?" If you are a robot, then chances are that you selected "improved organizational security." For the rest of you humans do not worry; chances are that improved organizational security is not the primary motivating factor in your life. It is important that you sit down and try to understand your intentions and motivations before you attempt to understand those of others. What you need to get out of this self-analysis is an idea of the items that you prioritize above the primary mission of your security efforts. This is where you will find the items that will tempt you into acts of primacy; and may compromise your attempts at achieving true security. For all of the items that you have placed ahead of organizational security, have you made decisions in support of those items that have actually compromised organizational security? Maybe you have, maybe you haven't, and we are not here to judge, just to help provide a tool that gives you the power of awareness.

A healthy communication, as illustrated in Figure 5.10, is a balance between the relationship and content component where both affect each other.

Step #2: What's in The Message?

As we learned in the prior section, negative messages are more likely to be taken personally by the recipient than positive messages. This factor becomes important when we consider that the human ego is a trigger point for acts of primacy.

What do we mean by a negative message? Good question. We categorize a negative message as anything that focuses on a deficiency. Think about that for a second. Because those of us in security deal almost exclusively in deficiencies, most of what we communicate is often negative. Either the organization is deficient, the department is deficient, the security controls are deficient, or maybe the manager running the department is deficient. We are deficient in that security always deals in identifying deficiency. After all, that is how we identify risk. Though this is a common form of communication between security professionals, it is viewed as negative by individuals outside of our professional domain. So, with that understood, let us take a look at the past security communications to the organization that have originated from your security program:

Organizational Group	Percentage of Last Five Communiqués That Were Negative (report, presentations, e-mail, meetings)
Board of directors	
Executive management	
Middle management	
Supervisory management	
Employees	
Consumers	
Security program	

If your self-assessment of recent communications indicates that the majority of messages contain a negative message, chances are that you have experienced some level of primacy from others. Our approach in these situations is to attempt to balance the negative message with some positive aspect or findings that are associated with the topic. Treat deficiencies as an opportunity for improvement and present them as recommendations. If you frame negative issues in the guise of a suggestion for improvement, it will achieve two things. First, it will expose the issue without any value statements associated with it. This is massively important if your objective is to avoid the recipients from personalizing the deficiency. The second thing that is achieved by this approach is appealing to the logical aspect of how humans process information. If you are making a suggestion, you cannot simultaneously be making an accusation. This will redirect the group mindset into solving the problem instead of assigning blame.

If, for some reason, there is not any way to spin a positive message, then try to balance the bad with the good. Include some information that may soften the blow for those who may personalize the negative information. A good rule of thumb is to begin positive, give the bad news, then end on a positive note. This may provide enough conversational gravity to avoid any unpleasant repercussions.

Another important consideration is to not take a personal position on negative information. For example, the sentence: "Our assessment of the data center showed that it was highly deficient" is very different from the sentence: "The data center is highly deficient."

The first one personalizes the negative message, while the other is more content focused. It is amazing how powerful even a small change like that can be for stoking or reducing primacy in your communications.

Up to this point we have only discussed the content portion of a message, but as we learned earlier, all messages have two components: content and relationship. When battling primacy, the content of the message will only get you halfway there. More often than not, the relationship will dictate both the amount of primacy that is exercised and the degree to which the content will be altered. Now stay with us, we almost melted our little pea brains working this one out.

In situations where the other party is overtly displaying primacy, you are in no situation to do anything other than take it and ride out the storm (see our example earlier in the chapter of the CISO who was getting highly influenced by primacy during a discussion with his CEO). However, in most situations, the nature of communication furnishes you with a tool for managing the relationship portion of a communication. That tool is the content.

The association between the two is bidirectional. A relationship within a communication can be manipulated through the content and the content can be manipulated through the relationship. The trick is to beat them to the punch. If you can accurately assess the audience and tailor the delivery of the content to influence the relationship, this can minimize the chances for a display of primacy. This concept works whether you are the subordinate or the superior in the communication relationship.

Let us reverse the roles and make you the superior in this communication. You have the choice of facilitating the communication through questions and honest exchange. In the situation where you foster a positive relationship, the other party is likely to provide honest, useful information. This is what Skye would refer to as a healthy system. For example, if you are having an earnest conversation with your best friend about a difficult subject, the content of your message is likely to be honest, civil, and uninhibited because the relationship portion has already been established and is safe.

The alternative course of action is that you possess the position of power in the communication and decide to exercise that power. The result is likely to impact the content of the information providing you with censored or limited information on the subject (see our example of the CISO talking with his CEO). For example, in a conversation with your children regarding the "birds and the bees," the child is less likely to be honest and forthright with information or questions if you take a Draconian approach.

Taking this concept into the world of business, whether you are in the subordinate or superior position in a communication, a positive spin on a message will serve to create open, honest, and accurate content in a comfortable atmosphere. After all, chances are that participants are more willing to have a productive communication with someone who presents their negative information in the context of recommendations rather than someone who is airing a laundry list of problems. Remember this analogy! You do not want to be the guy with the laundry list! Below is another tool to help identify how the relationship element of messages is impacting each organizational group in the true security model.

Exercise 15

This exercise can also be found in the Appendix with worksheets.

Objective

The objective of this exercise is to determine the level of impact that primacy has on your decisions and actions as they relate to security.

Exercise

For each of the messages that you send to a specific group, answer the following questions. If you do not interact with the group, simply answer "not applicable."

Organizational Group	Is the Relationship Influencing the Integrity of the Content of Your Messages? (circle one)	How?
Board of directors	Yes No	
Executive management	Yes No	
Middle management	Yes No	
Supervisory management	Yes No	
Employees	Yes No	
Consumers	Yes No	
Security program	Yes No	

Step #3: Be Gentle with Your Knowledge

Information is a form of commerce or power within most organizations and can be used as a display of primacy as much as position or title. When this power is used, we like to refer to this maneuver as the "stomp." This is a

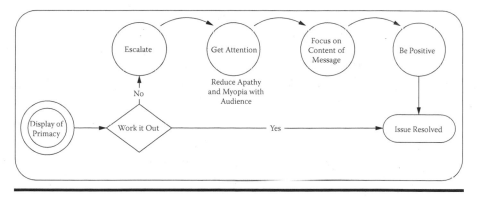

Figure 5.11   This figure presents the process for addressing displays of primacy.

situation where you employ your superior knowledge and expertise in a subject to gain control over the conversation. The only problem is that you wind up stomping the other person into the ground by pointing out his or her lack of knowledge on the subject. But more importantly, you will turn off those who do not understand you. How many times have you been party to a conversation with an engineer in the room where he or she goes "techie" on the group? Does the group stop and marvel at his or her knowledge? Nope, the group breaks the tension by making a techie or nerd reference and proceeds to ignore him or her.

As security professionals, you and your team will possess highly specialized knowledge that is expressed with its own unique nomenclature. This makes you prime candidates for employing the stomp on those outside of our domain. Don't do it! No matter how tempting, it is an act of primacy that will come back to haunt you in one fashion or another.

Step #4: Power Flows from the Top

When experiencing primacy, it is common to feel a sense of powerlessness, particularly if you are the subordinate. In these situations, you are given a choice: either work out the situation directly with that person or escalate the issue to someone who has more power and influence. It is always best to try to work out issues directly with the person you are having difficulties with, but in reality at some point as situations progress this might not be possible any longer. In these situations, if you have no recourse, it generally makes sense to escalate the issue. However, there are some caveats to this:

1. We will say this again. It is always best to work out things directly in a communication with the person displaying primacy when that is possible. Use escalation as a last resort.

2. Your goal is not to leave tread marks on the person with whom you are having difficulties. If you decide to go higher in the organization, be very careful about how you escalate past the other person.
3. When presenting a message to a higher-level audience in the organization, as always, your objective should be to reduce apathy and myopia at the higher levels in order to facilitate the audience's understanding of the security message and objective.
4. Focus on the content of the message, not the primacy that you encountered.
5. Start at the highest level possible, not the next higher level. This will reduce the potential of repercussions from the individual.
6. Do not make anyone look bad, even if they deserve it.
7. Be positive.

Conclusion

Unfortunately, there is no silver bullet for addressing primacy. Each individual will display it in different degrees and ways. The key is that no matter how it materializes, primacy will always affect either the content or the relationship of any communication. Your objective is to find a balance that allows for the unadulterated disclosure of security information while avoiding the potential influence of primacy. These tools and techniques have worked for us and hopefully they will do the same for you. The essential element is an accurate appraisal of the situation—both your motivations and those around you—and a tailoring of the message delivery to promote a free exchange of ideas (healthy system).

Chapter 6

Infancy

"Trust me, I have done this a thousand times!"

Overview

It seems as though nowadays you cannot turn on a television or pick up a newspaper without hearing a story about global warming. Talk about fear, uncertainty, and doubt (FUD)! These headlines illustrate issues ranging from the Earth running completely out of water to California falling off the continent and becoming an island (sweet, that would give us another coastline ... more surf!). Just as the rate of new prognostications has increased, so has the emergence of "experts" with their doom and gloom and their complicated climatological models, charts, and all kinds of stuff that we are supposed to believe. How can you go wrong trusting what Al Gore is telling you? After all, isn't he the inventor of the Internet?

In our opinion, the only fact that truly exists when evaluating weather is that the discipline of meteorology is not perfected just quite yet. How many times have you gone for that umbrella after watching a weather report only to become angered that you did not wear shorts that day, or vice versa? What a sweet job. As a weatherman, you are considered awesome if you are only wrong 80 percent of the time. What other job can you think of that allows for such high error rates? So, excuse us if we are somewhat skeptical of these so-called "weather experts." These are the same people who, 30 years ago, were convinced that we were entering another Ice Age (Figure 6.1).

This is why it is fascinating to us, when we are confronted by the same people who give us such trustworthy weather reports on the issues and causes of global warming, that so many people still seem to take their new prognostications as the coming reality.

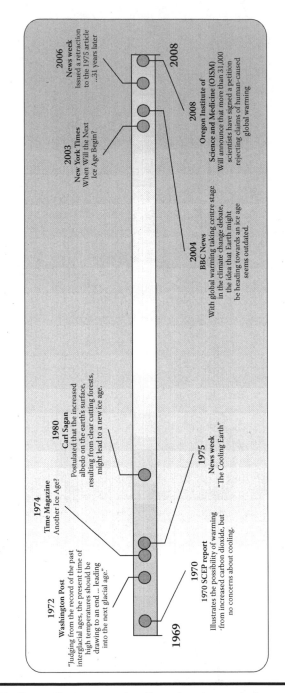

Figure 6.1 This figure illustrates a timeline of various weather predictions in recent history. Though these are considered to be reputable sources of information, they do not seem to have a very good track record.

Now, it is clear that the world's climate is changing. And it is likely that the billions of people and their daily activities have something to do with it. What we find amazing, and what is at the heart of this chapter, is the way in which this fairly new issue has people talking about it, and others believing these people like this issue has been studied and understood for 100 years. Ah! Welcome to the chapter on infancy.

At this point, we have covered three of the four constraints including apathy, myopia, and primacy. It should be apparent that the root causes for each of the three constraints discussed so far rest in different human tendencies that lead to different manifestations within an organization. The final constraint we are going to address, infancy, is caused by something very different: time. Though the discipline of security has been around for thousands of years—we have been building walls and moats for centuries—the modern discipline of security, and specifically information security, is a concept that is still fairly new and very complex.

A great deal of this complexity can be attributed to the rise and progression of technology. Technology has improved the ability for people that are very far apart to still communicate, leading to new and exciting ways of committing crimes. Today, an attacker can be sitting on a beach in Fiji and attacking a bank in Switzerland and still make his or her 11:00 a.m. tee-time. Even in the areas of physical security and process development, we now have cameras, card readers, biometric scanners, shredders, and the list goes on and on. The point is that there are now more ways in which organizations can be compromised and more ways in which these attempts can be

Organization, Framework, or Regulation	Description	Date Founded
ISC2	Security certification body	Founded in 1989
SANS	Security certification body	Founded in 1989
British Standard (BS) 7799-1	Security framework	First published in 1999
COBIT	Security framework	First published in 1996
PCI, DSS	First industry mandated security requirements	First published in 2004
CERT	Security research organization	Established in 1988
SOX	Major security legislation	Enacted in 2002
HIPAA	Major security legislation	Enacted in 1996

Note: DSS = Data Security Standards
CERT = Computer Emergency Response Team
ISC2 = International Information Systems Security Certification Consortium
SANS = System Administration, Audit, Network, Security
COBIT = Control Objectives for Information and related Technology
HIPAA = Health Insurance Portability and Accountability
SOX = Sarbanes Oxley

identified, qualified, and mitigated. The result is an alphabet soup of options and permutations.

This has created a bit of an issue for the modern chief information security officers (CISOs) and their teams. As clever attackers dream new and exciting ways to attack organizations using advanced technologies and tools, we are using techniques to combat these situations that are still very new. To demonstrate this, we have provided a snapshot of many of the organizations, frameworks, and security regulations that champion security and are on the mind of most security professionals today.

Regardless of which items we selected, you get the idea. Few would argue that these are not some of the most influential organizations, regulations, and standards in our field today. Yet, though they are powerful, not one of them is more than 20 years old. Compare this with other disciplines that are commonly found in most organizations, such as accounting, legal, finance, or human resources, and you start to see the discrepancy. To hit this point home, consider that the American Institute of Certified Public Accountants (AICPA) was founded in 1887. All of this is compounded by the fact that, as part of our complex world, our discipline must adapt and change as rapidly as the technologies and trends that support it.

Figure 6.2 demonstrates that the majority of our profession does not feel that security regulations are effective at addressing security; maybe the politicians might want to include the security profession in the process.

Figure 6.3 supports the precept that proper experience in security is difficult to locate and obtain for the majority of organizations; you're not alone.

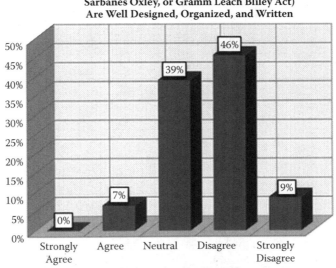

Figure 6.2   Figure 6.2 demonstrates that the majority of our profession does not feel that security regulations are affective at addressing security; maybe the politicians might want to include the security profession in the process.

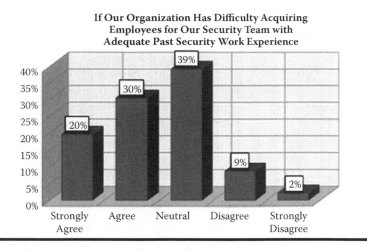

Figure 6.3 **Figure 6.3 supports the precept that proper experience in security is difficult to locate and obtain for the majority of organizations; you're not alone.**

If the modern incarnation of security is so new, how can it wield power within those same organizations? More importantly, how do immature practices hinder our ability to achieve true security? This is where our human tendencies arise and contribute to facilitating the negative aspects of infancy. That is the subject that we will address in this chapter.

This chapter will follow a similar format as the previous chapters on the other security constraints. We will begin with some information from Skye on how humans take in stimuli—read data, information, and knowledge—and how this may cause humans to be over-confident when trusting information they are receiving or presenting to others. She will then use systems theory as a lens to show how infancy can negatively affect an open system.

From there we will look at the causes of this phenomenon within organizations and then within your security program. One of the major concerns we will explore is the rapid nature of change within the modern organization. New ideas and ways of doing things arise quickly, are adopted even faster, and become a passing fad before you can blink. This creates a perfect environment for the proliferation of issues associated with infancy.

Once we have explained the causes of infancy-related issues, we will move into the cause and effect relationship of infancy within the True Security Model. This relationship will aid us in presenting some tangible manifestations of infancy that can set us up for solutions.

The final section, as always, will focus on some actionable solutions that can be applied to compensate for the effects of infancy in your environment. This will include a time machine that can be downloaded from the book's Web site at no extra charge (just kidding). Since we cannot alter time, we will focus on how to validate the information that is presented and when to trust the information that is received. It should be fun. With that, let us get started off to the races.

Causes of Infancy in Humans

The amount and availability of data has exploded in the past decade almost exclusively as a result of innovations in technology. This has also led to a recent increase in the amount of research that deals with how humans seek out, process, and distribute data or information to and from others. Fittingly, this domain of study is known as "human-information behavior." Though there is a great deal of research, focusing on a multitude of areas, we will try to identify some of the items that are interesting and relevant to our efforts in this chapter.

Humans are struggling with the volume and velocity of information. Although some days it seems as though humans are passive receivers of stimuli or information internally and externally, we are actually always processing stimuli. Can you imagine what would happen if we had to consciously tend to every cue? Blink, cough, walk, sneeze, walk, observe, use hands, etc. One could argue that we would go nuts! Thankfully, many of the cues are tended to without our notice. However, when we are bombarded with large quantities of data or information, we can run into trouble discerning what is important amongst all the clutter. Thus, it is important to consider how we take in information and make sense of our environment. The process of how we take in information is called "perception." Perception is the means of selecting, organizing, and making sense of stimuli in our environment. One of the most interesting aspects of perception is that it is the mechanism that ultimately determines how we internalize our environment and create our knowledge. Though this process is highly fallible, we tend to treat the related conclusions as truth. Furthermore, the stimuli that receive the greatest amount of our attention are generally based on our human needs and drives. If we are hungry, we invariably will tune into stimuli that will appeal to the hunger drive. If we are depressed ... well you get the point.

Furthermore, how we make sense of information is based on several factors such as culture, age, cognitive complexity, education, experience, gender, prejudice, bias, goals, prototypes—what you visualize or expect when you are presented with an individual with a title for example—and the list goes on. This is important because when you attempt to teach others information, what they receive or hear may not be the intended message even if you feel that the message you sent was very clear and even obvious. For example, if you say to your friend, "I will be home early tonight." Depending on your definition of early and your friend's definition of early, you might have two very different definitions and thus misunderstanding can occur. Of course, this is a simplistic example and one that might not cause damage to the relationship; however, depending on the number of people in your organization, the opportunity for misunderstanding and miscommunication is exemplified exponentially.

Some other areas of research of relevance to this chapter are the ways in which data is classified and consumed by humans. Figure 6.4 depicts the evolution of data as it is refined and understood.

One of the best ways we have found to differentiate data, information, knowledge, and wisdom comes from a researcher named Topsy Smalle. With her permission, we have adapted her material, which is built upon her expertise and that of others, and used it as a springboard

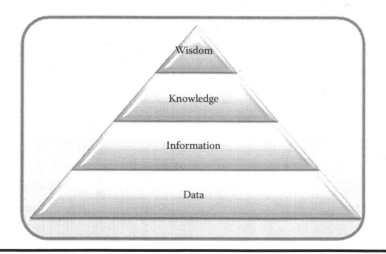

Figure 6.4 **This figure depicts the evolution of data as it is refined and understood.**

for our conversation. The bottom of the pyramid, the widest part, reflects the multitude of data available to an individual on a daily basis, via the media, newspapers, Internet, institutions, life experience, and culture; the list is infinite. The second tier reflects information. We constantly take in information from the environment, books, teachers, facilitators, mentors, experience, etc. and we connect that information to our prior understanding of the concept. Knowledge is constructed from information, which is pieced together by data. When we connect past knowledge with new information by making connections, associations, interpretations, and patterns, we continue to construct our personal knowledge. Knowledge involves comprehending and using data and information to make arguments, answer questions, construct meaning, and ultimately teach others and ourselves. The top of the pyramid is wisdom. You need the foundation of everything that falls below it to reach this space. Wise people exhibit curiosity, coupled with a zest for learning and a mindful state of mind. Wise people learn to evaluate resources, check primary resources, evaluate messages and information, and critically analyze data. Furthermore, they question the validity of information and learn to examine multiple sources to seek their truth. The reason that we bring this up is that not everyone is so wise. The manner in which we are able to consume, categorize, and utilize these items can vary wildly, leading to very different and often unpredictable situations.

Who Do Humans Trust?

As we mentioned in earlier chapters, humans will focus on both the content and relational elements of a communication. The relational components of a communication are of importance here when looking at how humans trust data and then make decisions with it. There is a direct correlation between the level of trust and the level of skepticism of the source. Humans have some interesting tendencies when it comes to trusting data or the people providing the data.

One point of interest is that humans often trust data from sources they can relate to. For example, information that a person may receive from a social networking Web site that deals with one specific type of issue, such as child abuse or a favorite baseball team. Their relationship will also impact the level of trust when comparing similar types of sources. For example, most people are more likely to trust data from a news organization such as *The Wall Street Journal* with which they are familiar than data they receive from a college newspaper. News organizations are highly aware of how important trust is, and this is why many television stations begin their telecast with a slogan such as, "Channel X News, your most trusted news source."

There is also research that suggests that humans trust data that comes from those that we view as authority figures. The most common authority figure we can all relate to is our parents or primary caretaker. We believe things like the Easter Bunny, the Tooth Fairy, and Santa Claus when we are young. Of course, at some point we grow out of this phase, where we do not trust everything our parents tell us, but these influences remain with us in some form or another for the remainder of our lives.

Another human condition that affects how we trust data is based on its age. We are more likely to trust data that is current than something that is ten years old. For example, you are more likely to trust an article from a 2007 *Newsweek* than from 1977.

Finally, it is logical that humans are most likely to trust themselves and their own knowledge, even when they should not. Our parents used to tell us that "a little knowledge is dangerous." They were not kidding. How many times have we sat in a meeting with people who possessed a small amount of knowledge regarding security, yet they believed that they understood the entire domain? The Dunning–Kruger effect suggests that humans who have little knowledge often believe that they know more than others around them who actually have much more knowledge.

Summary

There are obviously many items that can influence how humans receive, process, perceive, and make decisions with data. It is important to remember that there are both cognitive and emotional considerations that impact what we do with information. Cognitive influences include items such as the amount of data that we can process at a given time or our ability to differentiate between data, information, knowledge, wisdom, and understanding. Emotional considerations are just as important with items such as how we trust the sources of the data that we receive and our overconfidence in our own abilities.

Infancy within a System

We have discussed the primary principles of systems theory, which are: (1) wholeness, (2) interdependency, (3) nonsummativity, and (4) feedback. Furthermore, we have illustrated how a system takes in information from its surrounding environment and simultaneously interacts with its surrounding environment. Depending on how systems engage with one another and the environment will determine system effectiveness, growth, and ability to positively respond to change. Infancy within a system can be detrimental. When using systems theory as a tool, it enables one to see how too much information too fast causes instability in the system and moves the system toward ineffective communication exchanges within the organization and within the environment; a system can only be effective if it has sufficient time to process information. A system that does not have clearly defined processes (infancy) takes longer to consume, synthesize, and react to the information. If there is insufficient time to do so, the result is immature or ill-advised action in the best case. In a worst case, the system stops taking input (shutdown) in order to deal with the mass of information awaiting attention. Figure 6.5 represents

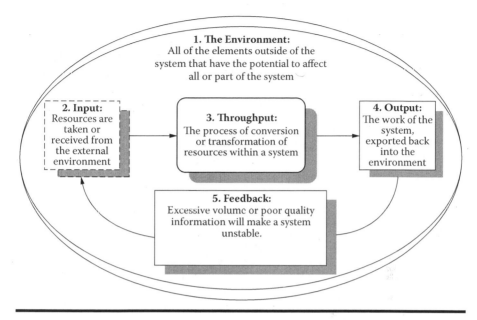

Figure 6.5 This figure represents the axiom of "garbage in, garbage out" as it pertains to systems theory. The quantity and quality of feedback are critical to a healthy functioning system.

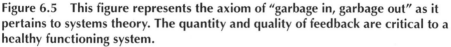

the axiom of "garbage in, garbage out" as it pertains to systems theory. The quantity and quality of feedback are critical to a healthy functioning system.

Infancy within an Organization

There are many elements within an organization that support the detrimental effects of infancy. This should seem logical since at the core of infancy is the exchange of information and ideas, something that happens constantly in the modern organization. Just as with many of the other constraints, the first influencer of infancy within an organization is its culture.

As we discussed in the human section in this chapter, trust is a major factor within the relationship component of any communication. More importantly, as humans, we have a tendency to trust data that comes from those who are in a position of authority. Therefore, the cultural authority model becomes relevant in our discussion. As you may recall, cultures generally range between vertical dictatorships on the left, to communal consensus environments on the far right.

In the vertical model, employees are more likely or, in some cases, forced to consume the information that they receive from those who are in power. If a message comes from the top, it is accepted by the audience without question. In this situation, infancy prospers through the dissemination and assimilation of information that may not be accurate.

Within horizontal organizations, skepticism of information is the norm. That questioning is part of the ritual that allows the various factions within an organization to flex their political muscle. After all, since everyone is in charge of their own little world, it would be a sign of weakness to simply accept the edict of someone else. This is the stuff that fuels all of the committee meetings that are commonly used in these organizations. In these models, debate of the information that is provided is expected; it is the foundation of the consensus model. In this situation, infancy may prosper due to the obfuscation created by all of the tangents, noise, and voices that are part of the consensus process. Organizational culture aside, technology has also proven to be a great facilitator of infancy.

The rapid improvements in technology have led to rapid changes in organizations as they adopt and utilize these technologies. For example, improvements in technology have led to a truly global economy where a business in London can easily communicate and sell products or services to an organization in Singapore. These changes lead organizations in a constant search for more information on different means of doing business. In many situations, the changes within the modern business happen faster than an organization's ability to find, process, and then make decisions to support that change.

A classic example was the move a couple of years ago of many organizations in the United States to farm out work to India. Many of the organizations in which we have worked took this path as soon as the technology could support the transfer. What they failed to consider was many of the other supporting processes and procedures that had yet to be developed and implemented to support this change. One of the most common issues to be forgotten or overlooked was security, of course. All of a sudden, data within key applications was shipped thousands of miles away to locations which few had ever visited. In these situations, members of the security team were forced to come up with new models and methodologies for implementing security. Over time, these models do become more effective as they move toward a more mature state. Until that time, they contribute to a security state of infancy.

No place is the technical advancement felt more strongly than in the means and manner in which communication occurs within organizations. Many of these new options have moved away from face-to-face interaction, enabling the focus of the message to be solely on the content of the message and less on the relationship component. It does not take a rocket scientist to see that a large portion of organizational communication now relies on items such as e-mail, instant messaging, or voice mail. All of these tools have limited the amount of information that can be gathered about the relationship component of a communication. For example, it is far more difficult to determine the mood and temperament of the author from a single e-mail versus a conversation with that individual in the room. So why is this important?

Earlier, we discussed that trust of the information source is a large component in determining how an individual reacts to the furnished information. Additionally, trust is usually transferred from the relationship component of a message, not the content portion. Therefore, as the use of content-focused technologies continues to increase, the amount of relationship elements to those communications will continue to decrease resulting in the use of information that should not be trusted or failing to employ information that should be trusted.

The last item to consider is how immaturity can be taken seriously. Would you believe your eight-year-old boy as he instructs you on how to meet girls in a bar? Not a chance. However, we follow that type of behavior within organizations. This stems from the basic nature of human beings to accept information from sources that we deem as authoritative.

For example, one of the most common questions that we get when we speak, and we mean all the time, goes like this: "My boss just read something from XYZ security research firm about ABC and no matter what I do I cannot get him to listen to anything else. How can I get him to listen to me about the DEF way of addressing this issue?"

The larger the research firm in the question, the higher the degree of clout that it often carries with executive management. Organizations love trusting information, in our opinion almost blindly, from what they perceive as authoritative sources on a subject. This is particularly fascinating when you consider that these research firms have in many cases never actually secured anything. They are, for the most part, academics sitting in their ivory tower, relying upon survey information to base their claims. Not exactly the same as a practitioner in the field who lives and breathes solutions on a daily basis. Once again, we are not knocking research firms. They perform a very useful function as research firms aggregating ideas, not as the final authority on solutions.

Research is not the only place where this blind trust occurs. Large consulting firms, such as the Big X, are another source that is blindly trusted by organizations relying on the authority that they have placed in these firms rather than to the actual content of the information they get from these establishments. Just look at how these firms justify a $300 an hour billing rate for the new college graduate assigned to your project: "You are not just getting Joe (the new college grad), you are getting the power of the entire XYZ organization." That statement is meant to instill confidence and trust … nothing else. So, why does this continue to happen in organizations even after they have been burned by it?

As we stated, this phenomenon has its roots in the human tendency to trust information from sources viewed as authoritative. The other factor to consider is the decisions and the associated costs that are made as a result of this information. In many cases, these decisions hold the individual's career or political stature in the balance. This is where timeless axioms such as: "No one ever got fired for buying IBM" have arisen. The statement speaks to deferring professional liability to an accepted authoritative entity, not necessarily the best source.

For example, it is much safer to select information from a large consulting firm from the Big X than a niche boutique firm. If something goes wrong as a result of that information from the Big X firm, then the answer from the person who selected the information is, "Hey, I got it from the Big X, everyone knows that they're experts." That is a very different answer than if the boutique firm was selected: "Hey, that was a small firm, you should have known better than to trust that information."

Summary

Infancy is something that is the result of an uncontrollable aspect of our reality: time. After reading this section though, it should be clear that there are many things occurring in organizations that allow immature elements to be treated as "adults" (remember the 8-year-old giving you dating advice). These aspects of our culture and lineage allow infancy to influence our security efforts. Let us move on to how security participates in the propagation of the effects that infancy produces.

Infancy within a Security Program

Because your security program is a system within an even larger system—the organization—it inherits the same issues and concerns that we addressed in the prior section on organizational infancy. However, because organizational security itself is one of the newer concepts in many organizations, it has several facets that magnify the effects of this security constraint. Figure 6.6 confirms that the majority of security professionals believe that our field has a long way to go and that it is still evolving.

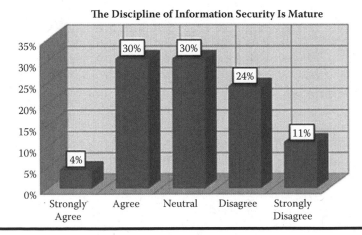

Figure 6.6 This figure confirms that the majority of security professionals believe that the security field has a long way to go and that it is still evolving.

Security is a discipline that mandates the need to review everything with a healthy dose of skepticism.

Nature of Security

When looking at how security contributes to the constraint of infancy, the first item to consider is the nature of security itself. Security is a discipline that requires the analysis of a ridiculously large set of data. In order to secure anything, all aspects and elements of a situation must be reviewed, evaluated, and categorized. The data surrounding any security analysis begins to grow exponentially as multiple permutations are derived for each identified instance of potential risk. That is why security assessments, vulnerability scans, audit findings, etc. are such large undertakings and generate so much raw data. When we go into organizations to help build security programs, it is not uncommon for us to look at reports that are easily 150 pages long. The message here is that security produces massive amounts of stuff. Referring back to the human section, individuals generally have difficulty differentiating between data, information, knowledge, and wisdom. There are other considerations as well when looking at the all-encompassing nature of security.

We have all heard it, security touches everything. There is truth in this. Security does touch many items from people, to processes, technology, facilities, and specific widgets within each of those categories. For example, look at this book. Hopefully, we are addressing the challenges you are now or will be facing in your security efforts and providing reasonable solutions. However, you may notice that we have not once mentioned any issues that are commonly found in the rest of the books on your security bookshelf. There are really no boundaries to security or how you can approach it. This provides the chief information security officer (CISO) and his or her team many potential paths to take on the journey. When you couple a diverse knowledge set with an unlimited array of options, and a discipline that is still very new, you are likely to make some wrong turns along the way.

Lack of Credibility

We do not believe that there are many people who would argue that security, specifically information security, is fairly new to the party in most organizations. We are like the new kid who has transferred to a different school in the middle of the semester. We are supposed to be accepted and recognized by the cool kids, but they just keep giving us a wedgie, calling us nerds, and stealing our milk money. In order to fit in, we do things such as create positions with powerful titles, just like other more respected groups in the organization. Do you think we are kidding? We always find it hilarious how most CISOs report at a middle-manager level, yet retain the "chief" portion of their titles. Note to everyone in security:

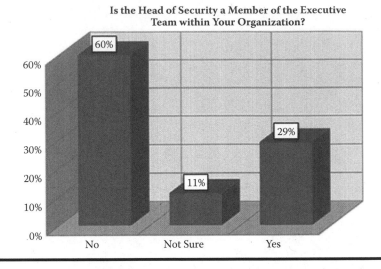

Figure 6.7 This figure shows that most security organizations suffer from the same fundamental issue: lack of representation at the executive level.

groups outside of security laugh at us for this, if they care enough to think about it (apathy). As we said, security is the new kid in school, and as a result does not carry the credibility of some of the more time-honored groups. This results in overcompensation by our community in an attempt to be heard and respected. However, just like the new kid in school, only time and deeds will earn the respect and status that we seek. But, we can't just accept that fact and act appropriately. Instead, we present the image that our tools and techniques are as good as other disciplines that are time tested. Look at some of the trappings associated with our profession today from our security certifications, to our research, frameworks, and the experiences that we draw from in order to solve important problems. As we mentioned at the beginning of this chapter, most of these items are less than 20 years old—not exactly field proven and time tested. However, you would never know that by the way most security professionals speak of them. Figure 6.7 illustrates that most security organizations suffer from the same fundamental issue: lack of representation at the executive level.

Now perhaps we do not have a choice. Though we promised a downloadable time machine, which can speed up our knowledge and experience, it was not ready at the time of publication. However, misrepresenting the maturity of organizational security is not the right approach either. Actually, that misrepresentation is having a devastating effect on the credibility of our profession. It makes us look foolish when we do things such as implement a regulation that is vague or considered infeasible, or blindly accept and implement a framework in one country because it was successful in a completely different hemisphere. A perfect example is the implementation of Information Technology Infrastructure Library (ITIL) security management. Though it was highly successful in Europe, implementations in the United States have not gone as well. To those outside of security, the only thing that we do in these situations is further deteriorate our credibility, not increase it. Going back to our new-kid-at-school analogy, this leads us to eating alone if we have any money that has not been stolen.

Pedaling Doom (or How Chicken Little Found His Calling in Security)

In our experience, the use of fear, uncertainty, and doubt (FUD) has been a popular means of furthering the cause of organizational security. After all, it is easy to use in that there is little understanding required on the part of the audience and it is convenient in that the facts can be adjusted to support the security agenda. And most of all it is fun; merely step back, think of the worst possible situation associated with an issue, and start scaring people (good times ... ah, yes ... good times).

The reason that we place the use of FUD here in the infancy chapter is because it is often used as a replacement for a sound approach or solution to a problem. A CISO gets stumped or does not have the experience to get the support of his or her audience, and out comes FUD. Or even worse, he or she only knows how to communicate in the language of FUD. Both of these methods of communication exacerbate the problems associated with infancy, allowing it to continue to spread.

Summary

Infancy is unavoidable. We have all gone through it personally, professionally, and spiritually. However, it is entirely different when your industry is going through adolescence and puberty and is forcing you to relive the experience. We think that the analogy of high school best fits our profession at this time:

1. We aren't as smart as we think we are.
2. We are always trying to make ourselves look cooler than we truly are.
3. Like the new kid, we are on the outside looking in.
4. No one understands us, but we do have a lot to say.
5. We are awkward and clumsy in our communication.
6. We still don't get the girls (or guys).

Now that we have shared our perspective of the security discipline, we will explore how infancy impacts the True Security Model. Figure 6.8 represents a graphical depiction of the human, system, organizational, and security program causes of infancy.

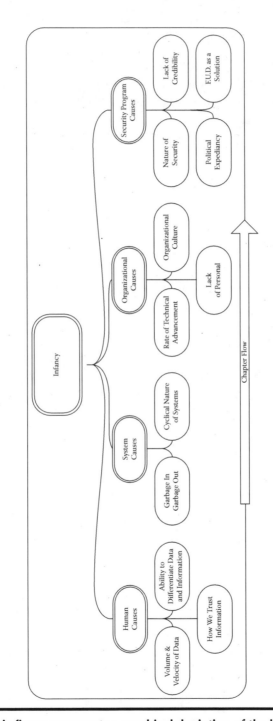

Figure 6.8   This figure represents a graphical depiction of the human, system, organizational, and security program causes of infancy.

True Security Model and Infancy

We have taken a good look at how infancy influences humans within systems, organizations, and security programs; we will move on to how it functions within our True Security Model. This is where we demonstrate how it impedes our ability to achieve true security.

We will again evaluate the influences and effects of infancy on each organizational group within the True Security Model. For each group, we will identify the tendencies and situations that allow infancy to propagate and grow. You will notice that similar to some of the other constraints, the influences on infancy grow as you move down the management chain within each organizational group.

After looking at the influences of infancy, we will move on to its effects on each group. Though many people enable the effects of infancy without even knowing it, this does not mean that the effects are not pronounced to those who are trained to look for them. That is exactly what we are going to do.

Finally, as with other constraints, we will finish each review on an individual group with a look at how that group or others around it participate in the security con. When considering how infancy grows and spreads, in many cases unknowingly by those within an organization, the con is less pronounced than with some of the other constraints.

We will begin with a quick review of the various organizational groups that comprise our True Security Model.

True Security Model

Below are the various groups commonly found within an organization and the desired actions that we hope to obtain from each group in order to achieve true security.

As a quick refresher on the True Security Model, refer to the target groups and desired behavior table below:

Organizational Group	Desired Action or Behavior
Board of directors	Endorsement
Executive management	Priority
Middle management	Resources
Supervisory management	Support
Employees	Diligence
Consumers	Trust
Security program	Execution

For each group, we will explore the cause and effect relationship that infancy can have on the desired action we need to obtain. We will begin by providing some common symptoms that are displayed when infancy is present, and then we will look at some of the more intangible effects. We will also discuss the ways in which some are compensating (security con) for the effects of infancy within each group. Of course, we will start at the top of the food chain with our pals on the board of directors.

Board of Directors

It is ironic that those who are often considered the most powerful and knowledge-able in an organization propagate infancy for exactly the opposite reasons. When it comes to security, generally those on the board are security neophytes. Most have no idea what security is, are generally not that interested in the subject (apathy), or have a perception of security that is oversimplified and narrow (myopia). This results in the inability to determine the validity or quality of information that is presented to them, thus allowing immature concepts, approaches, and ideas, to be accepted as wisdom instead of meeting it with skepticism.

As you would expect, this can have devastating effects on an organization. Though infancy, in and of itself, will not hinder the endorsement that is sought from the board, it does taint the validity of the endorsement. It would be akin to children obtaining their parent's permission to spend the evening at a friend's house when in reality they plan to attend a concert. In summary, if those on the board are coerced by the information or individuals by the use of immature approaches—to solve complex security issues—then there is a high probability for a faulty endorsement.

This is not a mistake that can be easily rectified once committed. Few are willing to recant prior statements or admit to making a mistake at the board level. We must also consider the fact that though these individuals are not security experts, it in no way diminishes any of their power and authority. Once they issue directives, based on the information that they receive about security issues, there is little that can stop those further down the management chain from being forced to implement those directives.

During our travels, we have seen some of the wackiest directives one could imagine issued from boards due to infancy. One of the most common is the constant change of where security reports within the organization.

Though elements of this behavior can be attributed to primacy, more often than not organizations simply have no idea where security belongs in their organiza-tion. They will move the department three times in a year—that is the record for us—based on various reports or articles that were reviewed at the board level. Sadly, many times these reports are created by individuals or other organizations that have no exposure or experience with the organization in which the information is applied. Yet once the board is convinced, the damage is done and the directive is issued.

The security con in this situation is perpetrated by those on the security team who take advantage of the trust and naïveté of the board of directors. This is a clas-sic case of information asymmetry, where one group, which is the security team, possesses a superior understanding of the subject matter of security than another group, which is the board of directors, allowing for the manipulation of data to meet the group's agenda and objectives. This situation is not unique to security; it happens in many professions such as real estate, law, or any other area where there is a knowledge or expertise imbalance between two parties.

Executive Management

Executive management has the unenviable position of executing the direction given by the board of directors. If this direction is misguided or wacky, executive management has little recourse but to follow such direction. This creates its own issues when placed in the context of security. As we have discussed, this group generally has a limited view of what constitutes security (myopia), is rarely interested in broadening that view (apathy), and is generally concerned with the potential for security to embarrass it (primacy). The net result is that any elements of infancy are rarely circumvented at this level; they are merely propagated down the chain of command.

As a result, the priority that is given to security by executives is directly correlated to the endorsement and type of security directives that are given by the board of directors. If the board issues misguided directives for security, these items will generally still be given priority by this group, and then will simply be passed down the line. This is how the effects of infancy continue to pick up steam as it heads down the management chain.

The con at this level is generally exercised by the executives themselves who can leverage the information asymmetry. That's right! You do not have be a security genius to pull this trick! You just need to be a little more educated than the next guy. We have seen many situations where the naïveté of the board is used to reduce its focus on security. We do not believe that this is done for gain or a dislike for security, merely to remove another "mandated" element from the board's already cluttered list of items that are vying for priority.

Middle Managers

When considering infancy and middle management, most of the influence comes from the availability and presentation of deficient or inaccurate security information. The first place that this group gets poor information from is the management. In these situations, poor security information or knowledge is provided to executives or the board. This information is then consumed and transformed into immaturely developed directives. These directives then proceed downstream to middle management to further their implementation. Therefore, if the initial information is misguided or errant, the end product meets with resistance, doubt, or sometimes open mutiny.

So, what is this management group to do? Many times the lack of a mature approach to organizational security leaves the group without a knowledgeable, authoritative resource with which to get clarification, guidance, or direction—specifically, when the direction from higher levels of management is flawed. This can create a great deal of frustration and resentment, since middle management truly needs an advisor that can translate the directives into an actionable set of tasks under these circumstances. The other alternative is that the organization provides sufficient security training to make informed, rational decisions. However, an organization that lacks a mature security program is likely missing the foundation element of a robust security training and awareness campaign. Either it provides limited ad hoc training, which is seldom targeted, or it does not provide any training at all.

The net result is for middle management to become reluctant to participate and provide the necessary resources for security initiatives, instead providing a token appearance of compliance rather than a truly committed effort to reduce the risk of the organization. After all, how can one realistically staff a directive that is vague or based on information that is known to be inaccurate? This is not so far-fetched. Up until this point, in the chain of command, all of the conversations are at a theoretical level by individuals who generally have little knowledge surrounding the intricacies of implementation.

The con at this level is very subtle. Most of the people involved are doing the best they can with the information and data at their disposal. The group that is far more culpable for the con at this level is executive management. That's right sports fans! They perpetuate the con at the middle management level. How? We are glad you asked. The answer is the executive reflex of cover your assets (CYA). They do not want to take the responsibility of interpreting vague or poorly founded directives that they receive from the board. Therefore, they redirect any conversation regarding their implementation into the realm of the theoretical rather than discussing the practical issues faced by middle management. Of course, this leaves middle management to wrestle with the issues and the liability of failure by themselves.

Supervisory Team

As we have said before, the supervisory team is those people in the trenches guiding subordinates to execute the tasks and directives that are issued from higher levels of management. As a result, these individuals must find a balance between incorporating the designated security practices, tools, and procedures of the organization into their daily activities, while at the same time maintaining the productivity and morale of their area. This is a very tough job and infancy does not help in the slightest. Organizations where the security efforts are immature spend little time working with this group, instead focusing on communicating with upper management, and then expecting them to distribute the information downstream.

Unfortunately, this approach leaves the supervisors out in the cold attempting to figure out the implementation of security on their own. You can imagine how this makes them feel. Couple this with limited security training and controls for the organization and you can see how frustrating it must be for this group to execute on security initiatives. We do not believe that it is much of a stretch to assume that these types of experiences produce a barrier to the level of support that is needed to execute the True Security Model. And though this is not always the case, it occurs on a fairly frequent basis leaving the existing security team wondering why this group does not wish to work with them.

The con at this level is generally instigated by security team members by avoiding this group in hopes of not having to explain some half-baked plan or concept. In this case, they do not want to be questioned on something to which they may not have answers, thus, damaging their professional credibility. We think that a healthy dialog with this group regarding concepts under development is a healthy form of litmus test that actually aids in flushing out flaws and accelerating the rate of adoption after it is introduced. This is why it is sad when this is not what happens.

Employees

Employees are a fairly simple group. As we mentioned above, immature security generally coincides with nonexistent, ad hoc, or deficient security training. As a result, employees receive little of the information required in order to make informed decisions regarding the employment of secure practices and tools in performing their daily tasks. This ignorance is translated into real consequences for the security effort. After all, how can you hope to gain an inspired level of security diligence from this group if it has not been given the requirements, tools, and reasons for such diligence? If you aspire to the True Security Model, the hearts and minds of the employees are a mandatory component for such a model.

The security con at this level is generally performed by members of the security team who use the employees or their procedures as a scapegoat for the lack of proper training. However, we also feel that the employees are complicit with the con when they fail to ask for direction or training—specifically when they know that there is risk associated with the means and manner in which they execute their job.

Consumers

It is fair to say that most consumers "do not know what they do not know." They are not aware of how important the security efforts of an organization are in keeping their private information secure; though, they are getting smarter. They also do not know how difficult a task it is to secure their information, and how many organizations are struggling with this issue. In actuality, how could they know? All of the emphasis on consumer security is focused on educating consumers on how they must protect their own personal information. A Google™ search on the term "consumer security" will get you items such as top ten lists for how to not fall for a phishing scam or how to protect your social security number. This stuff helps and is important, but it is only half of the equation. What is missing is the ability for a consumer to hold the organizations that house their personal information just as accountable. For example, there are few places consumers can go today that would show them how well an organization is doing at protecting their personal information once they have provided it. Instead, most consumers expect that it is the job of security regulations to handle this for them. Our message in Chapter 1 was that most regulations are not doing a very good job. As the security knowledge of consumers begins to mature, they will realize they must be proactive in assuring that their information is protected by any organization that comes in contact with it.

In the True Security Model, we need trust from this group. Obviously, this situation may lead to blind trust, but that is not the same thing as informed genuine trust. The difference between the two lies in the efforts of your security program behind the scenes. Security programs are both being diligent and adequately protecting the data of their consumers, or they are using the lack of visibility by consumers to let their deficient efforts remain unnoticed.

Obviously, the con with this group is carried out by members of the security program who choose the second option illustrated above. They are not adequately protecting their consumers' data and are using the lack of interest and visibility of consumers to front this activity.

Exercise 16

This exercise can also be found in the Appendix with worksheets.

Objective

The objective of this exercise is to determine how mature the security practices are within your organization.

Exercise

Take five minutes and think about how your organization secures the data of its consumers. Answer the following three questions:

1. Do you believe that your organization adequately secures the data of its consumers? Why?
2. On a scale of 1 to 10 (1 being vulnerable and 10 being highly secure), where would you place your organization when considering consumer security. Why?
3. Would you trust your organization to secure your personal data? Why?

Summary

Security in the modern organization is not easy. It is all the more difficult by the amount of time our profession has had to adapt to the rapidly changing legal, technical, and cultural landscape. This infancy presents a number of unique challenges that can be overcome with time and effort. This does not mean that the only recourse is to sit back and let time sort things out for us. Though maturing process takes time, there are things that can be done to combat the constraint of infancy now.

Security Solutions

Sorry folks, but the time machine still is not working. We thought we had it running, but the bearings on our trusty DeLorean prevented us from generating the required velocity. That and we could not figure out how to make it downloadable. So, we are turning to plan B for combating infancy.

Do not despair! There are many things within the control of a CISO to combat infancy that do not require mastery of the space–time continuum. All of these solutions are basic and simple. They begin with establishing open communication channels and obtaining access to the right information that will enable informed decisions for both you and then those around you. Sounds easy and, believe it or not, it is. The key is to take an organized approach to acquiring, consuming, and distributing the data. As always, we will start with some human and then systems theory considerations for combating infancy.

Humans Considerations

Because humans tend to pay attention to information, or stimuli, in their environment that supports their needs at a given moment, too much information that does not connect with their prior knowledge, or present needs and motives, might seem irrelevant to the present state of mind of the individual. For all of the information that you collect, you must answer the following questions: "Why do I need to know this?" and "How will this help me become better?". Furthermore, if the person does not understand why he or she needs to know the information or how it directly impacts his or her position in the organization, further ownership and application of the information gets filed in the "duly noted" part of the brain. In other words, the information is received but never placed into action. The employees of most organizations are flooded with information and cope by categorizing information that is not deemed as immediately important to their function as unnecessary, perhaps even "busy work."

Know Who and What to Trust

It is important to focus your energy on evaluating the sources from which you get your information, before assigning a level of trust to it. Be aware of human tendencies to become too trusting of some sources and to not trust enough of others.

Just as important as whom you trust, is to be cognizant of these same human tendencies when presenting information to other people. Be aware of their level of trust for you or the information you are presenting and what the repercussions of that trust level will be.

Systems Theory Considerations

When dealing with a system, it is important to recognize that if the inputs into a system are faulty, the outputs are also going to be faulty. So when a system is receiving faulty, incomplete, or obscure data as an input, this will lead to faulty throughput and obscure or ineffective final product as output; in other words, "garbage in, garbage out." Therefore, it stands to reason that the focus should be on obtaining the highest quality data and information possible to feed to your system. Furthermore, each individual within the system should independently and collectively seek data, information, and knowledge mindfully to cultivate wisdom. Imagine how powerful a system could become if you are your weakest link or, better yet, a weak link cannot be identified.

Just as important as strong inputs are mature processes within the throughput of a system. Even if the
inputs into a system are of sufficient quality and quantity, poor processes will yield substandard results. The
more refined and mature the throughput processes, the
better and more efficient the system will produce output. In systems that lack mature capabilities, the compensating factor is time. You will want to be considerate
of the increases in time and the additional effort that
will be required to produce a viable, useful output. It
should be noted that the use of time as a means of compensating for incomplete or immature processes has a
major downfall. In these situations, the system is easily
saturated by volume. This results in either a shutdown
of the system (closed) or an accelerated processing rate
that is incapable of yielding quality results. Either result
is highly detrimental to achieving true security.

Now we will move on to some solutions that are specific to CISOs and their team.
We will begin with measuring the effects of infancy in our own environment.

Infancy Breeds Doubt Which Leads to Skepticism

The easiest way to measure how immature your security efforts are is to measure
the level of skepticism of those around your security program. Now we could come
up with some complex mechanism for measuring this item, but instead we will
keep it simple. The best way we think you can get this information is to simply
ask them.

Exercise 17

The following exercise can also be found in the Appendix with worksheets.

Objective

The objective is to determine how the security efforts within your organization may
be proliferating security infancy.

Exercise

Ask the following three questions to each group within the True Security Model. In presenting these questions, make it so that the responses are anonymous. This will make the responders feel more at ease and open with their answers. Ask as many people to respond as makes sense in your situation.

1. Do you feel that the efforts of the security program within the organization utilize mature and fully developed techniques and approaches?
2. Please list five terms that best describe the efforts of the security program.
3. Do you feel that you have enough training, skills, or knowledge to understand what the security program is doing at your organization and why it is doing it?

If the responses come back predominantly illustrating that your security program is not perceived as mature, there is a good chance that there is some work to be done in mitigating the infancy constraint. If this is the case in your situation, do not fear; below are some more recommendations to help turn things around.

First Things First

Many security efforts embark on an intrepid journey to protect the organization from all forms of evil and menace. They go diving into the world of security with an intrusion detection system and firewall in hand, but forget to figure exactly what they are trying to achieve. With the exception of the idea of "security," they are operating without a clue as to their mission or the authority that is required to achieve success. What we are saying is that the fundamentals cannot be ignored. If you embark on your quest and your security program does not have an overall mission and mandate, or even worse, your individual role within that program is not defined, you are going to get into trouble. If you embark on your expedition and your organization does not have comprehensive security policies, you are in trouble. If you are off to the races and your security program does not have an effective risk-rating methodology or a solid training program, you are in trouble. Continuing to soldier forward with your security efforts without the proper foundation elements is tantamount to throwing gasoline on the infancy fire. These items work as a compass to provide consistent direction and guidance when you are faced with new issues, which is every day in security. In addition, keep in mind that a lack of these items within your security program will cause difficulty whether you are the CISO or a security analyst.

If you are a CISO, then you should be in a position to make these items happen if they are nonexistent. If you are not in a decision-making role, then you need to build a case and talk to those who are able to make these types of changes. If you think that either of these approaches is hopeless, then you need to reevaluate why you are still with the organization. Mom was right; first things first.

No One Likes Big Brother

There are very few organizations that benefit from security operating as big brother within the organization. This type of relationship creates barriers between your security efforts and the very people from which you need diligent adherence to security standards. Of course, you can intimidate or scare them into adhering to the rules, but that is nothing but reluctant compliance at best. If you are in the early stages of developing your security program, whatever those efforts may be, you will achieve far more with converts than with conquests. Remember that fighting infancy requires that everyone in the organization raise their personal level of security sophistication, and a security effort that is operating as big brother will make this task more difficult.

Find Good Sources

As we saw in the discussion of system theory, the quality of the source data is of paramount importance. If your sources for data are deficient or flawed, then you are doomed from the start. A nasty side effect of bad data is the burden that it places on the throughput of your security program system. The wasted effort and resources separating the useful morsels from the junk can seriously hinder your efforts. So, the key is to find sources that will provide the best fuel—data and information—for the machine—your security efforts. Here are some general rules about how to prospect effective sources for security data or information.

Do Not Blindly Trust Sources Just Because They Appear Authoritative

Timothy Leary once said, "Think for yourself and question authority." Question authority and measure their response to your questions. Though we are not in the habit of quoting certifiable loons such as Timothy Leary, he was right in this particular case. Our profession loves to trust sources that appear to be authoritative, from research firms to large security organizations to conference speakers. We want to believe in the people who appear to have the answers; it saves us a lot of unnecessary thinking and brain stuff. But before we take these people on blind faith, let us take a quick look at the facts regarding these sources.

Let us start with those at the security research firms. They generally possess very little practical field experience with security and more often than not have a background in literature. This makes sense since they spend most of their time writing. Many began life as a technical writer and got interested in our little security game of "cops and robbers." This leaves them in a position to rely on others for their information or the recitation of "security theory in the perfect world."

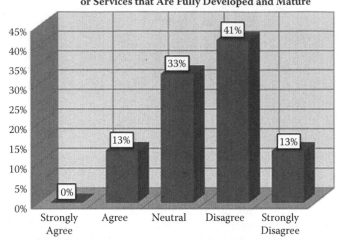

Figure 6.9   Figure 6.9 is fascinating in that the majority of individuals within the poll found that most products and services in the security space were incomplete or immature.

Large security service or product organizations are often large because of acquisition, not organic growth. As a result, the skill sets of the employees at these organizations tend to be very specialized (myopia), and very few will be experts across service or product offerings. You cannot necessarily blame them. These companies can have dozens of products to address a multitude of security issues. In order to implement and support these products, they require specialists.

Figure 6.9 is fascinating in that the majority of individuals within the poll found that most products and services in the security space were incomplete or immature. Yet, we as a profession continue to exert a great deal of resources—time, money, political goodwill—toward these products.

This can make locating the right person for a specific need, or even worse multiple needs, much more difficult. If you spend enough time with these folks (we certainly do), it is not long before you will hear the phrase: "That is a great question! I will have to get back to you on that topic … Bob Smith handles that … let us set up a meeting." Before you know it, you are 30 meetings deep before you arrive at an answer to the original question. All the while, you are in charge of making sense of all that diverse data and information that have been gathered in the interim.

Conference speakers are another group that is generally viewed as authoritative. We will let you in on a little secret. Very rarely are conference speakers chosen based on the content of their presentation, rather on the strength of their company brand or the amount of marketing dollars that their company pumped into the conference. Well, we had planned on making the conference rounds after this book … maybe not.

Our objective in this section is not to criticize research firms, large security organizations, or conference speakers, though it is a lot of fun. Instead, we are trying to convince you that scrutinizing these sources, prior to accepting their information, is healthy and responsible.

Any time you get data from someone, somewhere, or something, validate the source. Take the time to see if the research analyst behind the report has a creditable background on the subject. Or, when you meet with a large security organization, ask to see the resumés or bios of the individuals with whom you will be meeting. Ensure they have the experience and skills that you require prior to accepting the meeting. By the way, large security organizations are really not very fond of this particular maneuver. In our experience, there are only a few individuals in these organizations that are truly knowledgeable across the various products or service offerings. These are the folks you want, and they are there, you just need to fight for them.

Conference speakers are another area where verification is not difficult. If you get a chance, research the speakers whose presentations are of interest to you. We will let you in on another secret used by the experts; it is called "Google" … it is a search engine if there is anyone left on this earth who has not heard of it. It is amazing what you can learn about someone with just a little bit of effort.

These suggestions will not revolutionize the world and certainly do not take any specialized skills. And like most of our scathingly brilliant ideas, they are really nothing more than common sense. They are very easy and can be performed with minimal effort. This is why we are puzzled that many do not perform these steps before consuming the data and information of potentially unreliable sources. Take the time to verify your sources, and this will pay dividends by ensuring the quality of the data and information that you utilize in your security efforts.

Educate Yourself and Then Teach Others

Take time every day to advance your understanding of security. Be honest about your shortcomings and identify sources, mentors, and other appropriate sources that will help foster your understanding of the field. The quest for lifelong learning never ends, so if you think that you have it all mastered and do not need any more training on anything, go back and read the chapter on myopia. Message one here is that all of us can always get smarter; never stop learning. Message two is teach yourself and then teach others. Most find that until they teach what they know to others, they do not master the information. Verbalizing the message is powerful and additional viewpoints enable you to see things from multiple perspectives.

All of us are under pressure, in a rather fast moving world, to deliver more in less time. This situation can lead to times when you may have to teach others before you have the necessary expertise. Now instead of one person proliferating infancy (you), you have just spread the virus to another victim. Do not do this! We repeat, do not do this! Take the time to learn the information first or find others that are more knowledgeable on the subject who can teach you. Remember that security professionals do not let other security professionals teach while under the influence of infancy. Before we leave this section, here are other quick ideas that may help:

1. Any time you see a concept that is foreign to you and is something that you think is important to understand, take note of it. We generally write it down, but any way you can capture it for later review will work. Not a day goes by when we are not taking note of something.
2. Create a methodical approach for how you can learn more about that item. Everyone learns differently. Some people like to read about a concept, others like to talk it out with their peers, while others do a combination of both. Whatever the approach, find out what works best for you and then make it into a repeatable procedure. Over time, as you begin collecting items to study, you should see dramatic increases in your speed at learning new things.
3. Do not be afraid to ask others to teach you. Most people enjoy sharing what they know; do not let your ego keep you from asking for help if you need it.
4. Find the sources that work best for you and constantly be searching for new sources that can fill gaps in your knowledge. For example, we try to keep content experts in just about every facet of security. We have a database security issue, we call our database expert. We have a European regulation issue, we call that person. We also try to do the same thing with learning tools such as security Web sites, search engines (Google anyone?), or books that we come across that appear valuable. The key is to always be on the lookout for something that may help you improve your ability to learn new things quicker and more effectively when the need arises in the future. Do not wait until you have the new concept in front of you before establishing your available weapons for learning about it.

Organize Your Messages

Once you feel confident that you have useful information from credible sources and you yourself understand the material, then you are ready to teach others. The following tips will aid you in disseminating information to various audiences.

1. Know your audience. It is important that you learn to whom you will be speaking. This may require sending out a message to the people that comprise your audience asking some questions that will help you meet their needs beforehand. Once you know your audience, you can speak the same language or jargon. While you talk to the audience, use examples that make sense to that audience and show how what you are talking about is applicable to everyday life. Make your messages concise. Do not bombard your audience with too many details. Have your findings or conclusions detailed in a standard

linear outline. If further supporting material is required or asked for, have it attached as an appendix or available through another appropriate venue.

2. If you use PowerPoint, be sure to use it effectively. A visual aid should add something that words alone cannot; it should not have every single word you say, or have too many distracting bells and whistles. Your slides should be concise, font readable, and most importantly it should add something of value to your presentation.

   a. Consider using acronyms or other methods that will help your audience digest and recall your main points.

   b. Remember that most people are poor listeners and have a hard time recalling information, so quantity will only set you up for failure.

   c. Attempt to keep your audience engaged. Consider "chunking" information in 10 to 15 minute increments and then ask a question or engage the audience in an active manner.

3. Customize your messages. We have yet to identify any security framework, research report, or other security widget that is out of the box customized or applicable for an organization. When you want to use these types of items, we encourage it, but there are some caveats. First, identify differences between what is presented in these items and your unique situation. Highlight these differences to the audience in which you plan on using these types of tools. The advantage to this customization is that it will aid your audience in associating with your message since it will be given in the context of your organization, something hopefully everyone involved can relate to.

4. Use definitions for everything. If you use a term that even has the possibility of confusing your audience, then define it. Remember that the only wrong definition is the one that is not given. Providing definitions will aid your audience in understanding your messages, and get everyone on the same page.

5. Do not use FUD. FUD is often used as a substitute for knowledge or the ability to articulate an issue. Because FUD elicits an emotional response, versus one that is based in logic, it makes getting the attention of the audience easier. But this emotional response also has negative side effects. The first is that the reactions of the audience will be as varied as the emotions that the fear and anxiety of the message can evoke, resulting in highly unpredictable results. The other factor to consider is that the effect of FUD diminishes over time. FUD can only be effective over a long period of time if the prognostications that you provide are highly accurate—meaning you need to be right about 90 percent of the time. That is a pretty risky proposition. Think of FUD as a credit card. The purchase in this analogy is the attention and action of the target audience. The currency is your credibility and that of your security program. The enticement of FUD is the same as a credit card in that it provides the user with purchasing power right here and right now. It provides instant gratification by supplying the user with a tool for achieving a tactical

victory on a given subject. However, pushing the FUD button every time an issue requires attention or resources will bankrupt the security organization and its practitioners of political capital. Because, just like a credit card, the FUD bill has to be paid at some point. Raising the alarm over issues that never materialize or are not apparent to others only makes one an alarmist who people will eventually disregard. For those who glossed over during our rant on FUD here is the synopsis: FUD is bad. Do not use FUD!

Be Patient

Our final suggestion for combating infancy is to be patient. Do not try to gain credibility all in one shot. Take the time to determine the means of demonstrating competency in the skills required for your security efforts. If you are not ready to do something, do not wing it. Be honest and communicate the fact that you need additional time, training, or resources prior to delving into an issue.

Just as you should be patient in building your own expertise and the sophistication of your security effort, you should also exercise that same virtue with others. Resist frustration when others take a little longer to catch on to your security wisdom. Focus on how you can better communicate your messages, and take your time. In most situations, those around you will come up to speed if you only give them the opportunity and time to do so.

Summary

As we mentioned in the beginning of this section, the solutions for reducing the effects of infancy are simple. Take the time to get the right information to build your knowledge, and then organize your communications so that others can come up to speed with you. Throughout both of these steps, please be patient.

Chapter 7

Tying It All Together

"Everyone wants to do the right thing!"

Tales from the Security Consultant

Working as consultants in a large organization, we were assigned to work with the information technology (IT) group to perform a risk assessment that related to the systems within the human resources function. It should be noted that within this organization, the security program was located within this IT group, and the head of IT also served as the chief information security officer (CISO) for the organization.

At first glance, the project seemed very straightforward. The aforementioned IT group told us that it wanted this assessment because it did not believe that the systems were adequately protected and they were obviously critical components to the business. Soon after starting the engagement, it became clear why the IT function was having difficulties up to this point. The first issue was the head of human resources. This individual strictly prohibited anyone working on this project to only talk to a select group of people on topics which she deemed applicable to security (primacy). Furthermore, she insisted to be included in every meeting that had to do with the assessment (primacy)—not an easy thing to accommodate due to her busy schedule. And though this individual was very bright within her realm of expertise in human resources, her perspective of security was very limited. In her mind, the scope of security was limited to issues associated with access control (myopia). Making matters worse, the head of IT—our sponsor and also the CISO—also had a very limited view of security (myopia). His view of security only considered network elements, specifically firewall configurations and router security. As you can imagine, this created a substantial handicap to our efforts.

After we gained a better understanding of the inherent roadblocks within the project, we spent time exploring the history of this initiative. We quickly discovered that we were not the first team of consultants to be engaged; in fact there were three other groups of consultants preceding us. All of these previous efforts had failed. In all of these failures, it should be noted that from what we could tell, all of the consultants understood what needed to be reviewed and how to approach the assessment from a security perspective. Where the previous teams fell short was in addressing the primacy and myopia constraints that were intricately interwoven into almost every situation. Alas, each group failed and was then removed either by the head of human resources or the IT group. Further compounding the situation, as each round of consultants cycled in and out of the organization, their failure further emboldened the constraints, making it more difficult for each subsequent effort. Thus, by the time we had arrived, the situation resembled the battlefields of Omaha Beach on D-Day rather than a Fortune-500 company. At this point, you are probably no doubt wondering what we did in this situation. The first two weeks were spent educating the heads of the human resources and IT in an effort to alleviate the myopia issue. We did these sessions together with all of the members from each manager's team in order to build trust and teamwork between them, as well as to set up some initial communication channels. Next, sporting her newly found knowledge on the extent of security, we leveraged the head of human resources' need to exercise primacy in order to make the necessary changes to the evaluation process. This enabled access to the necessary people and elements of the system for a proper risk assessment. As we went along, we also provided daily debriefings to the head of IT and his team to ensure they were in the loop with our actions under this newly agreed on definition of security. Then came the easy part: the risk assessment.

Overview

When deciding on how to approach this book, we, the authors, all agreed that the most powerful thing we could do was to make the intangible complexities of security more tangible for the reader. We wanted you to be able to return to the earmarked pages and immediately implement the exercises and knowledge gained, thus putting theory into practice when you experience situations that are impacted by security constraints. This is why we introduced various models (e.g., the True Security Model), leveraged established works of science, such as systems theory, and gave careful attention discussing each of the constraints in isolation and in application. The goal is to provide a visibility of items that may have previously gone unnoticed, undefined, or misunderstood. As our story illustrates, three groups of consultants had attempted to perform a risk analysis without ever acting to mitigate the security constraints that almost certainly had doomed their efforts from the start. In contrast, we spent the majority of time on the engagement nullifying and leveraging the security constraints to achieve our objective rather than working around the constraints.

Metaphorically speaking, at this point in the book, you are at the top of the hill. We have identified and introduced the majority of core issues that we believe are impacting the security efforts of most CISOs and their organizations. We hope that you are now armed with a new perspective of the gremlins that plague many security efforts.

The goal of this chapter is to help you learn how to identify and analyze the concepts in this book and apply them in practical everyday situations. We will begin by providing simple techniques for measuring the security constraints within your organization. We have presented some of these tools already during the discussion on each specific constraint in isolation, but will further provide techniques for addressing these constraints in aggregate, specifically in both everyday business situations and within each group of the True Security Model. We feel that this is important for two reasons. First, it is rare to find a single constraint operating alone. Generally, constraints manifest themselves in bunches, making them more complicated to isolate, identify, and address. This compound effect leads to our second concern in that it creates a negative feedback loop. As we discussed in prior chapters, the feedback loop is a critical component within systems theory and your security program. The security constraints contaminate the inputs into the system, tainting and stressing the processing, resulting in unhealthy output. This pollution is dumped back into the environment, further reinforcing the constraints, and is recycled back into the system for processing again.

In our opening narrative, we illustrated the compound effect of two constraints (primacy and myopia) and how it created a death spiral for each subsequent group of security professionals. This concept is illustrated in Figure 7.1.

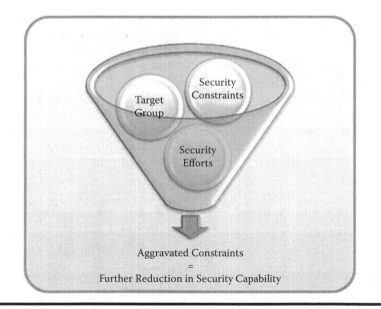

Figure 7.1 In our opening narrative, we illustrated the compound effect of two constraints (primacy and myopia) and how it created a death spiral for each subsequent group of security professionals. This concept is illustrated in Figure 7.1.

Once we address the identification of the security constraints, in the next section of this chapter we will direct our attention to the existence of the necessary elements of the True Security Model. This will include a review of both the tangible and intangible elements of the model. From an intangible perspective, we will identify if you possess the required elements from each group of the True Security Model. This is where we identify whether we have endorsement from the board or diligence from your employees. We will again provide tools that provide the identification of deficiencies from both a situational and organization perspective. For the tangible items, we will evaluate whether your security program has the six elements needed for a successful security effort. These include items such as a documented security strategy and mission and mandate (M&M). The goal of this review of the intangible and tangible elements of the True Security Model, coupled with the identification of security constraints within your environment, is to provide you an adequate knowledge of your current state.

With a clear view of the deficiencies within your environment, the final section of this chapter will focus on achieving the deficient elements of the True Security Model. We will employ the use of two tools to accomplish this task. The first and most powerful tool, which you now have as a result of reading this book, is awareness of the issues. Congratulations! The ability to identify the security constraints and their impacts will make them far more predictable. It is this predictability that will provide you a significant advantage in reducing their power and influence. Many of these techniques that you have read up to this point act as a precursor for the second tool: The R.E.A.P. Security Success Model. The R.E.A.P. (relate, educate, appraise and act, poised and patient) model represents the remaining emphasis of this section for both managing the security constraints and achieving any of the requirements—intangible and tangible—of the True Security Model. This tool is designed to serve as a guide that you can use in all of your daily interactions as a CISO.

The goal of this chapter is to provide you with as many tools as possible to enhance your security efforts and make them and you more successful. We want you to be able to measure the constraints that affect you, determine how these constraints are influencing your ability to achieve true security, and then provide tools for filling the gaps if they exist. You have worked very hard to get to this point, let us now put all of it into motion. We will begin with how to measure the security constraints in your environment from a global perspective.

Warning: Awareness and Comprehension of Previous Chapters Are Necessary to Read Past This Point

There is a reason that we dedicated a great deal of this book to exploring the True Security Model, the security constraints, and the security con. It was done to provide you with the ability to quickly identify these items within your own environment, given your unique situation. This knowledge and awareness is a prerequisite for everything else that we will address in this chapter, including the identification of gaps within your environment and the development of solutions to address these deficiencies. If you do not feel comfortable with your ability to identify these items quickly within your environment, please review the previous chapters to aid in strengthening that ability.

How to Measure Constraints within Your Environment

Before you can proceed and address the security constraints within your environment, you need to identify where these constraints exist and to what degree. We are going to look at this from two perspectives. The first is a tool for the identification of security constraints from a situational viewpoint. This will enable you to identify constraints as they might appear at a project level or through your daily interaction with others. Next, we will address the core focus of this section, which is the existence of the security constraints within the True Security Model. We will begin with a look at the situational techniques.

Localized Security Constraint Identification

As long as your job involves interaction with other humans, the security constraints inevitably exist. With that in mind, it is time to put your newfound awareness and understanding to work in identifying them within your environment. The good news is that the awareness and knowledge of the constraints which you have acquired by reading to this point, combined with your own personal experience, should make this process fairly easy. By completing the following exercise, you will be able to confirm and quantify the constraints within the situations of your choice in your work environment.

Exercise 18

This exercise can also be found in the Appendix with worksheets.

Objective

The objective of this exercise is to map the security constraints for situational analysis within your environment.

Exercise

Background: This tool is applicable either as part of your daily interaction with others or as a member in a project-based initiative. For each situation in which you would like to identify constraints, conduct the following four steps in this exercise.

Step 1: Identify All of the Participants. Identify all of the people that are involved within a given situation, including yourself. If you are analyzing a project, fill out the following table with each member of the project team, as well as all the people that team will interact with during the project. Where it makes sense, try to put people into groups so that your list is as compact as possible.

Step 2: Find the Constraints. For each individual in the list, identify whether he or she is demonstrating any of the security constraints. There is no magic potion for performing this task, simply take a moment and think about it. With your new awareness and visibility into the constraints, the table should start to populate rather quickly. Also, make note of the trends that start to develop. For instance, how certain people that work together often share the same constraints, or how in other situations there may not be any trends or relationships that can be identified.

Step 3: Score the Impact of the Identified Constraints. Once you have identified the constraints, the next step is to measure their effect on your individual situation. Again, we will keep this simple by employing a high, medium, or low rating system. Next to each individual that has been identified, simply go with your gut and give the impact of that constraint to your situational goals a rating.

Below, we have populated the table with the sample data from the example that we opened up this chapter with. Though we have done this using a table for demonstration purposes, you will find that after performing this exercise a few times it will become second nature. As a result, you will gain the ability to conduct this analysis on the fly.

Example

Situational Members	Demonstration of Apathy	Constraint Impact	Demonstration of Myopia	Constraint Impact	Demonstration of Primacy	Constraint Impact	Demonstration of Infancy	Constraint Impact
Head of human resources	No	N/A	Yes	High	Yes	High	No	N/A
Head of IT	No	N/A	Yes	High	Yes	High	No	N/A
Jenny Jones	No	N/A	Yes	Low	No	N/A	No	N/A
Stinky Pete	No	Low	No	High	Yes	High	Yes	High

Step 4: Add Detail for the High-Impact Elements. After completing the table, you will want to direct your efforts toward the individuals that are

demonstrating the constraints in a high-impact manner. According to our example, that would include everyone except Jenny Jones. For each of the people that were identified that produce a high impact, write a couple of sentences that illustrate why you believe the impact of this constraint is high and how this demonstration is affecting your situation.

Using the example from "Tales from the Security Consultant":

Example 1

Demonstrations of primacy by the head of human resources are limiting our access with the appropriate individuals, including her. This behavior is hampering our efforts to get the sufficient quantities of the "right" information to conduct a proper security assessment.

Example 2

The demonstration of myopia by the head of human resources is making it difficult to have meaningful conversations regarding the assessment or to convey security concepts beyond her limited understanding. The result is that the process, quality, and scope of the security assessment are compromised.

Identification of Security Constraints within the True Security Model

As you can see from the prior section, once you have achieved the awareness and understanding of the security constraints, identifying them and their effects is fairly easy (we told you that the hard part was over). And though the manner in which the process is presented is very formal, you will find that this exercise will become second nature after a very short period of time. More importantly, the goal of this process is to get you actively thinking about the security constraints just as much or more than the actual project itself. Now that you understand the basic concept, we will turn our attention to the identification of security constraints and their impacts within the True Security Model.

This process will be similar to the one we used for identifying constraints in a situational context, with one minor exception. Instead of focusing on the constraint associated with an individual behavior, we are now going to use this knowledge and apply it to group behavior. So if you are reviewing the board of directors, there is a strong likelihood that members will be demonstrating various levels of constraints at an individual level, but they will also participate in the shared trends of the group. It is these trends that are of interest for this exercise.

Obviously, this particular tool is geared specifically toward a CISO or security leader that is focused on a more global perspective. As a CISO, or other type of security leader within your organization, you should have had at least some interaction with the various groups within the True Security Model. If not, which is possible, you should take a moment and evaluate which constraints are causing this to happen. For the rest of you who do possess enough knowledge about each group, please continue on with this exercise.

Exercise 19

This exercise can also be found in the Appendix with worksheets.

Objective

The objective of this exercise is to map the security constraints for situational analysis employing the True Security Model.

Exercise

For this exercise, please follow the steps below:

Step 1: Identify the True Security Group. Take a moment and think about this group and the interactions that you have had with it. Obviously, as you move down the management chain within the True Security Model, the number of members will probably increase. Regardless of the size of the group, it will exhibit trends. The groups with the larger membership may take a little longer to identify and qualify, but in our experience those trends are always present.

Step 2: Find the Constraints. As you think about the group, what demonstrations of constraints come to mind? Again, there is no magic potion (though we have our staff alchemist working diligently on the project ... so far we only have a recipe for a really great martini) for performing this task, simply apply some brain cycles to the idea. Are there any trends or constraint relationships that are shared throughout the group? Is there a single constraint that appears to be dominant within the members of the group? Do not try to get them all at one time. It is similar to viewing one of those hidden picture posters. You have to step back, relax your eyes and focus on nothing in particular, and presto an image appears. Group constraints are similar in nature. You have to train yourself to eliminate a lot of the "noise" surrounding them.

Step 3: Score the Impact of the Identified Constraints. Once you have identified the constraints, the next step is to measure their effect on your ability to obtain the desired element defined within the True Security Model for the target group. Again, we will keep this simple, by employing a high, medium, or low rating system. Next to each group that has been identified, simply go with your gut feeling and give a rating for the impact of that constraint to your situational goals.

As a quick refresher on the True Security Model, refer to the target groups and desired behavior table below:

Organizational Group	Desired Action or Behavior
Board of directors	Endorsement
Executive management	Priority
Middle management	Resources
Supervisory management	Support
Employees	Diligence
Consumers	Trust
Security program	Execution

Example

True Security Group	Demonstration of Apathy	Constraint Impact	Demonstration of Myopia	Constraint Impact	Demonstration of Primacy	Constraint Impact	Demonstration of Infancy	Constraint Impact
Board of directors	Yes	N/A	No	N/A	No	N/A	No	N/A
Executive management team	No	N/A	No	N/A	Yes	High	No	N/A
Middle management	No	N/A	Yes	Low	No	N/A	No	N/A
Supervisors	No	Low	No	High	Yes	High	Yes	High
Employees	No	N/A	Yes	High	Yes	High	No	N/A

Complete the Steps 1–3 Worksheet

True Security Group	Demonstration of Apathy	Constraint Impact	Demonstration of Myopia	Constraint Impact	Demonstration of Primacy	Constraint Impact	Demonstration of Infancy	Constraint Impact
Board of directors								
Executive management team								

True Security Group	Demonstration of Apathy	Constraint Impact	Demonstration of Myopia	Constraint Impact	Demonstration of Primacy	Constraint Impact	Demonstration of Infancy	Constraint Impact
Middle management								
Supervisors								
Employees								
Consumers								
Security team								

Step 4: Add Detail for the High Impact Elements. After completing the table, you will want to focus on the groups that are demonstrating the constraints in a high-impact manner. Again, just as we did previously, write a couple of sentences that illustrate why you believe the impact of this constraint is high and how this demonstration can impact your ability to acquire the desired true security element from this group.

Example

Demonstrations of apathy by the board are making it difficult to get any security items on the board meeting agenda. This lack of visibility of security is making it difficult to get the board's endorsement of the security program.

Summary

Once again, as you repeat the exercise of constraint identification and rating, you will find that the process becomes faster and easier. In many cases, all it takes is a little bit of time and some focus for them to present themselves. As you train yourself in this technique, you will begin to notice how your attention in situations will begin to change. In most of our initiatives, we spend over 75 percent of the time in the beginning of a new engagement on the identification, prioritization, and reduction of the security constraints that will impact our security objectives. We call it "greasing the skids," but in reality we are removing the obstacles that will inevitably distract us from the required tasks of security.

GAP the True Security Model

Now that we have a good idea of the constraints that we are facing within the environment, the next step will be an evaluation of the tangible and intangible elements within the True Security Model. When addressing the intangible aspects, we are interested in measuring whether we have achieved each of the desired elements for each of the target groups within the True Security Model. For the tangible elements of the True Security Model, we are looking for items such as a documented security program strategy, mission and mandate (M&M), a comprehensive set of security policies, etc. We will begin with the six tangible elements of the True Security Model.

The Tangible Elements of the True Security Model

The goal, as you may have guessed, is to identify deficiencies and determine the relationship of these deficiencies to the security constraints. We will not address how to attain these items if they are missing from your security program. That information is available, for those interested, in our first book: *The CISO Handbook*. As a reminder, the six tangible elements of the model are:

1. Security strategy
2. Mission and mandate (M&M)
3. Roles and responsibilities
4. Security policies
5. Training and awareness regimen
6. Security risk project portfolio

Exercise 20

This exercise can also be found in the Appendix with worksheets.

Objective

The objective of this exercise is to evaluate the impact that the security constraints have on attaining the tangible elements of the True Security Model.

Exercise

For this exercise, please follow the steps below:

Step 1: Determine whether your program has each of these components: "Yes or No!"

Step 2: Is the quality of each of these components sufficient to meet the needs of the security program?

Step 3: For each of the items that are deemed as deficient, determine the security constraints that are interfering with their development.

Example

True Security Components	Does This Element Exist?	Is It Sufficient for the Organization?	Hindered by Apathy	Hindered by Myopia	Hindered by Primacy	Hindered by Infancy
Security strategy	Yes	No	No	Yes	No	Yes
Mission and mandate	Yes	Yes	No	No	No	No
Roles and responsibilities	Yes	Yes	No	No	No	No
Security policies	Yes	No	Yes	Yes	No	No
Training and awareness regimen	Yes	No	Yes	No	No	Yes
Formal security risk project portfolio	No	No	Yes	Yes	Yes	Yes

Step 4: As before, attempt to quantify the effect of the constraint by writing a quick sentence or two that is representative of the issue. We have always found that if we cannot write it down, we do not truly understand the issue. So, even if this step may seem unnecessary, it acts as a crucible that burns away all of the unnecessary noise that generally surrounds these issues.

In the example table, the security policies were deemed as existing, yet insufficient for the needs of the organization. The quantification of these items could look something like the following:

Example

Though the security policies for our organization exist, they are weak, and in many cases inapplicable to the lines of business. Though this issue has been raised with executive management, few seem to show any interest in the issue (apathy). When one of the executives is reasonably engaged, he or she asks general questions regarding the status of the company firewall or about antivirus and deem the situation under control (myopia).

As we mentioned above, we are not going to spend time on helping you attain the tangible elements of the model if they are missing. If you are interested in attaining those items (you should be), then our advice is focus on reducing the constraints that you have identified in this exercise, and then use our other books or some of the other resources that are now available to build these tangible components. Once you have the constraints identified and then minimized, building these components should be straightforward.

Measuring the Intangible Elements of the True Security Model

Again in this section, we will address the true security elements from two perspectives: situational and organizational. The situational presentation is provided for the use by all security professionals, where the organizational perspective is more applicable to those who are charged with leadership positions in security.

Situational Use of the True Security GAP Analysis

We will utilize the following exercise in order to measure true security within the most common situations within an organization that you choose to evaluate. Common situations for its use are on projects, management meetings, or team meetings—basically, any situation where groups of people must work together.

Exercise 21

This exercise can also be found in the Appendix with worksheets.

Objective

The objective of this exercise is to measure the intangible elements of the True Security Model in a project or workgroup environment.

Exercise

For this exercise, please follow the steps below:

> **Step 1:** For each group you are evaluating, identify the group members, the true security group to which they belong, and then whether these individuals are demonstrating the associated true security element.

Example

Individual Name	Title	Indentify Their True Security Group (board of directors, supervisor, etc.)	Have You Achieved the Desired Element? (circle one)
Joe Johnson	Operations manager	Middle management	Yes No
Sally Smith	Security analyst	Security program	Yes No

> **Step 2:** Since our objective is to make the intangible more tangible, for each individual where you answered "Yes," write a couple of sentences that identify

the evidence that you have to substantiate that you have achieved the desired true security element. Remember, this information is for your eyes only, so be honest with your answers. For each individual where you answered "No," write a couple of sentences that describe what evidence has led you to feel that the associated true security element is absent.

Example

Joe Johnson: Joe worked diligently to identify the appropriate resources that were needed for my identity management initiative. Once he assigned them to the project, he allowed them to operate without any distractions. Further, Joe has protected them from some of the other efforts that requested their participation in order to keep them focused on this assignment. Once again, this is demonstrating the attainment of the resources element we need from Joe as a middle manager.

Sally Smith: Sally is working hard but continues to demonstrate myopia through her continual reference to technical security controls. Her inability to grasp and apply the security risk elements associated with process development is hurting the team in that we cannot assign her to those areas. As far as she is concerned, everything in security is a result of "spoofing" packets.

Keep in mind as you go through this exercise that there are no incorrect answers. We are attempting to develop reasoning and intuitive deduction skills toward intangible issues. Therefore, do not be hard on yourself; just try to identify gaps within the True Security Model as you see them. Now we will move on to evaluating gaps from an organizational perspective.

Organizational GAP Analysis within the True Security Model

Since this exercise is enterprise focused, it is again more applicable for those who are in charge of developing or managing the entire security effort for an organization. We guess that is good since the majority of you reading this are CISOs. It deals with the hierarchy of management and obtaining specific elements to further the goals of security as a whole. This will once again call on you to observe and formulate trends within these various groups.

Exercise 22

This exercise can also be found in the Appendix with worksheets.

Objective

The objective of this exercise is to measure the intangible elements of the True Security Model within each of the true security target groups.

Exercise

For this exercise, please follow the steps below:

Step 1: For each group within the True Security Model, identify whether your organization has achieved the associated true security element. Use a Yes/No answer. Keep in mind that we are looking for a trended answer which reflects your opinion of the group as a whole. Once again, just go with your gut feeling; it will give you the answer rather quickly.

Example

True Security Group	Desired Element	Have You Achieved This Desired Element? (circle one)
Board of directors	Endorsement	Yes
Executive team	Priority	No
Middle management	Resources	No
Supervisory team	Support	Yes
Employees	Diligence	Yes
Consumers	Trust	No
Security program	Execution	Yes

Step 2: Remember the objective is to make the intangible more tangible. So for each group where you answered "Yes," write a couple of sentences that identify the evidence that you have to substantiate that you have achieved this element. Again, this information is just for your own edification, so be honest. For each group where you answered "No," write a couple of sentences that identify the evidence of why you feel that you have not achieved the true security element.

Example

A Board of Directors That Has Provided Endorsement: I believe that we have achieved endorsement from the board of directors in our organization due to the fact that the board has been actively initiating, monitoring, and then measuring the implementation of security directives. These directives seem to be timely, logical, and in the best interest of the organization.

A Board of Directors That Has Not Provided Endorsement: The board of directors in our organization is not endorsing security. The board has a limited visibility of the security posture of the organization and has never shown any interest in attaining such a view. The board's security directives are ad hoc and often misguided.

Summary

The information covered in this section, coupled with a review of the constraints from the prior chapters, should provide you a basic understanding for determining the current state for your individual environment. These techniques are designed to provide you with simple and quick tools that can be utilized in a variety of situations. We hope this enables you flexibility for using these tools as a CISO or in the other various roles your team may be performing within your security program. Of course, just identifying your gaps is not all we need to worry about; now comes the more complicated part: filling the gap.

Filling the Gap

This is where your determination and hard work pay off. Up to this point in the book, we have spent a great deal of time identifying and qualifying the nature and relationship of the security constraints to the True Security Model. Now it is time to take action! The following section will describe our approach for dealing with those nasty security constraints and serve as a guide for attaining true security. We have aggregated a series of techniques into the R.E.A.P. Security Success Model. We just love models!

R.E.A.P.—Security Success Model

We originally developed the R.E.A.P. (relate, educate, appraise, and act poised) model as a tactical tool for addressing, what we viewed at the time, as political situations. As our understanding of the security constraints grew (myopia), and we settled on the four constraints we have shared in this book, we found that the model was applicable for mitigating the effects of each of them. It ultimately evolved into an essential tool for us in developing security programs or just about any other type of initiative that was given to us by our clients. These practices will not be found in any CISSP training manual, but it is what we use to train our own team of consultants in our security practice as well as many of the security leaders that engage us.

R.E.A.P. allows for the modification of the only thing that is truly within your control: you! Just as we spent a large portion of this book building your awareness and ability to identify the security constraints, we must now turn our attention to you and your behavior. You are an integral part of the security "system." As such, the way in which you perceive, process, and produce information has a direct impact on the health of the system. That is where R.E.A.P. comes in. It alters the manner in which you process information received and produce the output that is returned into the environment. It serves as a guide as you make decisions and deal with the complex environment that surrounds us all as security professionals. Let us introduce each of the components.

Relate

> Relate (definition 1): "To have connection, relation, or reference."
> *The American Heritage® Dictionary of the English Language, Fourth Edition*

Relate means taking the time to view a situation from the other person's or group's perspective. It is the first step in developing empathy for those with whom you are dealing. Your mother may have told you not to criticize until you have "walked a mile in another man's shoes." There is a lot of wisdom in that sentiment. We seldom stop and consider the position of the other person before attempting to further our own positions which, as we mentioned in the chapter on myopia, can lead you to a mindless state. So, our prescription is to always, always be mindful and consider the person's or group's perspective on the issues with which you are communicating.

Relating to those that are around you is crucial because it provides you insights into how they view the world. As we mentioned earlier, security and many of its associated concepts are just that: concepts. They will be viewed and interpreted differently by each person based on *their* definition and perspective. Taking the time and energy to understand the viewpoint of others is critical for developing a meaningful dialogue regarding security. Engaging in this way will open you up to multiple perspectives and varying ways of understanding the world.

Another important aspect to relating to others is that it removes a sense of powerlessness from communication. When you demonstrate verbally and nonverbally that you have an investment and that you care about the opinions or feelings held by other parties, you are informing them that they are an active participant in the process rather than a victim of it. This approach is extremely effective, specifically if the person in question tends to be ignored frequently by others. The more you invest, the more the individual is willing and wanting to also invest in the process.

By finding the right way to connect with others, you are increasing the probability that others will better understand your messages. Through the careful application of your own messages, coupled with a genuine investment in your colleagues' input, you are paving the path for meaningful dialogue to take place.

As you may have guessed by now, the relate component is a powerful aid in the fight against apathy. It is designed to remove feelings of powerfulness and enable you and those you communicate with to understand each other's perspective. Most importantly, the relate process accelerates the development of the relationship portion of the communication model. Ultimately, that is the most powerful tool for addressing apathy.

Situational Application of Relate

Though relate seems like common sense, far too often it is overlooked by individuals who are in a hurry to get their job done. We have found that the additional effort pays dividends in the long run. Therefore, we believe that you should make every effort to relate to as many people as possible. The following exercise is meant to aid you in your efforts by serving as a guide. It is really not very difficult; it just takes a little awareness, time, and energy.

Exercise 23

This exercise can also be found in the Appendix: R.E.A.P. checklists.

Before distributing any communication, take a moment and ask yourself the following questions:
■ How might this message be interpreted by the reader? ■ Is my message clear and understandable? ■ Have I taken time to consider the possibility for multiple perspectives on this message? ■ Have I invested time and energy to understand the perspective of the person or group to whom I am addressing this message? ■ How can I improve my message and limit misunderstanding?

Application within the True Security Model

The following exercise is designed to help you with the relate component within the True Security Model:

Exercise 24

This exercise can also be found in the Appendix: R.E.A.P. checklists.

True Security Group	*Have I Taken the Time to Learn about the Perspective of the Person or People Who Are Going to Receive This Message? (circle one)*	*Have I Educated Myself on This Person's or Group's Viewpoint? (circle one)*
Board of directors	Yes No	Yes No
Executive team	Yes No	Yes No
Middle management	Yes No	Yes No
Supervisory team	Yes No	Yes No
Employees	Yes No	Yes No
Consumers	Yes No	Yes No
Security program	Yes No	Yes No

How Can I Relate to Those Around Me? (Look, Listen, and Learn)

One of the most powerful yet underutilized tools at your disposal is to listen. Just listen! Most people spend their nonspeaking time during a conversation determining what they are going to say next, and often interrupt the speaker to make their point. Don't! There's a reason why we have two ears and only one mouth! Once you have set your mind to listening, you are again investing in the relationship. Another tool that can help you further sculpt the environment you want is to use the "question."

Take a moment and ponder the question. The question is the second most valuable tool in the relate arsenal. Once again, most people spend the majority of their speaking time during a conversation making statements. Statements are generally not very interactive; quite the contrary, many times they are viewed as provocative or boastful. Neither of these descriptions sounds very helpful for nurturing a relationship. They are excellent at telling the world how you feel on a topic. They are excellent if you are attempting to establish boundaries or to provoke someone; however, they are a bad idea when it comes to relating. Questions on the other hand accomplish four things:

1. They allow you to find out more about the person with whom you are attempting to relate.
2. They allow the other person to speak so you can listen.
3. They demonstrate interest in the other person, which is key to relating.
4. They empower the other person by making their perspective the central issue.

A word of warning when using the question: it is the same tool used by interrogators. Be sure that your tone and manner are friendly. Furthermore, be certain that you do not disguise your judgment or point of view within the question. A simplistic example of this type of question is, "Don't you think you are driving too fast?" Lastly, when a person asks you a question, make sure that you do not answer a question with another question. You want to use questions to help other people dialogue and share their opinions and feelings in an environment that is safe and open. Remember that you are trying to foster trust within the relationship.

The last technique that we have is of course body language. The majority of our communication is nonverbal, anywhere between 65 to 95 percent, leaving only about 10 percent for the verbal interaction. Furthermore, if there is a discrepancy between what a person says and the manner in which he or she says it, we tend to believe the nonverbal message over the verbal. Imagine coming home late and your significant other will not look you in the eye, has his or her arms folded across the chest and coldly states, "I said I am not mad at you!" What message would you walk away with: angry or not angry? The manner in which people carry themselves and their tone when responding to you can provide feedback on the state of the relationship. Be aware of the messages that they are sending to you, most of which are not verbal, and adjust accordingly.

Educate

> Educate (definition 2): "To provide knowledge or training in a particular area for a particular purpose."
> *The American Heritage® Dictionary of the English Language, Fourth Edition*

If relate is the "listening" tool, then educate is the "speaking" tool. We expressed the need to first listen in order to relate to the perspective of the other person. Now we need to provide you with a means of sharing your opinions, ideas, and perspectives. The manner in which we suggest to accomplish this task is through the process of teaching.

The teacher–student relationship provides a fabulous means of presenting information and ideas without the appearance of provocation or pomposity. After all, you are in a position to teach because you are supposedly more knowledgeable on the subject of security. Well at least you better be! That is where we will begin: teaching yourself before teaching others. Developing the ability to sort through data, make sense of it, and then pass that along as knowledge is important within a discipline that is ripe with immature practices and techniques (infancy).

Educating yourself follows the same rules that were discussed in the chapter on infancy. We can obtain data, information, knowledge, or wisdom when learning about an issue. Each level brings with it a deeper understanding of the subject and its interrelationship with other elements within an environment. We believe that in order to teach, you must work past the data and information levels to obtain an understanding that constitutes knowledge—a familiarity, awareness, or understanding gained through experience or study. We hate to sound like a bad episode of Kung Fu, but only then will you be ready to educate others. Attempting to educate with only data and information will present a hollow image of a teacher or mentor. It may work once or twice, but will only be sufficient for passing along the "what" to the student. Eventually, they will want to know the "why" and "how" surrounding an issue as well. The ability to answer those questions is a certain demonstration of knowledge or perhaps even wisdom (grasshopper!). Therefore, during the process of educating yourself, it is in your best interest to search for the why and how for each topic. Now, if you are looking for some complex model for determining if you are properly educated on a subject, the bad news is that we do not know of one. The good news is that you do not need a complex model to answer this question. We all know when we have enough information on a subject; we can feel it. It is like when you know that you have studied enough for a test back in high school. Just take a moment and think about it, the answer will come to you. Of course, self-education is only the first step along the way to employing this educate technique.

If you accept the idea that educate is the means by which you can share your opinions and perspectives with others, then assessing their training requirements is the next step. If you have embraced the first step in R.E.A.P., this should not be too difficult because you have already spent time listening and learning about those around you. This assessment should provide an idea of the type of education that is required along with the most effective means of delivery. In other words, this is the manner in which you transform your knowledge into a consumable format in order to teach those around you.

This process will strengthen the relationship by increasing your comprehension of others and, of course, getting them to understand yours. Because education works on building your knowledge and that of others, it can diffuse many of the security constraints. When used to learn the perspective of others and to teach your own, it reduces apathy by raising awareness and eliminating the excuse of ignorance. The manner in which you increase your own knowledge regarding concepts and techniques provides a more comprehensive view that can then be passed along to others. This aids in the reduction of myopia. Finally, your ability to acquire knowledge, transform it, and then pass it on is critical to reducing the effects of infancy.

Situational Application

You should constantly make an effort to build your knowledge and then pass that on to others. The following simple exercise will help you with this effort and serve as a guide.

Exercise 25

This exercise can also be found in the Appendix: R.E.A.P. checklists.

> *Take a moment and ask yourself the following questions:*
>
> - What have I learned in the past week that increases my ability as a security professional?
> - Have I transformed this information to make it understandable to those around me?
> - How have I assessed who may need this new knowledge?
> - Have I passed this knowledge on?
> - Have I checked to see whether the message I intended to send is close to the receiver's interpretation? (This can be done by both asking questions, and asking for the other person to verbally paraphrase or share his or her understanding with you.)

Application within the True Security Model

The following exercise is designed to help you with the educate component within the True Security Model.

Exercise 26

This exercise can also be found in the Appendix: R.E.A.P. checklists.

True Security Group	Have I Appropriately Educated Myself on the Security Concepts Needed by This Group? (circle one)	Have I Appropriately Educated This Group? (circle one)
Board of directors	Yes No	Yes No
Executive team	Yes No	Yes No
Middle management	Yes No	Yes No
Supervisory team	Yes No	Yes No
Employees	Yes No	Yes No
Consumers	Yes No	Yes No
Security program	Yes No	Yes No

Appraise and Act

> Appraise (definition 2): "To estimate the quality, amount, size, and other features of; judge."
> *The American Heritage® Dictionary of the English Language, Fourth Edition*

We use the idea of appraise as the formulation tool within the R.E.A.P. model. It attempts to factor in all of the information that you gather into an actionable plan. The goal of this plan is the development of both the content and delivery mechanisms that will produce the desired results of minimizing the security constraints.

One of our hopes for this book was to provide you with an understanding and appreciation for the number of moving parts within most systems, and the diverse set of interactions among system components. As security professionals, whether CISOs or not, we are not merely casual observers, but active participants who are subject to the ebbs and flows within any system. As such, we need to appraise a situation from two perspectives: two sides of the same coin.

The first is to appraise the actions of others—not their words, but their actions. We are interested in their actions during the daily course of performing their job. What we are looking for are clues to their true motivations. Why people perform an action is as important as the action itself. It provides insights into predicting their potential range of responses to the introduction of new situations (security) and different mechanisms of delivering that information. The other side of appraise pertains to yourself. We are still interested in the same information, but for different reasons. Your motivation for any particular initiative needs to be understood in that it may impair your objectivity toward a subject. The other value that can be associated with this technique is in the insights into how others may perceive your intentions toward the same initiative.

Throughout the book we have illustrated how even subtle demonstrations of behavior by others and by you can be communicating massive amounts of information. It is critical that you:

1. Are aware of the verbal and nonverbal messages you are sending and conversely be aware of the messages others are sending to you—both intended and unintended.
2. Begin to recognize the patterns in the messages sent and received and assess their relevance.
3. Factor all of the above findings into your decision-making process.

The appraise element is designed to reduce many of the constraints that plague our security efforts. It can diffuse primacy by using your new understanding to change your approach, methods, delivery, and content. Opening yourself up to the subtle nuances in others (e.g., constant yawning, doodling, participation, etc.) provides information about the degree of apathy within others. Appraising the actions of others provides insights into their level of understanding, use, and trust of the security information that you have provided. This application and trust can aid in combating both myopia and infancy.

Situational Application

There are two aspects that need to be considered when appraising a situation. As we stated above, they are how you evaluate both yourself and others. The following exercise will help you with this effort and serve as a guide.

Exercise 27

This exercise can also be found in the Appendix: R.E.A.P. checklists.

> *For any meeting, ask yourself the following questions to better understand the motives (self and other) behind the meeting:*
>
> - Why did the other person agree to this meeting? What is in it for them personally?
> - Why am I attending this meeting? What is in it for me personally?
> - What personal agenda may be determined from question #1?
> - Is that agenda influenced by, or a manifestation of, one or more of the security constraints?
> - Which ones?

Remember that the constraints prosper when they go unidentified; therefore, our objective in appraise is to identify and apply what we have learned about counteracting the constraints as part of the formulation process.

Application within the True Security Model

We have emphasized the need to understand motivation as it affects the development of both your agenda and that of others. This is effective when addressing situations that involve individuals, but the group dynamic adds some additional complexity. This complexity actually works in our favor for a change by simplifying the appraise process.

The dynamic of any group of peers is that it acts as a filter and aggregator of personal agendas into a group agenda. For example, every player on the team has a personal agenda. Regardless of the player's personal agenda, the group agenda will always be the one to win the game. This is true among all of the groups within the True Security Model. The net result for appraise is that we only need to worry about the group agenda, rather than that of each individual. The following exercise is designed to help you with the appraise component within the True Security Model. The one exception to this rule, which once again benefits security, is if there is an individual within the target group whose personal agenda can be leveraged to gain the support of the group. This is the champion of our cause.

Exercise 28

This exercise can also be found in the Appendix: R.E.A.P. checklists.

Objective

The following exercise is designed to help you with the appraise component within the True Security Model.

Exercise

For any meeting that you will participate with a specific group within the True Security Model, answer the following questions:
■ Does the agenda for the group align with your agenda and motives? ■ Is there a potential champion in the group? ■ How can the message be tailored to circumvent or reduce the security constraints?

Complete the following table:

Example

True Security Group	Desired Element (your agenda)	Reason for Meeting	Does the Agenda for the Group Align with Your Agenda and Motives?	Is There a Potential Champion within the Group?	How Can the Message Be Tailored to Circumvent the Security Constraints?
Executive management	Priority	Security budget	No. Due to the time of year, this group will be motivated by overall budgetary reduction and the priority assigned to other issues. This may lead to acts of primacy or apathy.	Yes, it is Joe Smith. He had his identity stolen last year and is very sensitive to data handling.	Stress the cost-effective nature of training and process improvement for addressing security issues. Focus anecdotal references on data leakage and data theft.

Obviously, this is a unique situation, as will be yours with the various groups in the True Security Model. The details of this specific example are not important. What is important is that you develop an approach that:

1. Acknowledges their agenda and how it can produce the security constraints
2. Meets your agenda
3. Reduces or compensates for the security constraints

We are not fooling ourselves into thinking that this approach is foolproof. There are far too many variables involved when attempting to manage human interaction. What this approach does provide is a systematic means of improving your odds when dealing with these situations.

> Act (definition 1): "The process of doing or performing something."
> *The American Heritage® Dictionary of the English Language, Fourth Edition*

Act is simply the execution of the plan that was formulated during appraise. It embodies taking the information that you have learned from yourself and others through the relate, educate, and appraise components and then applying it in your actions. It represents the moves that you make on the chessboard of the organization.

Your thoughtful actions or planned inaction can reduce many of the negative demonstrations associated with primacy in yourself and others. By adjusting your level of interaction, you may also reduce apathy through empowering others and myopia through educating them. The manner in which you take information and then act on it can also reduce the impacts of infancy.

Situational Application

How do you plan to take action during your efforts as a CISO? The following simple exercise will help you with this effort and serve as a guide.

Exercise 29

This exercise can also be found in the Appendix: R.E.A.P. checklists.

Before attending your next meeting, take a moment and ask yourself the following questions:
■ Have you adequately appraised the situation? ■ How do you plan to take action?

Application within the True Security Model

The following exercise is designed to help you with the act component within the True Security Model.

Exercise 30

This exercise can also be found in the Appendix: R.E.A.P. checklists.

True Security Group	*Do You Have Enough Information to Take Action with This Group toward Achieving True Security?(circle one)*	*How Are You Going to Take Action?*
Board of directors	Yes No	
Executive team	Yes No	
Middle management	Yes No	
Supervisory team	Yes No	
Employees	Yes No	
Consumers	Yes No	
Security program	Yes No	

Poised and Patient

> Poised (definition 2): "Freedom from affectation or embarrassment; composure."
> *The American Heritage® Dictionary of the English Language, Fourth Edition*

Patient (definition 5): "Capable of calmly awaiting an outcome or result; not hasty or impulsive."
The American Heritage® Dictionary of the English Language, Fourth Edition

Life as a CISO and for those on your team as security professionals is challenging to say the least. There will be many factors, individuals, and situations that will try your patience and composure. We added the "P" to the R.E.A.P. model because it is the only tool that we have ever found that is capable of managing the negative feedback loop of the security constraints that was discussed in the chapter overview. It is analogous to passive resistance in that it provides nothing for the constraints to feed on (poise) and allows them to run out of energy (patience).

When addressing these two in the context of security constraints themselves, poise and patience are potent weapons. When dealing with infancy, they breed trust and allow for the growth of the individual or group at a rate they feel comfortable with. Maintaining your poise and patience addresses myopia in that it provides the time necessary to expand horizons of others without closing off the channels of communication that can result from actions associated with your frustrations.

Final Steps

To this point, we have identified the security constraints within your environment, as well as deficiencies of the desired elements within each group of the True Security Model. We did this in order to help you know where to focus your efforts. Next, we introduced the idea of R.E.A.P. as a tool for helping you alleviate escalated security constraints within your environment or attain missing elements within the True Security Model. You may have figured out by now that there is no way to provide exact instructions for attaining true security. Instead, as you implement these techniques you will become stronger at assessing your own situations, and using the tools we have provided in a manner that makes sense to you. We will, however, end this chapter with some of the practical applications of the R.E.A.P model that we have utilized over the years. These items are designed to serve as examples for you and your team to use in situations that you deem they will be helpful.

Management Suggestions	Board of Directors	Executive Management	Middle Management	Supervisors
Relate	Read and understand the backgrounds of each board member. Communicate using their nomenclature.	Conduct one-on-one meetings with executive managers on a regular basis to just listen to how you can help with their objectives. Take time to learn the background of each executive.	Conduct one-on-one meetings with middle managers on a regular basis to just listen to how you can help with their objectives. Establish definitions that are understood by all of the executives.	Conduct one-on-one meetings with supervisors on a regular basis to just listen to how you can help with their objectives. Conduct one-on-one meetings with their team members to learn how you can help them.

Management Suggestions	Board of Directors	Executive Management	Middle Management	Supervisors
Educate	Educate with short and concise security information that board members can review on their own time.	Take time to educate executives individually, then build consensus in group sessions with all executives.	Educate with group sessions that include their whole team.	Educate with group sessions that include their whole team. Provide the why and include definitions for all materials that are provided to this group.
Appraise	Review the actions of board members on past security decisions.	Use individual meetings to learn the motivations of each executive.	Use individual meetings to learn the motivations of each middle manager.	Use individual meetings to learn the motivations of each supervisor.
Act	Execute the plan.	Execute the plan.	Execute the plan.	Execute the plan.
Poised and patient	Be poised and patient in all of your actions with this group.	Be poised and patient in all of your actions with this group.	Be poised and patient in all of your actions with this group.	Be poised and patient in all of your actions with this group.

	Employees	Consumers	Security Program	You
Relate	Take the time to meet with field soldiers within your organization and understand their needs and concerns. Interactive training and awareness campaigns that include every employee; ensure that the "why" of security is addressed.	If possible, talk with the consumers of your organization's products and services about what is important to them about security.	Take time to meet individually with all of the members on your security team, regardless of level, to learn what is important to them about security.	Take time to evaluate how you can better relate to those around you.
Educate	Interactive training and awareness campaigns that include every employee and talk to the "what" of security.	Provide the ability to explain the "why" to interested consumers about the various security controls that impact them. Provide easy-to-understand information about your consumers' security responsibilities	Have team meetings at least weekly. Have specialists teach their craft to others among the team during team meetings. Create or suggest a program that enables structured research on emerging trends or concepts that are of importance to the team.	Constantly identify channels to build your knowledge as a security professional. This process should never stop.
Appraise	Select employees at random and meet with them individually to identify what is important to them.	If possible, try to develop surveys that can provide you insights into your impact with this group.	Use individual meetings to learn the motivations of each member of your team.	Take time weekly to evaluate your own motivations.

	Employees	Consumers	Security Program	You
Act	Execute the plan.	Execute the plan.	Execute the plan.	Execute the plan.
Poised and patient	Be poised and patient in all of your actions with this group.	Be poised and patient in all of your actions with this group.	Be poised and patient in all of your actions with this group.	Be poised and patient in all of your actions.

Summary

As you can see, the final prescription is direct and easily accomplished with a couple of subtleties worth noting. The first is that the approach requires interaction with each of the target groups. The successful implementation of security requires understanding and acceptance by every level of the organization; it is one of the few disciplines that touch everything in the organization. As such, it would be naïve to believe that interaction with a few of the groups can accomplish this objective. Unfortunately, that is exactly what we often see. A security program full of security professionals who spend 99 percent of their time working with executive management, or only with other security professionals, and can't understand why their efforts are not successful.

The other subtlety to note is that the combination of the True Security Model and R.E.A.P. is a reformulation of the axiom: plan the work and work the plan. The difference is that we are focusing on communication to enable the work versus focusing on the work to enable communication. It is a distinction that makes all the difference in the world. The True Security Model provides an outline for setting the objectives and identifying each group, while R.E.A.P. formulates the communication plan that provides the highest potential for success.

Chapter 8

Closing Thoughts

"We all have a choice!"

The Final Tale from the Security Consultant

We were engaged to help a very large loan provider based in the United States to enable access to its core databases from service providers located around the world. This move was driven by an enterprise business decision to farm out as many support services as possible in order to reduce the management cost of the systems. It is the same story that we are sure many of you have experienced. We will not go into the details of the security risks that this situation presented, though there were many. And though we were technically successful in our engagement by serving as a content expert and providing countermeasures to our sponsor, the team was not able to fully reduce all of the security constraints on this project. As a result, our sponsor, the CISO for the organization, was only able to have the team implement 60 percent of the recommended corrective actions that all of us deemed necessary. The final result was the security risks had been reduced, but a great deal of customer data had just become, in our opinion, far too exposed to exploitation or theft.

As has been a theme throughout the book, the security risks are not why we present this story. Instead, we are describing this situation because this time it is personal. You see, one of the databases in question on this project contained the personal loan information for a member of our consulting team. This situation left the group with some unresolved issues regarding the engagement. Those issues were the focus of the post-mortem meeting for the project. The issues revolved around the following three questions:

1. Did we do all that we could do on this engagement to reduce the security constraints?
2. Did we truly make a difference in the security of the client organization?
3. Did the existence of a teammate's data in this situation alter our approach to the engagement?

We present this story because the meeting that ensued following that engagement clearly illustrates the final three ideas and concepts that we want to leave you with in this book.

Concept 1: Recognize That the Security Constraints Are What Leads to All of the Failures on Security Initiatives and in Security Programs

Our team is trained to utilize R.E.A.P. (relate, educate, appraise, and act poised and patient) in every situation during any engagement. This helps us identify the security constraints and true security deficiencies that exist quickly and efficiently.

We do this because we have learned over the years that the security constraints are what makes security difficult and lead to true security deficiencies. This ultimately leads to failed security projects or overall security programs. As a result, our emphasis is always on first identifying and then reducing the constraints, creating an environment ready for success. Only then do we address the security issues. Though this may sound counterintuitive, we have never found any other way to be successful with security in a modern organization.

Concept 2: Be Reasonable in Your Approach to Mitigate the Security Constraints

It is important to push yourself and implement everything that you can think of to help reduce the security constraints. But this desire must be tempered with moderation. Remember the poise and patient portions of the R.E.A.P. model. The security constraints deal with the motivations, emotions, and actions of others around you. The wrong move with any of these items can place you in an undesirable situation that is potentially worse than before you started. Take action, but be reasonable and careful.

Concept 3: True Security Is an Ideal

It is a rare situation when the security constraints are completely eliminated and you achieve all the elements of the True Security Model. Success should be determined by the identification, measurement, and reduction of the security constraints and the resulting achievements this enables. The True Security Model can be a double-edged sword, providing an actionable framework while simultaneously setting one up for frustration and disappointment. Our message to you is that true security is an ideal; it may not be completely attainable in every situation. You need to be alright with the fact that you will not always, or more realistically not often, be able to reduce all of the constraints or fill all the gaps that they may create within the True Security Model. If you have reduced more of the constraints than before you started, and improved the security of a situation to the best of your ability, you need to be happy with that. Security is a very tough discipline. It deals with sociological, physiological, technical, and countless other elements that need to be considered in every situation. A victory in such a complicated environment is important regardless of its magnitude, but only if you have given your best effort.

Concept 4: Treat Security Personally

The benchmark to set for yourself, when identifying how much energy to exude in your security efforts, is to look at every situation as though you are protecting your own personal data or safety. Looking back at the narrative that opened this chapter, everyone on our project team should feel good about his or her efforts on the project. During our post-mortem meeting we concluded that there was nothing further that could have been done, nor would we have changed our approach. Does this mean that some of us may want to look for a different loan provider? Perhaps. But as far as the engagement was concerned, we did everything we reasonably could to secure this situation, regardless of whether it was our data or not. If you take this same approach to your work, there will never be a question as to whether you gave your best effort.

Summary

In reflection, we find it interesting how many of the topics that we have discussed are what is shaping the landscape of security and the individuals who inhabit it, but are topics that are rarely discussed among those in our profession. This book has been our attempt to change the popular notion of our discipline and bring attention to the concepts and issues that truly determine our fate in security—from what we are erroneously measuring to what we should be measuring and how to act upon that information. The intent was to take you from a potential state of victimhood to a state of empowerment where you understand and influence the environment, instead of the other way around.

In addition, though any security professional within an organization can make a difference at attaining true security, few possess as much an influence as the typical leader of the security program (CISO, CSO, etc.). As a security leader, you generally have the ability to directly interact with all of the various true security groups. Further, due to your position of authority, you can more effectively teach these skills to those on your team creating a whole force of true security zealots. This is why even though many of the exercises that we presented in this book can be applicable for any security professional, we still chose to focus on the security leadership role.

We know that as a security community, we all have a lot more work to do in order to mature our discipline. Hopefully, the concepts in this book have provided some new insights that will help you in your efforts as a security professional. In the end, that is all that we can ask for.

As always, please send us your feedback and comments on this book to www. CISOHandbook.com. Now, as is the case when we finish a book, it is time for our ceremonial beer. Please feel free to join in from wherever you are around the world.

And of course: "Good luck and *via con Dios*!"

Ron, Mike, and Skye

Appendix

Exercise 8: Apathy

Objective

The objective of this exercise is to evaluate how the actions of the security team are contributing to apathy within your environment.

Exercise

Ask at least ten people for their perceptions of your security office. Present the question in a format that allows for open-ended answers versus closed questions.

Considerations

Informal settings work best for off-the-record conversations.

Always make the answers anonymous—do not e-mail them out—and without repercussion. In other words, make it safe to tell the truth.

Be creative in your presentation, such as asking for a metaphor that best describes perception of the security office.

Honesty breeds honesty. Be upfront and you will have a greater chance of getting honest useful feedback.

If you are reading this after completing the book, employ the R.E.A.P. Model.

Examples
■ When you think of security, what is the first thing that comes to mind?
■ When you think of the security team at our organization, what is the first thing that you think of?

Exercise 9: Apathy

Objective

The objective of this exercise is to evaluate the level of apathy within your environment.

Exercise

List all of the areas within your environment where you have witnessed apathy. When engaging in this type of self-reflective activity, be mindful not to pinpoint particular individuals as apathetic—as a character flaw versus a situational response. Be specific or as general as you deem appropriate for your situation. For each area where you identify apathetic behavior, attempt to identify the "why," as well as the effects this will have on your security efforts. Remember, there are no wrong answers.

Example

Situation	Why	Impact on Security Efforts
Apathetic employees	Organization was just purchased by a new organization creating a feeling of powerlessness at the staff level	Employee activities when influenced by apathy lack diligence in applying necessary security processes and procedures

Situation	Why	Impact on Security Efforts

Exercise 10: Myopia

Objective

The objective of this exercise is to evaluate the level of myopia within your environment.

Exercise

Within your own organization, take a moment and think about your last two weeks on the job. How many demonstrations of myopia did you observe during your interactions with co-workers? By the way, it is okay to count yourself as a demonstrator as well. We will not tell anyone.

Situation #1

_____

_____

_____

_____

Demonstration #1

_____

_____

_____

_____

_____

Situation #2

_____

_____

_____

_____

Demonstration #2

_____

_____

_____

_____

Exercise 11: Myopia

Objective

Many organizations trust their vendors to provide them with detailed knowledge and understanding for many complex security issues. The objective of this exercise is to evaluate whether your vendors have a comprehensive view of security or one that is fairly narrow within their specialty. This is important in determining the level of credibility that you bestow on the vendors on a given topic, specifically if they claim to have a heuristic view of security.

Exercise

The next time that you find yourself in need of a security product, try this approach. Invite several product vendors to your company, preferably market leaders in that specific area, that offer multiple products that could meet several of your organizational security needs. This probably is not very different from your current process. Where we would like you to alter your tactics is in asking each vendor to come prepared with his or her sales pitch, as well as the ability to provide:

1. One person who can speak knowledgeably about how all of his or her products interoperate or leverage the features of each other
2. A high-level, one-page diagram that illustrates the idea to facilitate the conversation

Please list below which vendors were able to meet the criteria in both questions.

_____

_____

_____

_____

_____

Please list below which vendors attempted to use their standard sales pitch and disregarded your questions.

_____

_____

_____

_____

_____

Exercise 12: Myopia

Objective

The objective of this exercise is to evaluate your own level of myopia as it pertains to security.

Exercise

Follow the steps below for this exercise:

1. Brainstorm all of your security issues on a piece of paper.
2. Reflect on your security issues by writing down what issues fall into the following categories: people, process, technology, facilities, and miscellaneous.
3. Now, place your findings in the above categories or the categories that you came up with that we did not address.
4. Is there one particular category that disproportionately outweighs the others?
5. Assess your level of comfort for the following categories listed below or use your own self-created categories.
6. Honestly assess your findings. Do you find your ability to address security questions highly polarized or lacking breadth and depth in one or more areas?

Example

Category	Description	Level of Comfort (circle one)
People	This area represents the sociological controls that can be put into place to modify the behavior of individuals regarding security issues.	High, medium, low
Process	This area represents the ability to integrate secure processes into the organization's business practices.	High, medium, low
Technology	This area represents the ability to apply technical solutions to meet the security requirements of the organization.	High, medium, low
Facilities	This area represents the ability to evaluate and safeguard the physical components of an organization.	High, medium, low

Exercise 13: Primacy

Objective

The objective of this exercise is to review how the actions of the security team may provoke demonstrations of primacy by others.

Exercise

Look at the last six months of communiqués to areas outside of the security organization and determine if the tone of the messages was positive or negative. Next, review the means by which they were delivered. Was there a positive or negative response to the delivery mechanism?

Communiqué	Tone (circle one)
	Positive Negative
	Positive Negative
	Positive Negative
	Positive Negative
	Positive Negative
	Positive Negative
	Positive Negative
	Positive Negative
	Positive Negative
	Positive Negative
	Positive Negative
	Positive Negative

Overall Trend (circle one)	
Positive	Negative

Exercise 14: Primacy

Objective

The objective of this exercise is to evaluate how your own motivations may contribute to primacy within your environment.

Exercise

What is the fundamental motivation that drives you as a security professional?

Priority	Item	Primacy Index
	Notoriety	Increase
	Family happiness	Neutral
	Improved organizational security	Increase
	Larger budget (if you have one)	Increase
	Increased status	Increase
	Teaching others about security	Decrease
	Getting paid	Increase
	Other	N/A

As you may have noticed, there are more issues that will generate primacy than neutralize it. Reflect on the impact that your motivations may have on producing demonstrations of primacy.

Exercise 15: Primacy

Objective

The objective of this exercise is to determine the level of impact that primacy has on your decisions and actions as they relate to security.

Exercise

For each of the messages that you send to a specific group, answer the following questions. If you do not interact with the group, simply answer "not applicable."

Organizational Group	Is the Relationship Influencing the Integrity of the Content of Your Messages? (circle one)	How?
Board of directors	Yes No	
Executive management	Yes No	
Middle management	Yes No	
Supervisory management	Yes No	
Employees	Yes No	
Consumers	Yes No	
Security program	Yes No	

Exercise 16: Infancy

Objective

The objective of this exercise is to determine how mature the security practices are within your organization.

Exercise

Take five minutes and think about how your organization secures the data of its consumers. Answer the following three questions:

Do you believe that your organization adequately secures the data of its consumers? Why?

_____

_____

_____

On a scale of 1 to 10 (1 being vulnerable and 10 being highly secure), where would you place your organization when considering consumer security? Why?

_____

_____

_____

Would you trust your organization to secure your personal data? Why?

_____

_____

_____

Exercise 17: Infancy

Objective

The objective is to determine how the security efforts within your organization may be proliferating security infancy.

Exercise

Ask the following three questions to each group within the True Security Model. In presenting these questions, make it so that the responses are anonymous. This will make the responders feel more at ease and open with their answers. Ask as many people to respond as makes sense in your situation.

1. Do you feel that the efforts of the security program within the organization utilize mature and fully developed techniques and approaches? (Circle one)

Yes	No

2. Please list five terms that best describe the efforts of the security program.

_____

_____

_____

_____

_____

_____

_____

_____

3. Do you feel that you have enough training, skills, or knowledge to understand what the security program is doing at your organization and why it is doing it? (Circle one)

Yes	No

If the responses come back predominantly illustrating that your security program is not perceived as mature, there is a good chance that some work needs to be done in mitigating the infancy constraint. If this is the case in your situation, do not fear; below are some more recommendations to help turn things around.

Exercise 18: Tying It All Together

Objective

The objective of this exercise is to map the security constraints for situational analysis within your environment.

Exercise

Background: This tool is applicable either as part of your daily interaction with others or as a member within a project-based initiative. For each situation in which you would like to identify constraints, conduct the following four steps within this exercise.

Step 1: Identify All of the Participants. Identify all of the people that are involved within a given situation, including yourself. If you are analyzing a project, fill out the following table with each member of the project team, as well as all the people that team will interact with during the project. Where it makes sense, try to put people into groups so that your list is as compact as possible.

Step 2: Find the Constraints. For each individual in the list, identify whether he or she is demonstrating any of the security constraints. There is no magic potion for performing this task, simply take a moment and think about it. With your new awareness and visibility into the constraints, the table should start to populate rather quickly. Also, make note of the trends that start to develop. For instance, how certain people that work together often share the same constraints, or how in other situations there may not be any trends or relationships that can be identified.

Step 3: Score the Impact of the identified Constraints. Once you have identified the constraints, the next step is to measure their effect on your individual situation. Again, we will keep this simple, by employing a high, medium, or low rating system. Next to each individual who has been identified, simply go with your gut feeling and give the impact of that constraint to your situational goals a rating.

Below, we have populated the table with the sample data from the example that we opened up this chapter with. Though we have done this using a table for demonstration purposes, you will find that after performing this exercise a few times it will become second nature. As a result, you will gain the ability to conduct this analysis on the fly.

Example

Situational Members	Demonstration of Apathy	Constraint Impact	Demonstration of Myopia	Constraint Impact	Demonstration of Primacy	Constraint Impact	Demonstration of Infancy	Constraint Impact
Head of human resources	No	N/A	Yes	High	Yes	High	No	N/A
Head of information technology	No	N/A	Yes	High	Yes	High	No	N/A
Jenny Jones	No	N/A	Yes	Low	No	N/A	No	N/A
Stinky Pete	No	Low	No	High	Yes	High	Yes	High

Complete the Steps 1–3 Worksheet

Situational Members	Demonstration of Apathy	Constraint Impact	Demonstration of Myopia	Constraint Impact	Demonstration of Primacy	Constraint Impact	Demonstration of Infancy	Constraint Impact

Step 4: Add Detail for the High-Impact Elements. After completing the table, you will want to direct your efforts toward the individuals who are demonstrating the constraints in a high-impact manner. According to our example, that would include everyone except Jenny Jones. For each of the people who were identified that produce a high impact, write a couple of sentences that illustrate why you believe the impact of this constraint is high and how this demonstration is affecting your situation.

Using the Example from "Tales from the Security Consultant"

Example 1

Demonstrations of primacy by the head of human resources are limiting our access with the appropriate individuals, including her. This behavior is hampering our efforts to get the sufficient quantities of the "right" information to conduct a proper security assessment.

Example 2

The demonstration of myopia by the head of human resources is making it difficult to have meaningful conversations regarding the assessment or to convey security concepts beyond her limited understanding. The result is that the process, quality, and scope of the security assessment are compromised.

Complete Step 4

Situational Member #1

_____

_____

_____

Situational Member #2

_____

_____

_____

Situational Member #3

_____

_____

_____

Situational Member #4

_____

_____

_____

Situational Member #5

_____

_____

_____

Exercise 19: Tying It All Together

Objective

The objective of this exercise is to map the security constraints for situational analysis employing the True Security Model.

Exercise

Please follow the steps below for this exercise:

Step 1: Identify the True Security Group. Take a moment and think about this group and the interactions which you have had with it. Obviously, as you move down the management chain within the True Security Model the number of members will probably increase. Regardless of the size of the group, they will exhibit trends. The groups with the larger membership may take a little longer to identify and qualify, but in our experience those trends are always present.

Step 2: Find the Constraints. As you think about the group, what demonstrations of constraints come to mind? Again, there is no magic potion (though we have our staff alchemist working diligently on the project, so far we only have a recipe for a really great martini) for performing this task, simply apply some brain cycles to the idea. Are there any trends or constraint relationships that are shared throughout the group? Is there a single constraint that appears to be dominant within the members of the group? Do not try to get them all at one time. It is similar to viewing one of those hidden picture posters. You have to step back, relax your eyes, and focus on nothing in particular, and presto an image appears. Group constraints are similar in nature. You have to train yourself to eliminate a lot of the noise surrounding them.

Step 3: Score the Impact of the Identified Constraints. Once you have identified the constraints, the next step is to measure their effect on your ability to obtain the desired element defined within the True Security Model for the target group. Again, we will keep this simple, by employing a high, medium, or low rating system. Next to each group that has been identified, simply go with your gut feeling and give the impact of that constraint to your situational goals a rating.

As a quick refresher on the True Security Model, refer to the target groups and desired behavior table below:

Organizational Group	Desired Action or Behavior
Board of directors	Endorsement
Executive management	Priority
Middle management	Resources
Supervisory management	Support
Employees	Diligence
Consumers	Trust
Security program	Execution

Example

True Security Group	Demonstration of Apathy	Constraint Impact	Demonstration of Myopia	Constraint Impact	Demonstration of Primacy	Constraint Impact	Demonstration of Infancy	Constraint Impact
Board of directors	Yes	N/A	No	N/A	No	N/A	No	N/A
Executive management team	No	N/A	No	N/A	Yes	High	No	N/A
Middle management	No	N/A	Yes	Low	No	N/A	No	N/A
Supervisors	No	Low	No	High	Yes	High	Yes	High
Employees	No	N/A	Yes	High	Yes	High	No	N/A
Consumers	No	N/A	Yes	High	Yes	High	No	N/A
Security team	No	N/A	Yes	High	Yes	High	No	N/A

Complete the Steps 1–3 Worksheet

True Security Group	Demonstration of Apathy	Constraint Impact	Demonstration of Myopia	Constraint Impact	Demonstration of Primacy	Constraint Impact	Demonstration of Infancy	Constraint Impact
Board of directors								
Executive management team								
Middle management								
Supervisors								
Employees								
Consumers								
Security team								

Step 4: Add Detail for the High-Impact Elements. After completing the table, you will want to focus on the groups that are demonstrating the constraints in a high-impact manner. Again, just as we did previously, write a couple of sentences that illustrate why you believe the impact of this constraint is high and how this demonstration can impact your ability to acquire the desired true security element from this group.

Example

Demonstrations of apathy by the board are making it difficult to get any security items on the board meeting agenda. This lack of visibility of security is making it difficult to get their endorsement of the security program.

Complete Step 4

Board of Directors

_____

_____

_____

Executive Management Team

_____

_____

_____

Middle Management

_____

_____

_____

Supervisors

_____

_____

_____

Employees

_____

_____

_____

Consumers

_____

_____

_____

Security Team

_____

_____

_____

Exercise 20: Tying It All Together

Objective

The objective of this exercise is to evaluate the impact that the security constraints have on attaining the tangible elements of the True Security Model.

Exercise

For this exercise, please follow the steps below:

Step 1: Determine whether your program has each of these components: Yes or No.

Step 2: Is the quality of each of these components sufficient to meet the needs of the security program?

Step 3: For each of the items that are deemed as deficient, determine the security constraints that are interfering with their development.

Example

True Security Components	Does This Element Exist?	Is It Sufficient for the Organization?	Hindered by Apathy	Hindered by Myopia	Hindered by Primacy	Hindered by Infancy
Security strategy	Yes	No	No	Yes	No	Yes
Mission and mandate	Yes	Yes	No	No	No	No
Roles and Responsibilities	Yes	Yes	No	No	No	No
Security policies	Yes	No	Yes	Yes	No	No
Training and awareness regimen	Yes	No	Yes	No	No	Yes
Formal security project portfolio	No	No	Yes	Yes	Yes	Yes

Complete Steps 1–3 Worksheet

True Security Components	Does This Element Exist?	Is It Sufficient for the Organization?	Hindered by Apathy	Hindered by Myopia	Hindered by Primacy	Hindered by Infancy
Security strategy						
Mission and mandate						
Roles and responsibilities						
Security policies						
Training and awareness regimen						
Formal security project portfolio						

Step 4: As before, attempt to quantify the effect of the constraint by writing a quick sentence or two that is representative of the issue. We have always found that if we cannot write it down, we do not truly understand the issue. So, even if this step may seem unnecessary, it acts as a crucible that burns away all of the unnecessary noise that generally surrounds these issues.

In the example table, the security policies were deemed as existing, yet insufficient for the needs of the organization. The quantification of these items could look something like the following:

Example

Though the security policies for our organization exist, they are weak, and in many cases inapplicable to the lines of business. Though this issue has been raised with executive management, few seem to show any interest in the issue (apathy). When one of the executives is reasonably engaged, he or she asks general questions regarding the status of the company firewall or about antivirus and deems the situation under control (myopia).

Complete Step 4

Security Strategy

_____

_____

_____

Mission and Mandate

_____

_____

_____

Roles and Responsibilities

_____

_____

_____

Security Policies

_____

_____

_____

Training and Awareness

_____

_____
_____

Formal Security Project Portfolio

_____

_____
_____

Consumers

_____

_____
_____

Security Team

_____

_____
_____

Exercise 21: Tying It All Together

Objective

The objective of this exercise is to measure the intangible elements of the True Security Model within a project or workgroup environment.

Exercise

Please follow the steps below for this exercise:

> **Step 1:** For each member of the group you are evaluating, identify the group members, which true security group they belong to, and then whether this individual is demonstrating the associated true security element.

Example

Individual Name	Title	Indentify Their True Security Group (board of directors, supervisor, etc.)	Have You Achieved the Desired Element? (circle one)
Joe Johnson	Operations manager	Middle management	Yes No
Sally Smith	Security analyst	Security program	Yes No

Complete Step 1 Worksheet

Individual Name	Title	Indentify Their True Security Group (board of directors, supervisor, etc.)	Have You Achieved the Desired Element? (circle one)
			Yes No
			Yes No
			Yes No
			Yes No
			Yes No
			Yes No

> **Step 2:** Since our objective is to make the intangible more tangible, for each individual where you answered "Yes" write a couple of sentences that identify the evidence that you have to substantiate that you have achieved the desired True Security element. Remember, this information is for your eyes only, so be honest with your answers. For each individual where you answered "No," write a couple of sentences that describe what evidence has led you to feel that the associated True Security element is absent.

Example

Joe Johnson: Joe worked diligently to identify the appropriate resources that were needed for my identity management initiative. Once he assigned them to the project, he allowed them to operate without any distractions. Further, Joe has protected them from some of the other efforts that requested their participation in order to keep them focused on this assignment. Once again, this is demonstrating the attainment of the resources element we need from Joe as a middle manager.

Sally Smith: Sally is working hard but continues to demonstrate infancy through her continual reference to technical security controls. Her inability to grasp and apply the security risk elements associated with process development is hurting the team in that we cannot assign her to those areas. As far as she is concerned, everything in security is a result of "spoofing" packets.

Individual #1

_____

_____

_____

_____

Individual #2

_____

_____

_____

_____

Individual #3

_____

_____

_____

_____

Individual #4

_____

_____

_____

_____

Individual #5

_____

_____

_____

_____

Exercise 22: Tying It All Together

Objective

The objective of this exercise is to measure the intangible elements of the True Security Model within each of the true security target groups.

Exercise

Please follow the steps below for this exercise:

Step 1: For each group within the True Security Model, identify whether your organization has achieved the associated true security element. Use a yes or no answer. Keep in mind that we are looking for a trended answer that reflects your opinion of the group as a whole. Once again, just go with your gut feeling; it will give you the answer rather quickly.

Example

True Security Group	Desired Element	Have You Achieved the Desired Element? (circle one)
Board of directors	Endorsement	Yes
Executive team	Priority	No
Middle management	Resources	No
Supervisory team	Support	Yes
Employees	Diligence	Yes
Consumers	Trust	No
Security program	Execution	Yes

Complete Worksheet for Step 1

True Security Group	Desired Element	Have You Achieved the Desired Element? (circle one)
Board of directors	Endorsement	Yes No
Executive team	Priority	Yes No
Middle management	Resources	Yes No
Supervisory team	Support	Yes No
Employees	Diligence	Yes No
Consumers	Trust	Yes No
Security program	Execution	Yes No

Step 2: Remember, the objective is to make the intangible more tangible. So each group for which you answered "Yes," write a couple of sentences that identify the evidence that you have to substantiate that you have achieved this element. Again, this information is just for your own edification, so be honest. For each group that you answered "No," write a couple of sentences that identify the evidence of why you feel that you have not achieved the true security element.

Example

A Board of Directors That Has Provided Endorsement: I believe that we have achieved endorsement from the board of directors within our organization due to the fact that they have been actively initiating, monitoring, and then measuring the implementation of security directives. These directives seem to be timely, logical, and in the best interest of the organization.

A Board of Directors That Has Not Provided Endorsement: The board of directors within our organization is not endorsing security. They have a limited visibility of the security posture of the organization and have never shown any interest in attaining such a view. Their security directives are ad hoc and often misguided.

Complete Step 2

Board of Directors

_____

_____

_____

_____

Executive Management Team

_____

_____

_____

_____

Middle Management

_____

_____

_____

_____

Supervisors

_____

_____

_____

_____

Employees

_____

_____

_____

_____

Consumers

_____

_____

_____

_____

Security Team

_____

_____

_____

_____

R.E.A.P. Templates: Exercises 24 to 30

Exercise 16

Relate Checklist

Before distributing any communication, take a moment and ask yourself the following questions:
■ How might this message be interpreted by the reader? ■ Is my message clear and understandable? ■ Have I taken time to consider the possibility for multiple perspectives on this message? ■ Have I invested time and energy to understand the perspective of the person or group to whom I am addressing this message? ■ How can I improve my message and limit misunderstanding?

Exercise 17

The following exercise is designed to help you with the relate component within the True Security Model:

True Security Group	*Have I Taken the Time to Learn about the Perspective of the Person or People That Are Going to Receive This Message? (circle one)*	*Have I Educated Myself on This Person's or Group's Viewpoint? (circle one)*
Board of directors	Yes No	Yes No
Executive management	Yes No	Yes No
Middle management	Yes No	Yes No
Supervisory management	Yes No	Yes No
Employees	Yes No	Yes No
Consumers	Yes No	Yes No
Security program	Yes No	Yes No

Exercise 18

Educate Checklist

Take a moment and ask yourself the following questions:
■ What have I learned in the past week that increases my ability as a security professional?   ■ Have I transformed this information to make it understandable to those around me?   ■ How have I assessed who may need this new knowledge?   ■ Have I passed this knowledge on?   ■ Have I checked to see whether the message I intended to send is close to the receiver's interpretation? (This can be done by both asking questions, and asking for the other person to verbally paraphrase or share his or her understanding with you.)

Exercise 19

The following exercise is designed to help you with the educate component within the True Security Model:

True Security Group	Have I Appropriately Educated Myself on the Security Concepts Needed by This Group? (circle one)	Have I Appropriately Educated This Group? (circle one)
Board of directors	Yes No	Yes No
Executive team	Yes No	Yes No
Middle management	Yes No	Yes No
Supervisory team	Yes No	Yes No
Employees	Yes No	Yes No
Consumers	Yes No	Yes No
Security program	Yes No	Yes No

Exercise 20

Appraise Checklist

For any meeting, ask yourself the following questions to better understand the motives (self and other) behind the meeting:
■ Why did the other person agree to this meeting? What is in it for him or her personally? ■ Why am I attending this meeting? What is in it for me personally? ■ What personal agenda may be determined from question #1? ■ Is that agenda influenced by, or a manifestation of, one or more of the security constraints? ■ Which ones?

Exercise 21

The following exercise is designed to help you with the appraise component within the True Security Model:

For any meeting that you will participate with a specific group within the True Security Model, answer the following questions:
■ Does the agenda for the group align with your agenda and motives? ■ Is there a potential champion in the group? ■ How can the message be tailored to circumvent or reduce the security constraints?

Complete the following table:

Example

True Security Group	Desired Element (your agenda)	Reason for Meeting	Does the Agenda for the Group Align with Your Agenda and Motives?	Is There a Potential Champion within the Group?	How Can the Message Be Tailored to Circumvent the Security Constraints?
Executive management	Priority	Security Budget	No. Due to the time of year, this group will be motivated by overall budgetary reduction and the priority assigned to other issues. This may lead to acts of primacy or apathy.	Yes, it is Joe Smith. He had his identity stolen last year and is very sensitive to data handling.	Stress the cost-effective nature of training and process improvement for addressing security issues. Focus anecdotal references on data leakage and data theft.

Exercise Template

True Security Group	Desired Element (your agenda)	Reason for Meeting	Does the Agenda for the Group Align with Your Agenda and Motives?	Is There a Potential Champion within the Group?	How Can the Message Be Tailored to Circumvent the Security Constraints?

Exercise 22

Act Checklist

Before attending your next meeting, take a moment and ask yourself the following questions:
■ Have you adequately appraised the situation?   ■ How do you plan to take action?

Exercise 23

The following exercise is designed to help you with the act component within the True Security Model:

True Security Group	Do You Have Enough Information in Order to Take Action with This Group toward Achieving True Security? (circle one)	How Are You Going to Take Action?
Board of directors	Yes No	
Executive team	Yes No	
Middle management	Yes No	
Supervisory team	Yes No	
Employees	Yes No	
Consumers	Yes No	
Security program	Yes No	

References

Overview Chapter

R. Collette, M. Gentile, and T. August (2005). *The CISO Handbook, A Practical Guide to Securing Your Company*. CRC Press, Boca Raton, FL

B. Schneier (2003) *Beyond Fear: Thinking Sensibly about Security in an Uncertain World*. Springer, Warren, MI

P. Watzlawick, J. Beavin, D. Jackson (1967). *Pragmatics of Human Communication*. W. W. Norton & Company, New York, NY

Chapter 3

R. Collette, M. Gentile, and T. August (2005). *The CISO Handbook, A Practical Guide to Securing Your Company*. CRC Press , Boca Raton, FL

D. Goldman (1995). *Emotional Intelligence: Why It Can Matter More Than IQ*. Bantam Books New York, NY

P. Watzlawick, J. Helmick Beavin, D. Jackson (1967). *Pragmatics of Human Communication*. W. W. Norton & Company, New York, NY

Chapter 4

E. Herrmann, J. Call, M. Hernàndez-Lloreda, B.Hare, M. Tomasello1 (2007). Humans Have Evolved Specialized Skills of Social Cognition: The Cultural Intelligence Hypothesis. *Science, Washington D.C.,*7 September 2007

P. Drucker (1992). *Age of Discontinuity*. Harper and Row, New York, NY

P. Drucker (2003). *Managing in the Next Society*. Macmillan, New York, NY

D. Goleman, R. Boyatzis, A. McKee (2004). *Primal Leadership*. Harvard Business School Press, Boston, MA

E. Langer (1989) *Mindfulness*. Da Capo Press, Cambridge, MA

A. Mack and I. Rock (1998). *Inattentional Blindness* The MIT Press, Cambridge, MA

A.Toffler (1970). *Future Shock*. Random House, New York, NY

Index

A

Accountability
  and authority, 75–76
  perceived undesirability of, 5
Accountants, as security auditors, 26, 27
Act element, 231–233, 282–283
  applying within true security model, 230
  in security success model, 229
  situational application, 230
Adaptive approach, 77
Annual budget, subsuming security
    measurement under, 9–10
Apathy, xxii, xxvi, 4, 5, 29, 59–60.
    See also Employee apathy
  and accountability-authority equilibrium,
    75–76
  and authoritarian model, 67
  and board of directors, 83–84
  and boredom, 69
  and budget cuts, 69
  cause and effect on true security
    model, 80–86
  causes within security programs, 69–70
  causes within systems, 62–64
  change as catalyst of, 64, 69
  and communal model, 67–68
  and consumers, 88–89
  defined, 31
  and employees, 87–88, 93
  and executive team, 84–86
  exercise, 239–240, 241–242
  and futility, 69, 78
  hiding places of, 96

human causes, 60–62, 81
and ineffective leadership styles, 69
and job role authority and responsibility, 95
and lack of recognition, 69
and middle management, 86
miscellaneous factors promoting, 69
and missing tangible security elements, 79
and monotony, 69
as negative synergy, 63
organizational causes, 64–69, 81
and organizational culture, 94
organizational/security approach, 93–94
and organizational security interaction
    points, 76–78
and overambitious security initiatives, 78–79
and positive aspects to extreme cultural
    archetypes, 66–67
and powerlessness, 61
reducing through empathy, 89
and reorganization, 69
role of communication in stemming, 79–80
and security event interaction choices, 95
in security gap analysis, 216
and security personality model, 71–75
security program causes, 81
and security program personality, 94–95
security solutions to, 92
and self-serving bias, 87
and sexy security initiatives, 95–96
solutions, 89–96
and supervisory management, 86–87
systems theory perspectives, 90
touchy-feeling considerations, 90–92
and true security model, 82–89

Appraise element, 231–232, 281
  applying within true security model,
    228–229
  in security success model, 226–227
  situational application, 227
Audits. *See* Security audits
Authoritarian model, 65
  and apathy, 67
  organizational symptoms, 68
Authority
  and accountability, 75–76
  and apathy, 61
  and blind trust, 199–201
  of conference speakers, 200
  questioning, 199
  and trust, 183
Authority figures, and trust, 179
Automatic pilot, 100
Availability, 3

B

Bertalanaffy, Ludwig von, xxv
Big brother, 199
Big picture thinking, and myopia, 125
Black box, security as, 13
Blind trust, 124, 183
  avoiding with authority claims, 199–201
  by consumers, 160
  of large consulting firms, 183
Board of directors
  and apathy, 83–84
  defined, 44
  endorsements form, 219
  and infancy, 190–191
  lack of endorsement from, 220
  limited expertise in security, 119
  and myopia, 119–120
  and primacy, 156
Boredom, and apathy, 69
Budget cuts, and apathy, 69
Busy work, 196

C

Change, as catalyst of apathy, 64, 69
*Chief Information Security Officer (CISO)
  Handbook,* xix
CIA triad, 3
CISO Handbook survey, xxiv

Closed systems, xxvi
  and myopia, 102
Collette, Ron, xv–xvi
Communal model, 65
  and apathy, 67–68
  organizational symptoms, 68
Communication
  cyclical nature of, 161
  and organizational myopia, 110
  political determinants of acceptable
    content, 148
  positive spins on, 167
  relationship and content in, 163, 165, 178
  of security procedure rationales, 79–80
  as solution to myopia, 130–132
Communication behaviors, learned
    nature of, 60–61
Communication skills, of generalists
    vs. specialists, 113
Compartmentalization, 105, 123
  among supervisory managers, 122–123
  by consumer thinking, 124
  and myopia, 105
Competition
  and hierarchy, 136
Complexity
  as accessory to infancy, 173–174
  and myopia, 105–106, 106
Conference speakers
  authority of, 200
  verification of, 201
Confidentiality, 3
Consumer security, 193–194
Consumers
  and apathy, 88–89
  and infancy, 193–194
  and myopia, 123–124
  need for trust by, 48
  self-centered nature of, 124
Content-focused organizations,
    primacy in, 144–148
Contract workforce, 108
  and myopia, 106–108, 107
Costs
  of poor security policies, 16
  of poor security project portfolios, 22–23
  of poorly defined roles/responsibilities, 18
  of weak training curriculum, 20
Credibility, lack of, and infancy, 185–187
Cultural archetypes, positives in, 66–67
Cultural intelligence, 99

D

Data
    age of, and trust in, 179
    evolution of understanding, 177
Death march projects, 79
Desired action definitions, in true security
        model, 44–45
Diligence
    defined, 46
    role in achieving true security, 47
Documented procedures, noncompliance
        with, 88
Doomsaying, and infancy, 187
Doubt, and infancy, 197
Dunning-Kruger effect, 179

E

Educate element, 231–232, 280
    applying within true security
        model, 225–226
    in security success model, 224–226
    situational application, 225
Emotional intelligence, 91
Empathy, 91
    reducing apathy through, 89
Employee apathy, xx, 87–88, 93.
        See also Apathy
Employee myopia, xx. *See also* Myopia
Employee primacy, xx. *See also* Primacy
Employee responsibility, 133
Employees
    defined, 44
    and infancy, 193
    myopia and, 123
Endorsements
    by board of directors, 50
    as requirements for achieving true
        security, 55
Environment, in systems theory, 53, 54
Escalation, as response to primacy, 169–170
Evolution of data, 177
Execution, role in achieving true security, 48
Executive management
    and apathy, 84–86
    defined, 44
    employee dissatisfaction with, 66
    and infancy, 191

    insulation from security issues, 120
    myopia and, 120–121
    and primacy, 156–157
Executive ostrich maneuver, 34
Executives
    comfort level with audits, 25
    concern with security appearances, 24
Exercises
    apathy, 241–242
        apathy, 239–240
    infancy promotion, 257–258
    maturity of security practices, 255–256
    measuring intangibles in True Security
        Model, 271–274
    measuring intangibles within target groups,
        275–278
    myopia self-assessment, 243–244
    myopia self-evaluation, 247–248
    myopia vendor evaluation exercise, 245–246
    primacy impact, 253–254
    primacy provocation, 249–250
    primacy self-evaluation, 251–252
    security constraints mapping, 259–262
    True Security Model constraints
        mapping, 263–266

F

False security, 1, 11. *See also* false perception
        of; Security
    and limited training and awareness
        efforts, 20
    in management security portfolios, 84
    and poorly defined roles/responsibilities, 18
    and vague mission and mandate
        statements, 13
    and weak security polities, 16
    and weak security project portfolios, 22
Fear, uncertainty, and doubt (FUD), 171, 187
    avoiding in training and awareness, 203
Federal Information Security Management
        Act (FISMA), 25
Feedback, 207
    in systems theory, 54, 180
Firewalls, belief in security as, 6
Ford, Henry, 104, 113, 114
Futility, 79
    and apathy, 69, 78
Future shock, 106

G

Game of inches, security as, 112
Garbage in, garbage out (GIGO), 181, 196
General systems theory, xxv. *See also*
        Systems theory
Generalists, 114
    need for in security, 113–114
    using in security programs, 132
Gentile, Mike, xvi
Gentile, Skye, xvii
Global economy, 182
Government agencies, achieving true
        security in, 51

H

Health Insurance Portability and
        Accountability Act (HIPAA),
        14. *See also* HIPAA
Hegel, Georg, xxv
Hierarchy, 136
    and primacy, 169
HIPAA, 14–15
    security con example, 36
    security policies requirements, 15
HIPAA reviews, example, 36–39
Homeostasis, in systems theory, 56
Horizontal organizations
    and primacy, 142–143
    skepticism in, 182
Human interactions, role in security, xxiv

I

Identity theft, veterans' records, x
Immaturity. *See also* Infancy
    of security products, 200
Inattentional blindness, 100, 101
Industrial Revolution, 104
Infancy, xx, xxvi, 4, 5, 29, 171–175
    big brother cautions, 199
    and board of directors, 190–191
    causes in humans, 176–178, 188
    combating with patience, 204
    and consumers, 193–194
    defined, 32
    and doomsaying, 187

    and doubt, 197
    and employees, 193
    and executive management, 191
    human considerations in solving, 195–196
    and importance of self-education, 201–202
    and lack of credibility, 185–187
    and message organization, 202–204
    and middle managers, 191–192
    and nature of security, 185
    organizational causes, 181–184, 188
    organizational promotion exercise, 257–258
    and perception, 176
    and progression of complex
        technology, 173–174
    in security programs, 184–188
    security solutions, 195–204
    and skepticism, 197
    and source data quality, 199
    and supervisory management, 192–193
    systemic causes, 180–181, 188
    and systems theory, 196–197
    and true security model, 189–194
    and trust, 196
    vs. clearly defined processes, 180
    weather predictions example, 171–172
Information asymmetry, 119, 190, 191
Information mapping, 129
Information security
    constraints hindering, ix
    infancy as discipline, xx
Information Technology Infrastructure
        Library (ITIL), 187
Input
    requirements for true security, 55
    in systems theory, 53, 54
Integrity, 3
Intended message, 177
Interactions, role in systems theory, 57
Interdependence, in systems, 180
International Organization for Standardization
        (ISO), 42
ISO27001-2, 128

J

Jargon
    avoiding, 130
    importance of avoiding, 114
Job role, reviewing authority and
        responsibility, 95

K

Knowledge economy, 106
Knowledge management, and organizational
   myopia, 109–110
Knowledge workers, 107

L

Leadership styles
   and apathy, 69
   primal leadership, 146–147
Listening skills, 223

M

Management responsibility, and endorsement
   of security policy, 45
Mature processes, 197
Measurement
   basing on government funding, 11
   deficiencies in, 29
   faulty, xx, 7
   flaws in, 35
   improper application of, 7
   lack of accepted means, 7
   security certifications counts, 24
   security device counts, 23
   security event counts, 23–24
   security framework correlation, 28–29
   of threats du jour, 27–28
Message content
   political determinants of, 148
   and political pressure, 146
Message organization, quelling infancy
   through, 202–204
Middle management
   and apathy, 86
   conflict between education and executive
      perspective, 122
   defined, 44
   and infancy, 191–192
   and myopia, 122
   and primacy, 157–158
Mindlessness, 101
   and specialization, 99–100
Miscommunication, human reasons for, 177
Mission and mandate, 43, 198, 215

costs associated with, 13–14
defined, 8
and false sense of security, 13
and faulty measurement, 12–13
lack of formal, 12
of security programs, 11
Monotony
   and apathy, 69
   and myopia, 104
Myopia, xxii, xxvi, 4, 29, 97–98, 211.
      See also Employee myopia
   based on fear, 121
   causes in humans, 98, 99–101, 117
   causes within security programs, 110–118
   causes within systems, 98, 102–103
   communication as solution to, 130–132
   compound effects with primacy, 207
   and consumers, 123–134
   defined, 31
   determining one's own level of, 126–127
   domain-boundary, 32
   effects on security professionals, 207
   effects summary, 125
   and employees, 123
   event-driven, 32
   and executive team, 120–121
   as filter to all inputs, 103
   and history of specialization, 104–105,
      113–114
   as limited perspective, 125
   by management, 35
   measuring, 128
   measuring others', 128–130
   and middle management, 122
   organizational causes, 98, 103–110, 117
   and professional pedigree, 113
   real-world example, 205, 206, 218
   as safe haven from complexity, 106
   in security gap analysis, 216
   security program causes, 117
   security solutions, 126–133
   and security training deficiencies, 116
   self-assessment exercise, 243–244
   self-evaluation exercise, 247–248
   solutions, 125–133
   and supervisory team, 122–123
   touchy feely considerations, 126
   and true security model, 118–125
   vendor evaluation exercise, 245–246
   and vendor specialization, 115–116
   vicious circle of, 114–115

N

National Institute of Standards and Technology
(NIST), 42–43, 128
Needs and drives, and primacy, 140, 161
Negative feedback cycle, 57
managing with poise and patience, 231
Negative information, personal processing
of, 162, 165, 167
Negative synergy, 63
effects on systems, 64
New-hire orientation, security training
limited to, 19
Noncompliance, and apathy, 88
Nonsummativity, 63
in systems, 180

O

Office politics, as security constraint, xx
Open systems, xxvi
Organizational compartmentalization, 105
Organizational culture, 94
archetypes, 65
basis in job title *vs.* performance, 143
causes of apathy within, 64–66
highly segregated organizations, 144
horizontal organizations, 142–143
and primacy, 141
protection of sacred cows, 144
vertical organizations, 142
Organizational GAP analysis, 218–220
Organizational groups, in true security
model, 44
Organizational myopia, 103
and complexity of systems, 105–106
and history of specialization, 104–105
and knowledge management, 109–110
and professional fraud, 108–109
role of workforce in, 106–108
Output, in systems theory, 54
Overload, 176
and myopia, 106

P

Participants, identifying, 210
Passwords, gift card offer tactics, ix–x

Patience, in combating infancy, 204
Payment Card Industries Data Security
Standards (PCI DSS), 14–15
People element, managing in information
security, x
Perception, and infancy, 176
Poised and Patient element, 230–231, 231–232
Political pressure, impact on security, 146
Powerlessness
and apathy, 61
and primacy, 169–170
PowerPoint, effective use of, 203
Primacy, 4, 5, 29, 135–136, 211
and board of directors, 156
cause and effect in true security model, 155
causes in humans, 139, 154
causes within security programs, 148–153
compound effects with myopia, 207
in content-focused organizations, 144–148
and defensive responses to information, 162
effects of, 155–156
effects on security professionals, 207
ego as trigger point for, 165–168
escalation in response to, 169–170
and executive management, 156–157
and extremes, 143
in highly segregated organizations, 144
in horizontal organizations, 142–143
human considerations, 161
and human needs and drives, 140
and human responses to
information, 162–163
impact exercise, 253–254
and middle management, 157–158
organizational causes, 141–148, 154
and organizational culture, 141–148
in organizations protecting sacred cows, 144
in organizations valuing job title over
performance, 143
and power issues, 169–170
as primitive reaction, 153
process for addressing displays of, 169
provocation exercise, 249–250
real-world example, 205, 206
security professionals' view of, 150
security program causes, 154
security solutions, 163
self-assessment, 163–165
self-evaluation exercise, 251–252
solutions, 160–163
and stomping practices, 168–169

and supervisory management, 157–158,
    158–159
systems theory considerations, 161
tune-up, 136–138
in vertical organizations, 142
Primacy tune-up, 136–138
Primal leadership, 146–147
Prioritization
    role in achieving true security, 45–46
    underutilization in security efforts, 21
Private organizations, achieving true
    security in, 51
Proactive techniques, xxi, 77
Professional fraud, links to myopia, 108–109
Public corporations, achieving true
    security in, 51

R

Reactive approach, 77
R.E.A.P. Security Success Model, xxi, xxvii,
    220–221
    Appraise and Act elements, 226–227
    Educate element, 224–226
    Poised and Patient element, 230–231
    Relate component, 220
    templates, 279–284
Recognition, lack of, and apathy, 69
Regulations, 25, 173, 194
    poor framing of, 174
Regulatory compliance, lack of penalties, 37
Regulatory effect, 26
Relate component, 231–233, 279–280
    application within true security model, 222
    look, listen and learn technique, 223
    in security success model, 221
    situational applications, 221–222
Remediation, 25
Reorganization, and apathy, 69
Resources
    role in achieving true security, 46
    and systems theory, 57
Rigid categories, and myopia, 100
Risk assessment, real-world example, 205–206
Risk-rating methodology, 198
Roles and responsibilities, 16–18, 43, 215
    costs of poorly defined, 18
    defined, 8
    and false sense of security, 18

    lack of documented, 17
    security deficiencies in, 18

S

Sacred cows, organizations protective of, 144
Security
    big brother approach, 199
    as black box, 13
    CIA triad definition, 3
    as complex topic, 116
    defined, 3–6
    dictionary definition, 4
    differing perceptions of, 35
    difficulty in defining, 2
    difficulty in obtaining proper experience
        in, 175
    documented definitions of, 6
    evolving nature of, 184
    exponential data production by, 185
    failure to define, and myopia, 111
    false perception of, xix–xx, 1, 11, 13, 16,
        18, 20, 22
    functional definitions of, 5
    as game of inches, 112
    identification of deficiencies by, 166
    immaturity as field, 184
    impact of politics on, 146
    importance of continued learning, 201
    inability of current regulations
        to address, 174
    intangible negative influences on, xxi
    lack of representation at executive level, 186
    nature of, and infancy, 185
    overlaying systems theory onto, 54–55
    political uses of, 152
    solutions for infancy, 195–204
    as specialized language, 114
    technocentric, 111–112
    treating personally, 237
    ubiquitousness of, 97, 131, 185
    as universal responsibility, 133
Security auditors, roots in accounting, 26
Security audits, 24–27
Security certifications, counting, 24
Security Committee, Board of Directors true
    security example, 50
Security con, xx, 35, 120, 124
    congressional role in, 37

Security con (*continued*)
consultants' role in, 38
consumers' role in, 38–39
defined, 35, 36
example, 36
example analysis, 36–37
and HIPAA, 37
and infancy, 191, 192, 193
management role in, 37
and myopia, 118, 119
and primacy, 155, 157, 158, 159
U.S. Government role in, 37
Security constraints, xx, xxvi, xxvii, 29–33,
35, 207
as cause of all failures, 236
counteracting, xxi
difficulty of measuring, 35
effects on intangible elements of true
security, 52
identification, remediation, and
compensation, xxvii
identifying, 212
impacts of, 56
importance of understanding, 58
lack of discussion about, 33–34
localized identification, 209–211
management responses to, 34–35
mapping exercise, 259–262, 263–266
mapping impact on True Security
Model, 267–270
measuring, 209–214
pressures exerted by, 30
reasonable approach to mitigating, 236
scoring impact of, 210, 212–213
within true security model, 211–214
Security consultants, real-world tales, 205–206,
235–236
Security deficiencies, 1–2
executive concerns over, 24
Security device counts, 23
Security event counts, 23–24
Security framework correlation, 28–29
Security gap analysis, 214–215
intangible elements, 216–218
situational use, 218
tangible elements, 215–216
Security interaction points, 76–78
Security leadership, 238
Security measurement, 8
and false sense of, 11
lack of accepted means, 7

miscellaneous methods, 23–29
mission and mandate, 11–14
reasons for faulty, 10
roles and responsibilities in, 16–19
and security con, 35–39
and security constraints, 29–35
and security policies, 14–16
and security program strategy, 8–11
and security risk project portfolio, 21–23
training and awareness for, 19–21
Security personality model, 71–72, 94–95
architect type, 72
auditor type, 72
businessperson type, 73
cop type, 72
hacker type, 73
policy-wog type, 73
random type, 73
Security pipeline, 76, 77
Security policies, 14, 43, 215
costs of poor, 16
deficiencies in, 14–15
defined, 8
and false sense of security, 16
and faulty measurement, 16
importance of comprehensive, 198
lack of documented, 14, 15
Security posture, misleading representations
of, xxiv
Security practices, maturity exercise, 255–256
Security professionals
as authority figures, 76
death spiral of primacy and myopia for, 207
employee views of, 74
fundamental motivations of, 164
impacts of primacy and myopia on, 207
obtaining perceptions of, 74–75
pedigree and myopia, 113
professional backgrounds of, 71–72
Security program strategy, 8–9, 43, 215
components of complete, 9
defined, 8
failure to document, 10
and faulty measurement, 10
infancy and, 184–188, 188
links to annual budget, 9–10
missing tangible items in, 79
Security programs
causes of apathy in, 69–75
causes of primacy in, 148–153
reactive nature of existing, 25

Security research firms, 199
Security risk project portfolio, 21–22, 21–23,
    43, 215
    costs of poor, 22–23
    defined, 8
    and false sense of security, 22
    and fault measurement, 22
    political falsehoods in, 84
Security success model, 220–233
Security theatre, xix
Segregated organizations, 144
Self-serving bias, 87, 100, 150
Skepticism
    and infancy, 197
    and trust of source, 178
Source data quality, 199
    and infancy, 199
Speaking skills, 224
Specialization, 102, 106
    and ability to use tools, 99
    achieving efficiency through, 104
    and audit myopia, 27
    as cause of organizational myopia, 104–105
    and mindlessness, 99–100
    by vendors, 115–116
    vs. generalists, 113–114, 114
Specialized language
    avoiding, 130
    of security vendors, 131
    and stomping behaviors, 169
Staff level, role in successful security, 11
Stomping practices, and primacy, 168–169
Strong inputs, importance of, 196–197
Supervisory management
    and apathy, 86–87
    avoidance by security team, 193
    defined, 44
    and infancy, 192–193
    and myopia, 122–123
    need for support from, 46
    and primacy, 157–158, 158–159
Support, role in achieving true security, 46
Synergy, and apathy, 63
System continuum, xxvi
Systems
    defined, xxv
    open *vs.* closed, xxvi
Systems theory, xxiv, xxv
    applying to social organizations, xxvi
    components of, 53–54
    environment in, 53

    feedback in, 54, 207
    and GIGO, 181
    global considerations, 56–57
    homeostasis in, 56
    and infancy, 196–197
    inputs in, 53
    interactions in, 57
    and myopia, 102–103
    outputs in, 54
    overlaying security onto, 54–55
    perspectives on apathy, 90
    and primacy, 161
    and solutions to myopia, 125–126
    throughput in, 53
    and true security model, 53
    wholeness, interdependence, nonsummativity,
        and feedback in, 180

T

Target audience, xxiii, 130, 202
Tasking, perceptions of meaninglessness, 62
Team meetings, as training gold, 132
Technocentric security, and myopia, 111–112
Threat du jour, 27–28
Throughput, in systems theory, 53
Tools, 101
    and development of myopia, 99
    as relational element, 99
Training and awareness, 19, 43, 215
    as accessory to myopia, 116
    costs of poor, 20
    customizing messages in, 203
    defined, 8
    employing as security tool, 96
    and false sense of security, 20
    through team meetings, 132
    underutilization of, 19, 20
    use of definitions, 203
Transportation Security Agency (TSA), true
        security model example, 49–50
True security
    defined, 41–42
    endorsement requirements, 45
    as ideal, 236–237
    modeling intangible elements of, 43–47
    role of diligence in achieving, 47
    role of execution in achieving, 48
    role of resources in attaining, 46

True security (*continued*)
  role of support in achieving, 46
  role of trust in achieving, 47–48
  summary, 51
  tangible elements of, 42–43
True security group, identifying, 212
True security model, xx, xxvii, 41
  Act element within, 230
  and apathy, 82–89
  and board of directors, 119–120
  Board of Directors Security Committee
    example, 50
  cause and effect of apathy in, 80–82
  cause and effect of myopia in, 118
  cause and effect of primacy in, 155
  constraints mapping exercise, 263–266
  desired action definitions in, 44–45
  as double-edged sword, 237
  identifying constraints within, 211–214
  and infancy, 189–194
  inheritance and, 47
  intangible components, 42
  mapping constraint effects on achieving
    tangible elements, 267–270
  mapping intangibles for target
    groups, 275–278
  measuring intangible elements in, 216–218
  measuring intangibles exercise, 271–274
  myopia and, 118–125
  organizational GAP analysis
    within, 218–220
  organizational groups in, 44
  role of diligence in, 47
  role of endorsements in, 45
  role of execution in, 48
  role of inheritance in, 47
  role of priority in, 45–46
  role of resources in, 46
  role of support in, 46
  role of trust in, 47–48
  step-children groups in, 47–48
  and systems theory, 53–54
  tangible elements, 42–43, 215–216
  TSA example, 49–50
  using, 51–53
Trust
  and authority, 183
  by consumers, 124
  and infancy, 178–179, 181
  informed, by consumers, 194
  knowing whom to, 196
  and reaction to information, 183
  role in achieving true security, 47–48
  in self, 179
  and skepticism of source, 178
  TSA example, 49–50
Tunnel vision, 32
  of contract workers, 108

U

Unexpected events, and inattentional
  blindness, 101

V

Vendors, limiting training by, 131
Vertical organizations
  primacy in, 142
  trust in, 182

W

Weather predictions, unreliability of, 171–172
Wholeness, in systems, 180